SWAMI VIVEKANANDA'S CONTRIBUTION TO THE PRESENT AGE

PHOTOGRAPH COURTESY CANADIAN PACIFIC

The C.P.R. steamer Empress of India, Capt. Marshall, arrived at 7 o'clock last evening with a full passenger and freight list. The voyage over was quiet and uneventful, with fair weather, and the trip was made on schedule time.

(Vancouver *Daily News-Advertiser,*
Wednesday, July 26, 1893)

Swami Vivekananda . . . left behind all that was dear and familiar to him and, on May 31, 1893, set sail from Bombay for America. After stopping in China and Japan, he re-embarked at Yokohama. As far as can be learned, he crossed the Pacific on the SS. Empress of India, *a 6,000-ton ship of the Canadian Pacific Line, which left Yokohama on July 14 and landed in Vancouver on the evening of Tuesday, July 25.*

(Marie Louise Burke, *Swami Vivekananda in America New Discoveries,* pp. 13-14)

Works by Swami Satprakashananda

- METHODS OF KNOWLEDGE: ACCORDING TO ADVAITA VEDANTA
- HINDUISM AND CHRISTIANITY
- SRI RAMAKRISHNA'S LIFE AND MESSAGE IN THE PRESENT AGE: WITH THE AUTHOR'S REMINISCENCES OF HOLY MOTHER AND SOME DIRECT DISCIPLES
- MEDITATION: ITS PROCESS, PRACTICE, AND CULMINATION
- THE GOAL AND THE WAY: THE VEDANTIC APPROACH TO LIFE'S PROBLEMS
- THE UNIVERSE, GOD, AND GOD-REALIZATION
- SWAMI VIVEKANANDA'S CONTRIBUTION TO THE PRESENT AGE

and other Vedantic treatises

SWAMI VIVEKANANDA'S CONTRIBUTION TO THE PRESENT AGE

By

Swami Satprakashananda

THE VEDANTA SOCIETY OF ST. LOUIS

ISBN 0-916356-58-2
LC 77-91628

205 South Skinker Boulevard
St. Louis, Missouri 63105

Printed in the United States of America

CONTENTS

FRONTISPIECE — EMPRESS OF INDIA 1
PREFACE 7
NOTE ON THE PRONUNCIATION OF TRANSLITERATED SANSKRIT ALPHABET 9
ABBREVIATIONS 11

I. Introduction: The Unification of the World — How? 13
II. The Buddha, Śrī Śaṅkarācārya, and Swami Vivekananda 23
III. The Ramakrishna-Vivekananda Vedanta Movement 111
IV. Swami Vivekananda's Universality 135
V. A Classified Survey of Swami Vivekananda's Message 160
VI. (Supplement) Swami Vivekananda's Brother Disciple, Swami Brahmananda, as a Spiritual Teacher 178

Appendix A The Buddhist Scriptures 209
Appendix B The Vedic Scriptures 249
Appendix C Folk Festivals in India 213
Appendix D The Origin and the Restoration of the Handwritten Manuscript of Swami Vivekananda's "Song of the Sannyāsin" 223
Appendix E How a King Became a Saint 231

BIBLIOGRAPHY I English Works quoted from and consulted in the book 241
BIBLIOGRAPHY II Sanskrit and Pāli Works quoted from and referred to in this book 243
INDEX 247
ENDPIECE — EMPRESS OF INDIA 251

PREFACE

Swami Vivekananda's special contribution to the present age is the deliverance of a universal message conducive to man's moral and spiritual upliftment throughout the world and to the harmonious living of all human beings irrespective of differences of color, creed, sex, age, social rank, cultural standard, political outlook, and so forth.

The Swami's personal experience of East and West, his penetrating insight, his erudition, his boundless compassion, his immaculate life, and, above all, his realization of the Ultimate One, the Truth of truths beyond all diversities, made him specially qualified for the Divine Commission — the reconstruction of humanity on the spiritual foundation. No doubt, there will be warm response from all who are ready for the message.

It is true the reader will come across certain repetitions in perusing the book. In support of this I can mention what Sarvepalli Radhakrishnan says in the Preface of his book *Eastern Religions and Western Thought:*[1] "There is inevitably a certain amount of repetition in a book of this kind. I have made no serious attempt to avoid it, partly because it would have tended to spoil the construction of individual lectures [essays] and partly because a certain amount of repetition of general principles in different connexions has some value in itself."

I am thankful to the publishers who brought out my essays in Chapters II, III, and IV in the original form. Their names are mentioned at the beginning of the relevant chapters. I deeply appreciate the earnest efforts of my Vedanta students in the preparation of the typescript.

SATPRAKASHANANDA

The Vedanta Society
St. Louis, Missouri
July 24, 1974

[1]S. Radhakrishnan, *Eastern Religions and Western Thought,* 2d edn. (London: Oxford University Press, 1940), preface, p. ix.

NOTE ON THE PRONUNCIATION OF TRANSLITERATED SANSKRIT ALPHABET

a	as in all	ñ	n (palatal)
ā	as in far	ṭ	as in tool
i	as in tin	ṭh	as th in boat-house
ī	as ee in deep	ḍ	as in dog
u	as in full	ḍh	as in Godhood
ū	as oo in loop	ṇ	n (cerebral)
ō	as in note	th	as in thin
ṛ	as ri in prick	d	as th in then
ṁ	as ng in Hongkong	dh	as in Buddha
ḥ	as in oh!	n	(dental) as in noun
g	hard as in good	ph	as in loophole
ṅ	as ng in king	bh	as in abhor
c	as ch in church	v	as w
ch	as chh in thatch-hut	ś	as in short (palatal sibilant)
jh	as geh in hedge-hog	ṣ	(cerebral sibilant)

ABBREVIATIONS

BG	*Bhagavad-gītā*
Br.U.	*Bṛhadāraṇyaka Upaniṣad*
BS	*Brahma-sūtras*
Ch.U.	*Chāndōgya Upaniṣad*
CW	*The Complete Works of Swami Vivekananda*
GSR	*The Gospel of Sri Ramakrishna*
Is.U.	*Īśa Upaniṣad*
Ka.U.	*Kaṭha Upaniṣad*
Ma.U.	*Māṇḍūkya Upaniṣad*
Mu.U.	*Muṇḍaka Upaniṣad*
S.com.	*Śaṅkara's commentary*
SB	*Śrīmad-bhāgavatam*
Sv.U.	*Śvetāśvatara Upaniṣad*
Tai.U.	*Taittirīya Upaniṣad*
VC	*Viveka-cūḍāmaṇi*

CHAPTER I

INTRODUCTION: THE UNIFICATION OF THE WORLD — HOW?

A special characteristic of the present age is the general tendency of the human mind to conceive mankind as a whole. Man's mental vision is no longer confined to his family situation, civic conditions, social status, racial characteristics, or nationality. It is focused on the world at large, nay, it extends beyond this globe to the solar universe, even reaches the stellar. Some go so far as to dream of colonizing one of the adjacent planets in order to solve the menacing problem of population explosion on the earth.

This expansion of vision is accelerated by the interconnection of the remotest parts of the world (as far as the lunar surface) by wonderful facilities of transportation and communication brought about by the advancement of scientific knowledge and technology. Simultaneously, there has been intermingling of human beings of various countries, races, cultural standards, economic conditions, and political systems. Not only have they come to know each other intimately, in many cases they have come to live together. This has created the possibility of amicable relationship and also of disharmony among human beings.

Any serious conflict among men in these days is unthinkable, inasmuch as their power of damage and destruction far outbalances their power of self-defense or self-preservation. It is imperative that they should bring about complete harmony among themselves. This needs the unification of diverse individuals and groups of individuals constituting the human race. Consequently, comparative methods of study have been in vogue in the fields of religion, philosophy, arts, science, economics, politics, and so forth. A modern man knows much more about other races and countries than his forebears and is eager to know more.

Human beings in general have come to realize more than ever before that the interests of one country are invariably interwoven with the interests of other countries, that they have to live in the world as one family, that they must rise or fall together. It is also a recognized fact that the unification of the world has to be achieved despite all diversities — economic, political, religious, cultural, racial and so forth. The pattern for world unity is not uniformity, but unity in diversity. The world should move with the coordinated efforts of individuals and of groups of individuals in the largest scale possible. To accomplish this, mutual understanding and appreciation are indispensable.

The fundamental principle to be observed is how the interests of individuals and nations can be in conformity with the interests of humanity at large. Consequently, various organizations, national and international, are being formed. There are international academies of science, international academies of arts, international academies of law and so forth. Evidently, the foremost of the international organizations is the United Nations, which by means of its various organs is trying to bring about political, economic, and cultural relationship among countries, nations, and races. It is the hope of the leading men and women that this will fulfill man's dream of one world. How can there be one world in which all the varied interests of human beings are integrated? How can the nationals belonging to different countries regard themselves as world citizens?

That these organizations can help considerably to harmonize diverse human interests, there is no question. But the efficient working of an organization, vast or small, does not depend primarily on its constitutional laws and agreements but on the sincerity, the self-sacrifice, and the enthusiasm of its individual members. Nothing great can be achieved by mere sagacity, tactfulness and diplomacy.

No organization can function smoothly and achieve its end without mutual trust and cordial relationship among the members themselves. What but the inner goodness of the individual members can insure this? Negotiations, regulations, pacts among international organizations are necessary but not adequate for world-unity. The basic problem of world-unity is a moral problem. The integrity of a nation depends on the integrity of its individual members. Similarly, world-unity depends on the integrity of the nations and their fair dealings with one another.

Leading men and women of today generally expect to establish national unity and international harmony by the precept of enlightened self-interest. For the peace and progress of his community each individual member has to conform his own interests to the interests of the community as a whole. He should do what he can to promote the growth of the community and avoid what is detrimental to its interests. In the same way individual interests should subserve national interests; similarly the interests of different nations have to be coordinated in view of the international unity and well-being. But the precept of enlightened self-interest falls short of our expectations. It is after all self-interest, and not unselfishness. According to this, a person has to care for others' interests for the sake of his own interests. It can be of some help in normal circumstances when life's course flows smoothly, but it cannot meet the exigencies of human situations when an individual has to sacrifice his own interests for the sake of others. In such cases a man of enlightened self-interest is likely to have recourse to expediency. What ethics and religion teach is not self-interest but self-sacrifice as the ideal of man. This is efficacious and uplifting.

Morality exists in human life in many different forms. The

highest standard of morality means unselfishness for the sake of unselfishness; it considers goodness as a value; it teaches universal love without any distinction of merit, color, status, or creed. If we look for such a high ethical standard as universal love, which transcends all barriers between man and man, then it must be based on the spiritual oneness of mankind. It is the spiritual reality that is all-comprehensive and all-pervading. It goes beyond all limitations. There is, according to all religions of the world, a spiritual basis of the universe, which is the very perfection of existence. It sustains and manifests everything. It is the Light of lights. That Soul of the universe is the soul of each and every one of us. That is manifest in human beings as the inmost self, as conscious spirit. It is the pure-minded that perceive this truth and develop universal love.

In this progressive age Swami Vivekananda pointed out more than once that the world's basic need is not economic, political or cultural development, but the goodness of man. It is man that makes war, it is man that makes peace; it is man that makes laws, laws do not make man. What the world needs most is the right types of human beings.

In an interview with the correspondent of the *Sunday Times*, London, in 1896, Swami Vivekananda pointed out the world's basic need of right types of human beings:

> But the basis of all systems, social or political, rests upon the goodness of man. No nation is great or good because Parliament enacts this or that, but because its men are great and good.[1]

In his view the final solution of human problems rests upon the individual's moral and spiritual development. Without the spiritual ideal man's moral life is not well-grounded. In his lecture on "The Mission of Vedanta" delivered at Kumbhakonum (S.

[1] CW V:122.

India) early in 1897, on his return from the Western world, he said:

> No amount of political or social manipulation of human conditions can cure the evils of life. It is a change of the soul itself for the better that alone will cure the evils of life. No amount of force, or government, or legislative cruelty will change the conditions of a race, but it is spiritual and ethical culture alone that can change wrong racial tendencies for the better.[2]

What is the secret of man's moral and spiritual development? It is his faith in himself. This is the remedy for all weaknesses and the secret of his strength. Weakness is degenerative, while strength is uplifting and elevating. How to arouse man's faith in himself? By making him aware of his potential divinity. So Swami Vivekananda urges in the same address:

> Teach yourselves, teach everyone his real nature, call upon the sleeping soul and see how it awakes. Power will come, glory will come, goodness will come, purity will come, and everything that is excellent will come when this sleeping soul is roused to self-conscious activity.[3]

The potential divinity of man is the universal ground of human relationship, because it transcends all differences between man and man. Unity of mankind has to be achieved by fellow-feeling between man and man, the world over, despite all differences of caste, color, creed, sex, age, social status, and economic conditions.

The potential divinity of man is the fundamental teaching of religion, irrespective of doctrine or dogma, but without inner purity this truth does not shine within a person. Religion is the manifestation of the divinity already in man. To realize this divinity is the goal of human life. According to every theistic religion, God is infinite, eternal. Not only is He the omnipotent, omniscient Ruler of the universe, He is the all-pervading Self of

[2]CW III:182. [3]CW III:193.

the universe underlying every form of existence. He dwells within every individual as the innermost self, the central principle of consciousness, ever-shining within the psychophysical garb. "Be ye therefore perfect, even as your Father which is in heaven is perfect," says Jesus Christ.[4] What is imperfect intrinsically can never be perfect. Further, "Behold, the Kingdom of God is within you."[5]

The more you recognize your inmost self and your relationship with the Supreme Being, the more you feel your relationship with your fellow-beings, because the same Supreme Being dwells in all as the inmost self. With spiritual development love for all grows. You love your neighbor as yourself. As you recognize your unity with the Supreme Self, you find yourself in all. Thus, spiritual insight makes moral life spontaneous.

Inner purity is indispensable to spiritual development. Unselfishness is the basic moral virtue. It removes all disharmony between man and man. A person whose main interest in life is secular gain can hardly be consistently moral. His moral observance must be subservient to his secular interest. In this life in the economic, in the political, in the cultural and in the social field, moral scruples are often found to be in the way of material gain. Whenever there is conflict between the two, a seeker of temporal values will naturally be prone to sacrifice his moral principles.

On the contrary, a person who holds to the spiritual ideal cannot but be firm in moral observance. Without moral purity spiritual light does not shine within a person. So long as he cares for the spiritual goal, spiritual enlightenment, he has to cultivate inner purity, that is to say, he has to be consistently moral. And when a person is consistently moral, standing on the spiritual oneness of humanity, on the spiritual relationship between man and man, he cannot but have universal love. He recognizes his spiritual self, he recognizes the spiritual self of others, he

[4] Matt. V:48. [5] Luke 17:21.

recognizes the unity of all spiritual selves with the Supreme Self. He holds to the ideal of realizing that. Naturally, he can never sacrifice moral principles because his ideal is Self-realization. He will gladly sacrifice any other value — all his temporal pleasures and possessions for the sake of the ideal.

Man's moral nature is closest to his spiritual self. It is through his moral goodness that his spiritual self, which is ever pure, free, and illuminative, finds expression in other levels of life, such as intellectual, volitional, emotional, aesthetic, sensory, physical. It is man's moral nature that determines his dealings with others in collective life. In the pure-minded the luminous self maintains the clarity of vision, by which they find the right way of living.

Clarity of vision is also indispensable to man's success in secular life, inasmuch as it enables a seeker of temporal values to make the right use of his resources, internal and external. After realizing from experience the inherent incompetence of power and prosperity to lead man to unmixed blessing he turns to the Eternal.

The religion and philosophy of Vedanta, usually called Hinduism, is based on the central truths that underlie all the religions of the world. So says Swami Vivekananda in his lecture on "The Freedom of the Soul" delivered in London on the 5th November, 1896:

> There is no one system in the world, no real religion, which does not hold the idea that the human soul, whatever it be, or whatever its relation to God, is essentially pure and perfect, whether expressed in the language of mythology, or allegory, or philosophy. Its real nature is blessedness and power, not weakness and misery.[6]

To apply this truth for the development of man's life — physical, intellectual, aesthetic, moral and spiritual — was his mission.

Apparently, Swami Vivekananda taught a particular religion

[6]CW II:193.

called Hinduism; but he really delivered a message of universal truth. His conception of religion is most comprehensive. In his lecture on "The Necessity of Religion" delivered in London in May, 1896, he said:

> Religion is the greatest motive power for realizing that infinite energy which is the birthright and nature of every man. In building up character, in making for everything that is good and great, in bringing peace to others and peace to one's own self, religion is the highest motive power, and therefore, ought to be studied from that standpoint. . . . All narrow, limited, fighting ideas of religion have to go. All sect ideas and tribal or national ideals of religion must be given up. That each tribe or nation should have its own particular God and think that every other is wrong, is a superstition that should belong to the past. All such ideas must be abandoned.
>
> As the human mind broadens, the spiritual steps broaden too. The time has already come when a man cannot record a thought without its reaching to all corners of the earth; by merely physical means we have come in touch with the whole world . . .
>
> The religious ideals of the future must embrace all that exists in the world that is good and great, and at the same time have infinite scope for future development. All that was good in the past must be preserved; and the doors must be kept open for future additions to the already existing store. Religions must also be inclusive, and not look down with contempt upon one another, because their particular ideals of God are different.[7]

The universal truths underlying all religions despite differences of doctrines and dogmas may be stated as:

1. One infinite all-pervading Supreme Being (Pure Consciousness) underlies all things and beings. This is the Self of the universe.
2. Its special manifestation is in human beings because of the development of the mind that has transparency to transmit consciousness.

[7]CW II:67.

3. Man's inmost self is luminous, being of the nature of consciousness. It is pure, free, immortal.
4. It is ever united with the Supreme Self. To realize this unity is the Goal of human life.
5. The more a person grasps this unity with the Supreme Self the more he feels his kinship with all human beings. This is the sure way to universal love.
6. Man's moral life begins with the cultivation of fellow-feeling towards his fellow beings. This is the preliminary step toward the realization of this unity and consequent universal love.

These are the truths that form the common background of human life, Eastern and Western, ancient and modern. They unify all the aspects of man's life. In Swami Vivekananda's view there is no inherent contradiction between Eastern and Western ways of living and between one aspect of life and another, inasmuch as they can be attuned to the fundamental truths.

The world-progress of the present age as visualized by Swami Vivekananda shall be the onward movement of the entire human race as one body, as in an orderly procession in which every individual plays his part while moving ahead.

Swami Vivekananda was the personification of his message. He spoke from his realization of the oneness of all multiplicity. To him this oneness is the common ground of all metaphysical ideas, of all religious doctrines, of all ethical principles, of all scientific truths. This is where ancient and modern and also East and West meet. In his view there should be one humanity, neither Eastern nor Western.

His universal love was the outcome of his Self-realization, realization of the identity of the self with the Supreme Self. His brother disciple, Swami Turiyananda, remarked more than once, "Swamiji does not use the word 'I' in the sense of an individual separate from others." Truly, Swami Vivekananda never cared for his own salvation. In his letter to Mary Hale of Chicago dated 9th July, 1897, he wrote:

> May I be born again and again, and suffer thousands of miseries so that I may worship the only God that exists, the only God I believe in, the sum total of all souls — and above all, my God the wicked, my God the miserable, my God the poor of all races, of all species, is the special object of my worship.[8]

None but a free soul can speak in such terms.

Swami Vivekananda interpreted the fundamental spiritual truths in modern terms so as to enlighten mankind on the problems of human existence. He is the person who has built a bridge between the old and the modern, between East and West. He has fulfilled the vital need of the present-day world. It is the need of a universal message and a comprehensive view of life. The secret of his universality is not just a broad intellectual sweep or grasp; it is not mere humanitarian or philanthropic feeling; it is the realization of the essential identity of his own self with the Supreme Self that dwells within every individual as the inmost self.

The advent of Swami Vivekananda toward the close of the Nineteenth Century signalizes the dawn of spiritual consciousness on the horizon of human thought. Those who can read the signs of time know that for more than a century the world has been witnessing a spiritual rebirth, human minds have been recognizing the spiritual foundation of life and the world. Human thought is veering to spiritual idealism. As we shall see, Sri Ramakrishna is the pioneer in this spiritual renovation and Swami Vivekananda is his standard-bearer. Their mission is the reconstruction of humanity on a spiritual foundation, which consists of universal truths that underlie not only all religions but all phases of life.

[8]CW V:106.

CHAPTER II

THE BUDDHA, ŚRĪ ŚAṄKARĀCĀRYA, AND SWAMI VIVEKANANDA

1. *How the three great spiritual leaders are related.*

The Buddha, Śaṅkara, and Vivekananda stand out as three great revivalists in the religious history of India. Each has brought about significant changes in the religious life and thought of the country. Each has made a distinct contribution to world-culture. Each has delivered a message of universal significance and can be entitled a teacher of humanity. Like Śaṅkara and Vivekananda the Buddha realized the Supreme Being (Brahman) in nirvikalpa samādhi, though he did not declare Godhead or God.[1] This state is the acme of spiritual experience, the immediate apprehension of the ultimate Reality as Pure Consciousness undivided and undiversified. In Buddhism it is called *bōdhi* (enlightenment or illumination). Usually it is termed *nirvāṇa* (lit. blowing out). It means the extinction of the ego, the empirical self rooted in ignorance, by the knowledge of Truth. The Buddha's early names

An abridged form of this article was presented at the Parliament of Religions held in Calcutta on the occasion of the Birth Centenary Celebration of Swami Vivekananda, 1963-64, and included in the book *Parliament of Religions* (Calcutta: Swami Vivekananda Centenary Committee, 1965), pp.23-58.

[1]As regards the Buddha's experience of nirvāṇa, Dr. Law remarks: "According to the Buddha's claim, this is the ninth stage of *samādhi,* reached for the first time by him. This is a state of trance when outwardly a man who reaches it is as good as dead, there being nothing but warmth *(uṣmā)* as a sign of life. In this state, a level of consciousness *(citta)* is reached where consciousness is ultimately thrown back on itself, completely void, being devoid of subject-object relation *(grāhya-grāhaka-bhāva-rahita).*" "Nirvāṇa" by Bimala Churn Law, in *The Cultural Heritage of India,* 2nd rev. ed., 4 vols. (Calcutta: Ramakrishna Mission Institute of Culture, 1953-62), 1:550.

were Gautama (or Gōtama) and Siddhārtha. After the attainment of nirvāṇa or bōdhi he became known as the Buddha, the illumined one. He is also called "Tathāgata," he who has attained "suchness," the Truth or Reality which is ever the same, or such as it is. Buddhist nirvāṇa is in fact Brahma-nirvāṇa[2] mentioned in the *Bhagavad-gītā.*[3] It does not mean annihilation, but the attainment of full freedom and beatitude consequent on the realization of oneness with Brahman. All the three leaders lived as free souls working incessantly for the guidance and upliftment of mankind.

While Śaṅkara and Vivekananda were avowed Advaitists (nondualists), the Buddha was an Advaitist at heart.[4] His noncommital attitude with regard to the ultimate Reality implies its inexpressibility rather than its negation. According to the Upaniṣadic tradition, silence is the final answer to all inquiries as to the nature of Nondual Brahman beyond the range of word and thought (avāṅgmanasōgōcaram). Śūnyatā (lit. voidness or vacuity) in the Mādhyamika school of Buddhism pioneered by Aśvaghōṣa (poet and philosopher and the celebrated author of *Buddhacarita,* who lived in all probability in the first century A.D.) does not mean nonexistence, but nonrelational Reality beyond description: "Śūnyatā is the synonym of that which has no cause, that which is beyond thought or conception, that which is not

[2]In *Itivuttaka* (one of the fifteen divisions of *Khuddaka-Nikāya* of *Sutta-Piṭaka*) a Buddha or an Arhat is often spoken of as *Brahma-bhūta* — "one who has become Brahman." The expression *Brahma-prāpti* (attainment of Brahman) has also been used. Buddhist commentators, however, interpret these expressions in the sense of "most excellent," "attainment of the highest state."

[3]Says Śrī Kṛṣṇa, "The yōgī who finds happiness within, rejoices within, and is illumined within attains freedom in Brahman becoming one with Brahman. The sages whose wrong tendencies are eliminated, whose doubts are dispelled, and the senses controlled, and who devote themselves to the welfare of all beings, attain freedom in Brahman. The men of renunciation who are free from attachment and aversion, whose minds are disciplined, who have realized the self, become one with Brahman here and hereafter." (BG V:24-26.)

[4]The great lexicographer and poet, Amara-siṁha (circ. sixth century, A.D.), calls the Buddha *Advayavādī* (nondualist) in his lexicon, *Amara-kōṣa:* "Sarvajñaḥ Sugataḥ Buddhaḥ. . . . Advayavādī Vināyakaḥ."

produced, that which is not born, that which is without measure."[5]

The teachings of the Buddha, like those of Śaṅkara and Vivekananda, have the Upaniṣads as their source. "Early Buddhism, we venture to hazard a conjecture, is only a restatement of the thought of the Upaniṣads from a new standpoint," says Dr. Radhakrishnan.[6] But while Śaṅkara and Vivekananda accepted the Upaniṣads as the authoritative source of suprasensuous knowledge and acknowledged their allegiance to them, the Buddha did not. As a result, his religion became completely separated from the Vedic religion (later known as Brāhmaṇism and Hinduism).

All three were itinerant monastic teachers and formed new monastic organizations on the basis of the old. The monastic tradition is as old in India as the institution of marriage. From the earliest days the monks lived individually and would wander from place to place. (At times they lived together in the forests even in large numbers.) They generally followed the principles of the ascetic life as enjoined by the scriptures and enunciated by their teachers. It was the genius of the Buddha to organize the individual monks into a community or order under a set of common rules and regulations. Henceforth the monastic organization came into being and monasteries were founded to shelter the monks. Usually, the monks of the same order formed a fraternity and lived together in monasteries devoting themselves mainly to contemplation, meditation, study, and teaching. Some of them, however, chose the solitary life of a recluse or a wandering ascetic. The Buddha also instituted an order of nuns. Before him, we find solitary instances of individual nuns.

Śaṅkara belonged to the time-honored Vedic line of Sannyāsins, which had continued from time immemorial through a

[5] *Aṣṭasāhasrikā-Prajñāpāramitā,* Chap. XVIII.

[6] S. Radhakrishnan, *Indian Philosophy,* 2nd ed.rev., 2 vols. (London: George Allen & Unwin, 1929-31), I:361.

succession of teachers and disciples. He organized the ancient monastic body prevailing in his day under ten main heads. His monastic order is altogether separate from the Buddhist, although in establishing it he might have been influenced by the Buddhist idea of monastic organization. He restored the Vedic religion after its decline during the rise of Buddhism. The monastic institution formed by Swami Vivekananda in the modern age and named the Ramakrishna Order after his master, Sri Ramakrishna, is allied with Śaṅkara's Vedantic order of Sannyāsins and is virtually an offshoot of the same. It was initiated by Sri Ramakrishna, who was a Sannyāsī disciple of Tōtā Purī, an illumined teacher of the Advaita school of Śaṅkarācārya.

The Buddha was born near Kapilavastu[7] in Nepal in the foothills of the Himalayas in 623 B.C.,[8] and lived eighty years. Śaṅkara was born at Kalady in Kerala State in Southwest India in 686 A.D.[9] and lived only thirty-two years. Vivekananda was born in the modern city of Calcutta in Bengal in 1863 A.D. and lived but thirty-nine years. Thus, between the Buddha and Vivekananda there is a distance of about 2400 years and Śaṅkara stands almost midway between them. The Buddha's message points to ethical idealism, Śaṅkara's to spiritual idealism, and Vivekananda's to the

[7]About 100 miles northeast of Varanasi (Banaras). A stone pillar erected there 375 years later by Emperor Aśōka has this inscription: "Twenty years after his coronation, King Priyadarśī, Beloved of the Gods, visited this place in person and worshiped here because the Buddha, the Sage of the Śākyas, was born here. He ordered a stone wall to be constructed around the place and erected this stone pillar to commemorate his visit." N.A. Nikam and Richard McKeon, eds. and trans., *The Edicts of Aśōka* (Chicago: University of Chicago Press, Phoenix Books, 1959),p.69.

[8]According to the Therāvāda Buddhism. See the article of C.V. Joshi on the Buddha's "Life and Teachings" (pp. 20-34) and also Dr. Radhakrishnan's "Foreword" in P.V. Bapat, ed., *2500 Years of Buddhism,* (Delhi, India: Government of India, Publications Division, 1959).

[9]See Rajendranath Ghose's Preface to the Works of Śaṅkarācārya, Pt. I (Bengali edition), Calcutta, 1927. In the opinion of Sir R.G. Bhandarkar, Śaṅkara was born in 680 A.D., if not earlier. See S. Radhakrishnan's *Indian Philosophy,* II:447. Some modern scholars consider 788 A.D. as the year of Śaṅkara's birth.

conjoined practice of the two in all spheres of life. By instituting the service of man as the worship of God Swami Vivekananda has combined the love of man with the love of God; in other words, the ethical ideal with the spiritual ideal.

2. *The Buddha's early life, renunciation, and Enlightenment.*

The Buddha came of a royal family of the Śākya clan belonging to the Kṣatriya class. He is also called *Śākya-siṁha* ("the lion of the Śākyas") and *Śākya-muni* ("the sage of the Śākyas"). His father, Śuddhōdhana, ruled over a small kingdom in Nepal. It was prophesied at the prince's birth that he would renounce the world with his heart touched by human suffering. In order to prevent such an eventuality, which he considered to be a calamity, the king carefully guarded the son and kept him surrounded with the charms of life, so that no trace of human misery could cross his path.

At the age of nineteen the prince was married to a beautiful young girl. He received training in military and other arts according to the tradition of the royal family. There were, however, evidences of his strong tendency to be quiet and contemplative at times. At the age of twenty-nine a son was born to him. There was jubilation in the royal palace. It so happened that, while being driven in a royal chariot on three successive days, the prince witnessed human sufferings in the form of disease, decrepitude, and death, and was deeply moved. Then he happened to see a monk, whose serene and blissful countenance convinced him that there was an end of sorrows. Firmly resolved to find for humanity a way of deliverance from all miseries he tore himself from his family and left the palace in the stillness of night, soon after the birth of the son.

Having discarded his princely apparel, he put on the garb of an ascetic and travelled on foot for six long years from one place to another, with the sole object of finding the root-cause of human sufferings and the means of its extirpation. He met different religious teachers, studied different systems of thought, followed different courses of discipline, but found no satisfaction. Then he lived a very rigid and austere life, until his flesh dried up; yet his mind did not receive the light of Truth. A relaxation of severities followed as he dragged himself from the verge of death. At last with a firm determination to see the Light that removes all darkness he sat down under a tree for intense meditation on the innermost being, where shines the "Light of lights," and finally attained illumination (bōdhi). The tree, though replaced by a scion, is called to this day the Bodhi-Tree, and the place is known as Bodha-Gaya, being situated near the holy city of Gaya in Behar.

3. *The promulgation of the Message.*

With his face beaming with the radiance of Truth the Buddha proceeded to the Deer Park at Sarnath near Varanasi (Banaras). There he met five of his former companions and delivered to them his first sermon, which contained the gist of all his teachings. After hearing the sermon they became his first five disciples. Then the Buddha visited other places promulgating his message. Soon his fame extended far and wide and the number of followers increased. When the number of disciples rose to sixty he sent them to different directions with these words: "Go forth, O monks! on your journey for the weal and welfare of many, out of compassion for the world, for the weal and welfare of angels and mortals. Go no two of you the same way."

The Buddha is, indeed, the world's first great missionary. He is the first religious teacher to start evangelism out of sheer compassion. His followers carried his message far and wide without bigotry, intolerance, or coercion, let alone persecution. For nearly forty-five years he travelled back and forth in Behar, the United Provinces, and Nepal, imparting his teachings to one and all, without any distinction of caste, rank, merit, or sex. The rich and the poor, the learned and the ignorant, the righteous and the unrighteous, the young and the old, men and women — all received his grace alike. Among his disciples can be counted the Brāhmaṇa Kāśyapa, the King Bimbisāra, the merchant-prince Anāthapiṇḍaka, the barber Upāli, the robber Aṅgulimāla, and the courtesan Ambāpāli. The success of his mission was due to the lofty moral tone of his precepts, his wonderful power of presentation — simple, pleasant, and persuasive, and above all his gentle, serene, compassionate and radiant personality. Even in his dying hour he did not refuse to instruct Subhadrā, a wandering Brāhmin ascetic, who came for solace and guidance, and was received as his last disciple. Addressing his personal attendant, Ānanda, for the sake of the Order (saṅgha), the Blessed One said:

> Therefore, O Ānanda, be ye lamps unto yourselves. Rely on yourselves, and do not rely on external help.
>
> Hold fast to the truth as a lamp. Seek salvation alone in the truth. Look not for assistance to anyone besides yourselves.[10]

It is to be noted that in the Buddha's religion there is no room for Divine grace in man's struggle to get beyond all sufferings.

It was on the eightieth anniversary of his blessed birthday that the Buddha entered into parinirvāṇa (the nirvāṇa attended with the release from the body) with the welfare and happiness of all in his heart, while showering blessings upon all far and near.

4. *The teachings of the Buddha.*

The basic teachings of the Buddha are the Four Noble Truths (caturārya satya), which can be stated as follows:

[10] *Mahāparinibbāṇa suttanta.*

There *is* suffering in life, namely, in birth, in old age, in illness, in death, in contact with the disagreeable, in separation from the agreeable, in not getting what is desired. Suffering is inevitably associated with the holding of the psychophysical organism.

There *is* the cause of suffering. The root cause of man's suffering is the ignorance of the true nature of himself. Because of this a person is attached to the psychophysical organism. This attachment leads to rebirth through a succession of cause and effect, involving the law of karma. Thus, ignorance of the true nature of the self, attachment to the psychophysical organism, and rebirth are the three major links of the causal chain that turns on the wheel of life — from birth to death and death to birth — ever attended with suffering.

In the Buddha's view every individual is responsible for his own suffering. No supernatural agency is involved in it. Neither fatalism nor accidentalism can account for it.

There *is* the cessation of suffering. Since suffering is due to a cause, the removal of the cause means the cessation of suffering. This explanation is in accordance with the Buddha's theory of universal causation. All events, physical and psychical, are held by a law of cause and effect. Nothing happens by chance. Everything has a cause and as the cause is, so is the effect. Just as the plant originates from the seed under certain conditions, even so, whatever exists arises from certain causes and conditions and is impermanent. These (causes and conditions) being there it becomes; in the absence of these it does not arise. This is the Buddha's theory of Dependent Origination (pratītya-samutpāda, lit. "arising in correlation with").

There *is* the way to the cessation of suffering. All sufferings cease when their root-cause, ignorance, is eradicated by nirvāṇa, that is, by the attainment of perfect knowledge (bōdhi). Negatively, nirvāṇa is the extinguishing of all flames of desire (tanhā) with their root-cause, and, positively, it is the attainment of illumination attended with peace and bliss and love for all beings.[11] The way to nirvāṇa is the Noble Eightfold Path (aṣṭāṅgika-mārga). It is also called the Middle Path (madhya panthā), being characterized by the avoidance of the two extremes of self-indulgence and self-mortification. It is open to the lay disciples as well as the monks.

The following are the eight stages of the path:

1. Right view (samyak dṛṣṭi) — the true understanding of the Four Noble Truths.
2. Right resolution (samyak saṅkalpa) — firm determination to live the life accordingly.
3. Right speech (samyak vāk) — abstaining from lying, slandering, saying unkind words, and gossiping.
4. Right conduct (samyak kriyā) — abstaining from killing, stealing, drinking intoxicants, and adultery.
5. Right means of livelihood (samyak ājīva) — abstaining from trades in arms, flesh, living beings, intoxicants, and poison.
6. Right effort (samyak vyāyāma) — banishing evil thoughts and entertaining good thoughts.
7. Right mindfulness (samyak smṛti) — constant remembrance of the impermanence of the body-mind complex.
8. Right concentration (samyak samādhi) — practice of contemplation and meditation until the mind is perfectly tranquil. It is then that the Truth shines.

The Buddha combines in this Eightfold Path sound reasoning, ethical conduct, meditation and enlightenment.

[11]The Buddha's disciple and personal attendant Ānanda, speaks of nirvāṇa both in its negative and positive aspects: "This is a state of consciousness indicated by the Lord who knows and sees, the Arhat all-enlightened, whereby an almsman who lives the strenuous life purged of self both finds Deliverance from his prisoned heart, and sees the extirpation of the Cankers hitherto rampant, and wins at last that utter peace which was not his before." "The Portals of Nirvāṇa," *Sacred Books of the Buddhists,* vol. V, pt.4, from *Aṅguttara nikāya Sutta-piṭaka.*

A distinctive mark of the Buddha's message is the emphasis laid on complete self-abnegation and loving compassion for all living beings. And he himself was a personification of both. What boundless compassion of the teacher finds expression in such precepts as:

> May creatures all abound in weal and peace; may all be blessed with peace always; all creatures weak or strong; all creatures great and small; creatures unseen or seen, dwelling afar or near, born or awaiting birth — may all be blessed with peace!
>
> Let none cajole or flout his fellow anywhere; let none wish others harm in dudgeon or in hate.
>
> Just as with her own life a mother shields from hurt her own, her only, child — let all-embracing thoughts for all that lives be thine — an all-embracing love for all the universe in all its heights and depths and breadth, unstinted love, unmarred by hate within, not rousing enmity.
>
> So, as you stand, or walk, or sit, or lie, reflect with all your might on this; — 'tis deemed 'a state divine.'[12]

Never before perhaps was the practice of the non-resistance of evil recommended with such earnestness and in such strong terms as we find in the Parable of the Saw:

> Yea, disciples, even if highway robbers with a two-handed saw shall take and dismember you limb by limb, whosoever grow darkened in mind thereby would not be fulfilling my injunctions. Even then, disciples, thus must you school yourselves: Unsullied shall our minds remain, neither shall evil word escape our lips. Kind and compassionate ever, we will abide loving of heart nor harbor secret hate. And those robbers will we permeate with a stream of loving thought unfailing; and forth from them proceeding, enfold and permeate the whole wide world with constant thoughts of loving kindness, ample, expanding, measureless, free from enmity, free from ill will! Yea, verily, thus my disciples, thus must you school yourselves.[13]

[12]*Sutta-Nipāta* of the Sutta-piṭaka (Sermon-Basket). Eng. version from E.A. Burtt, ed., *The Teachings of the Compassionate Buddha* (New York: New American Library, Mentor Book, 1955), pp.46-47.

[13]*Majjhima-nikāya,* Sutta 21. Saw-simile Sutta.

5. *The Buddha's ethical teachings have a metaphysical foundation implicit.*

In one respect the Buddha's religion differs from all other religions of the world. While other religions rest on the recognition of some suprasensuous reality or realities, such as God, man's immortal self, heaven, hell, Buddhism as taught by the Buddha does not. The Buddha did not acknowledge any scriptural authority for the knowledge of the unseen. He depended solely on perception and inference. He took a practical view of things. He wanted men and women to accept what was evident and indubitable instead of inquiring after what was dubious and with regard to which no decisive answer could be expected. He laid stress on two important points: (1) the right understanding of the problem of suffering, and (2) the right way of living to get out of all suffering. To him metaphysical speculation counted little, so far as right living was concerned.

One main reason why he avoided answering such questions as — Does God exist? What becomes of an arhat (lit. worthy; he who has attained the ideal of his religion) after death? What is the nature of nirvāṇa? — was that he did not consider any discussion of them helpful to the edification of life and the attainment of nirvāṇa. On being asked what becomes of an arhat after death he once said: "And why, Maluṅkyaputta, have I not revealed these things? Because, O Maluṅkyaputta, this is not edifying, nor connected with the essence of the norm, nor tends to turning of the will, to the absence of passion, to cessation, to rest, to the higher faculties, to supreme wisdom, nor to Nibbāṇa; therefore have I not revealed it."[14] Another reason why the Buddha did not encourage metaphysical investigation was that in his time people were far more interested in this than in living the life to realize the Truth.

[14]*Majjhima-nikāya* I, Sutta 63; (Sutta-piṭaka). See also Oldenberg: *Buddha* (Eng. Tr.) pp.204-5.

It is true that the Buddha does not deny or affirm metaphysical truths. Nevertheless, they are implicit in his teachings. Even his own words corroborate this: "There is an unborn, an unoriginated, an unmade, an uncompounded; were there not, O mendicants, there would be no escape from the world of the born, the originated, the made and the compounded."[15] Nirvāṇa is the attainment of the Highest, the ultimate Reality, beyond name and form, beyond word and thought, where is the culmination of all knowledge, where is the cessation of all sufferings. It is the same as the realization of Nirguṇa Brahman, Pure Being-Consciousness-Bliss declared by the Upaniṣads. "The knower of Brahman attains the Highest."[16] "He who experiences the Bliss of Brahman has nothing to fear from."[17] For forty-five years after the attainment of nirvāṇa the Buddha lived the blessed life of a knower of Brahman.

That all-embracing love which the Buddha urges his disciples to strive after has its basis in the spiritual oneness of the universe, the unity of all individual selves in the all-pervading self. No relation is possible between one individual and another without a common meeting ground. "He who sees all beings in the very Self and the Self in all beings, in consequence thereof abhors none," declares the Upaniṣad.[18] A person can feel for one and all only by perceiving the innermost relationship with each one, the relationship that transcends all distinctions of the world of phenomena. The Buddha declares the impermanence or falsity of the psychophysical self, but not of the metaphysical Self.

6. *Buddhism is a variant of Hinduism.*

Though the Buddha did not acknowledge the authority of the Vedic testimony, he accepted the basic teachings of the Upaniṣads, but presented them in a new form to suit the socio-religious

[15]Udāna VIII:3. (Sutta-piṭaka.)
[16]Tai.U. II:1.3.
[17]*Ibid.* II:4.1.
[18]Is.U. 6.

conditions and the psychological atmosphere of his age. He did not found a new religion, but invented a novel garb for the old religious ideas. It is evident from his own words as well: "I have seen the ancient way, the Old Road that was taken by the formerly all-awakened, and that is the path I follow."[19] Dr. Radhakrishnan and Dr. Moore rightly observe: "The Buddha takes up some of the thoughts of the Upaniṣads and gives to them a new orientation. The Buddha is not so much formulating a new scheme of metaphysics and morals as rediscovering an old norm and adapting it to the new conditions of thought and life."[20]

The Buddha had his own reasons, as we have noted, for not declaring the Upaniṣadic Brahman, but he made the Upaniṣadic doctrine of karma and reincarnation and the liberation from the wheel of birth and rebirth the cornerstone of his religion. He adapted to his scheme of life the ethical principles of the Upaniṣads, and took up their ideal of renunciation. His doctrine of the "Middle path" is quite in accord with the Upaniṣadic teaching of self-discipline (tapas). Self-torture is against the spirit of the Vedic religion. The *Bhagavad-gītā* emphatically condemns it and enjoins moderate living.[21]

Buddhism in common with other religio-philosophical systems of India has taken into account the existence of human sufferings. This does not mean however that the advocates of these systems are pessimistic in their outlook and do not recognize the existence of happiness in human life. They do recognize the pleasures of life; but they discern at the same time their limitations. All these pleasures — physical, intellectual, or aesthetic, even at their

[19]Saṁyutta-nikāya II:16 (Sutta-piṭaka).

[20]Sarvepalli Radhakrishnan and Charles A. Moore, eds., *A Source Book in Indian Philosophy* (Princeton, N.J.: Princeton University Press, 1957), p.272.

[21]Cf. "Yōga is not for him who eats too much nor for him who eats too little. It is not for him, O Arjuna, who sleeps too much nor for him who sleeps too little. For him who is temperate in his food and recreation, temperate in sleep and waking, yōga puts an end to all sorrows." (BG VI:16,17. See also XVII:5,6,19.)

highest, are transitory, and by no means unmixed blessings. They cannot satisfy man's inmost yearning for unalloyed joy and unending happiness; whereas it is the fulfillment of this very longing that the propounders of Indian systems aim at. At any rate, man aspires to go beyond all sorrows. Religion promises this fulfillment.

While all other pursuits of life are occupied with the temporal, religion is the only human pursuit that is concerned with the eternal. Pleasures do not solve the problem of human sufferings. Man has to go beyond the relativity of pleasure and pain to reach the supreme Goal. The Sāṁkhya system of Kapila, who lived before the Buddha, opens with the proposition that the supreme purpose of human life is the complete eradication of all the three kinds of suffering.[22] According to Vedanta the ultimate end of life is the cessation of all sufferings and the attainment of Supreme Bliss.[23]

As observed by Dr. Radhakrishnan, "Buddhism, in its origin at least, is an offshoot of Hinduism."[24] Buddha was a Hindu reformer. "He also, like Jesus, came to fulfill and not to destroy," says Swami Vivekananda. Buddha was opposed to dogmatism prevalent at the time. This may be the reason why he did not acknowledge the authority of the Vedas and established his religion on perception and inference. But in so doing he cut off his religion from its ancient moorings. Though the reliance on authority does not necessarily mean the rejection of reason, yet, it is likely that the followers of the Vedic religion of his time were led primarily by dogmatic faith. As a monk, the Buddha was particularly interested in the jñāna-kāṇḍa (knowledge-section) of the Vedas. He did not care for the karma-kāṇḍa (work-section),

[22]These are (1) ādhyātmika — arising from the psychophysical organism, (2) ādhibhautika — caused by living beings and inanimate objects, and (3) ādhidaivika — caused by cosmic forces. See *Sāṁkhya-darśanam* I:1.

[23]*Vedānta-paribhāṣā* VIII, conclusion.

[24]S. Radhakrishnan, *Indian Philosophy,* I:361.

and even condemned the sacrificial rites, which were meant for the fulfillment of men's secular desires here and hereafter. He laid special emphasis on ethical conduct and attached no importance to rites and ceremonies. He wanted to rid religion of priesthood. The Vedic sacrificial rites were intended to lead the worldly-minded gradually from the search of the temporal to the search of the eternal. The seekers of Liberation were urged to turn away from all these ceremonials. "The foolish who revel in them as the Highest Good succumb again and again to old age and death," says the *Muṇḍaka Upaniṣad.*[25] The *Bhagavad-gītā* also has denounced them.[26]

It is apparent that in the Buddha's time the Vedic fire-sacrifices had turned into elaborate, ostentatious ceremonies performed with or without piety or faith. These also involved the immolation of animals. It was too much for the Compassionate Buddha to bear this brutal custom. He even offered to give his own life to save the life of a goat. Kindness to all living beings became a distinctive mark of his religion. During the Buddha's time, as we noted, the religious atmosphere of the country was rife with subtle metaphysical speculation having little relevancy to the way of life. The Buddha endeavored to avoid, on the one hand, the meaningless rites and ceremonies and, on the other, the vain metaphysical inquiries, and to draw the attention of the people to right living. He also wanted to wean the bigots from the excesses of asceticism involving self-torture. Further, he raised his voice against the fossilized caste-system dependent on parentage, but he did not decry the original caste-order based on *guṇa* and *karma* (natural aptitude and the social role in accordance with it).[27] Nor did he revolt against the existing social organization. The Buddha and his followers always respected the true Brāhmaṇas. "Not by

[25]Mu.U. I:2.7.

[26]See BG II:42-45.

[27]"The fourfold caste is created by Me by the differentiation of guṇa and karma," says Śrī Kṛṣṇa. (BG IV:13.)

birth, but by conduct does a man become a Brāhmaṇa or an outcast," says he.[28] He was opposed to all claim of unwarranted superiority and undue privileges either in social or in monastic life.

7. *Early Buddhism is Hinduism made dynamic. How it spread in India and abroad.*

The Buddha made the Upaniṣadic religion dynamic. He broke its age-old exclusiveness and freely circulated religious ideas through the common dialect of the people. Before this Sanskrit was used in all formal teaching of religion. It was a literary language known to the cultured class. Religious books were written in Sanskrit. It was the Buddha who for the first time delivered sermons in Pāli, the spoken dialect of a vast majority of the people in the central part of northern India, where he travelled as a preacher. He imparted religious teachings without any distinction whatsoever. He had both monastic and lay disciples. He also sent his disciples in all directions as missionaries. As a result, religious and moral ideals permeated all strata of society and brought about a transformation in social conditions and in the lives of the people in general. Buddhist monasteries became centers of education. The humanitarian deeds of the Buddhists improved the material conditions of the country. Arts, literature, and commerce developed. References to work for public good (Pūrta karma) are to be found in the Upaniṣad.[29] Though philanthropic activities, such as digging wells, tanks, etc., constructing roads, planting trees for shade, establishing temples and almshouses, prevailed in India from very ancient times, they received great impetus from the teachings of the Buddha.

For about two hundred years after Buddha's Parinirvāṇa (543 B.C.), his religion was confined within the borders of India. It

[28]*Sutta-nipāta* 641.
[29]See Mu.U. 1:2.10.

prevailed mostly in the northern part of the country and developed side by side with Hinduism. There was no antagonism between the two religions that grew out of the same main stem; rather they influenced each other. As noted by Sir Charles Eliot, "The development of Brāhmaṇism and Buddhism was parallel: if an attractive novelty appeared in one, something like it was soon provided by the other."[30] Buddhist evangelism received a fresh impetus under the patronage of the Emperor Aśōka (273-232 B.C.), who made it a state religion and whose sovereignty extended almost all over India. Himself a Buddhist convert and an ardent follower of the new religion, he made vigorous efforts to propagate Dharma (the moral and religious ideal taught by the Buddha) as widely as possible for "the welfare and happiness of the people" in India and outside. Throughout his empire, he founded monumental pillars engraved with edicts setting forth Dharma and his own objectives; and similar edicts were engraved on rocks and caves. In Pillar Edict VI he says:

> Twelve years after my coronation I ordered edicts on Dharma to be inscribed for the welfare and happiness of the people, in order that they might give up their former ways of life and grow in Dharma in the particular respects set forth.
>
> Since I am convinced that the welfare and happiness of the people will be achieved only in this way, I consider how I may bring happiness to the people, not only to relatives of mine or residents of my capital city, but also to those who are far removed from me. I act in the same manner with respect to all. I am concerned similarly with all classes.
>
> Moreover, I have honored all religious sects with various offerings. But I consider it my principal duty to visit [the people] personally.
>
> I command this edict on Dharma to be inscribed twenty-six years after my coronation.[31]

[30]Charles Eliot, *Hinduism and Buddhism: An Historical Sketch,* 3 vols. (New York: Barnes & Noble, 1921), I:xxx.

[31]Nikam and McKeon, *The Edicts of Aśōka,* p.36.

As regards Aśōka's religious missions we quote the following account:

> One learns from Buddhist literary sources that such missions were sent to the land of the Yavanas (Ionian Greeks), Gandhāra, Kashmir, and the Himalayan regions in the North; to the western part of India such as Aparāntaka; the southern parts such as Vanavāsī and Mysore, and farther south to countries as far as Ceylon and Suvarṇa-bhūmi, the land of gold (Malaya and Sumatra). These records dwell at length particularly on the mission to Ceylon, where Aśōka had sent his son Mahendra and his daughter Saṅghamitrā.
>
> This information is confirmed and further supplemented by Aśōka's thirteenth rock edict wherein it is stated that he tried to spread the Dhamma not only in his territory or among the peoples of the border lands but also in kingdoms far off, such as those of Antiochus (Antiyoko) II, King of Syria, and the kingdoms of four other kings, still farther off, i.e., Ptolemy (Turameya) of Egypt, Antigonos (Antakini) of Macedonia, Alexander (Alikasundara) of Epirus, an ancient district of Northern Greece, and Magas of Cyrenia in North Africa. He has also mentioned the names of Yavanas, Kambojas, Pāṇḍyas, Colas, Andhras, Pulindas, Ceylon, etc., in this context. In the second rock edict we are told that in practically all these countries, Aśōka had opened hospitals, both for men and beasts, had dug wells and tanks and planted trees and medicinal plants for the welfare and happiness of all beings.[32]

It is clear that the efforts of Aśōka were largely responsible for the popularization of the teachings of the Buddha in and outside India. It is he who paved the way for the Buddhist missionaries — occasionally helped by later kings like Kaniṣka[33] — to take Buddhism to central Asia, China, Japan, and Tibet in the north, and to Ceylon, Burma, Thailand, Cambodia and other countries in the south. Obviously, Buddhism did not spread in the wake of

[32]Bapat, P.V., "Aśoka and the Expansionism of Buddhism," in Bapat, ed., *2500 Years of Buddhism*, pp. 59-60.

[33]Ruler of a vast territory extending from Central Provinces in India to Central Asia during the last quarter of the first century, A.D. Like Aśōka he was a Buddhist convert. He belonged to the Kusan branch of the Yuehchi tribe, which originally inhabited Chinese Turkestan (modern Sinkiang).

military conquests; it was the moral fervor of its messengers that paved the way for its expansion. The Buddhist evangelists won the people wherever they went by example as well as by precept. They respected the indigenous faith and culture of the land and worked for their fulfillment. Above all, it was their solicitude for the material and the moral well-being of the people that made an irresistible appeal.

Buddhist monasteries in India turned into great seats of learning. Students from Tibet, China, and other Asiatic countries came to study at the universities of Nalanda, Valabhi, Vikramasila, Odantapuri. In northwest India Taksasila (Taxila, near Rawalpindi in Pakistan) was a Buddhist university town, where Greek, Persian, and Indian scholars met.

It may not be out of place to mention here that though Hinduism was not a missionary religion, yet Hindu religious teachings and cultural traits were conveyed into various Asiatic countries and into Greece and Rome by Brāhmaṇa teachers, travellers, merchants, and immigrants. These came by land and sea routes in the wake of the commercial relation that existed between India and the outside world from very ancient times. This happened before as well as after the rise of Buddhism. There are evidences of Hindu cultural expansion and religious influence in the architectural monuments, iconography, inscriptions, literature, religious and social institutions of many lands, particularly, Cambodia (Kambuja), Annam (Champa), Java, Sumatra, Bali. Two Sanskrit inscriptions of south Cambodia deciphered in 1931 and accepted by the epigraphists as belonging to the 4th or early 5th century A.D., acquaint us with the fact "that Vaiṣṇavism as well as Buddhism flourished side by side with the cult of Śiva in this realm." The Viṣṇu Temple, Aṅgkōr Vat (lit. City Temple) of south Cambodia, is said to be one of the largest (if not the largest) religious structures of the world. Further south on the island of Bali is Borabodur, a whole hill carved into a stupendous Buddhist stupa (7th century A.D.), another masterpiece of ancient Indian architecture.

8. *The Pāli canons and the early Sanskrit texts.* (See Appendix A, "The Buddhist Scriptures.")

Buddha did not write any book nor did he ever refer to any authoritative writing. Immediately after his death his followers felt the necessity of an authentic text for guidance and held a council at Rajagriha (near Patna) for the collection of his teachings. Approximately five hundred monks assembled. Mahākassapa presided over the council. Two important collections in Pāli were made. They are known as the *Vinaya-piṭaka* (Discipline-basket) and the *Sutta-piṭaka* (Sermon-basket). Upāli took the lead in the compilation of the *Vinaya-piṭaka,* Ānanda in the compilation of the *Sutta-piṭaka.* To these two was added a third compilation, the *Abhidamma-piṭaka* (the Metaphysical basket) at the third Buddhist council held at Pataliputra (Patna) under the aegis of the Emperor Aśōka. These three Pāli compilations or baskets (Tripiṭakas) compose the Buddhist canonical literature. The *Vinaya-piṭaka* has five books, the *Sutta-piṭaka* five, and the *Abhidhamma-piṭaka* seven as shown in the following table:

Vinaya-Piṭaka (Discipline-Basket)	*Sutta-Piṭaka* (Sermon-Basket)	*Abhidhamma-Piṭaka* (Metaphysical-Basket)
Mahāvagga	Dīgha-nikāya	Dhamma-saṅgaṇi
Cullavagga	Majjhima-nikāya	Vibhaṅga
Pācittiya	Saṁyutta-nikāya	Dhātu-kathā
Pārājika	Aṅguttara-nikāya	Puggala-paññatti
Parivāra	Khuddaka-nikāya[34]	Kathā-vatthu
		Yamaka
		Paṭṭhāna

[34]This book consists of fifteen minor works, e.g., Khuddaka-pātha, Dhammapada, Udāna, Itivuttaka, Suttanipāta, Vimāna-vatthu, Peta-vatthu, Thera-gatha, Theri-gāthā, Jātaka, Niddesa, Paṭisambhidā-magga, Apadāna, Buddhavaṁsa and Cariyā-piṭaka. Of these *Dhammapada* is widely recognized as a compendium of the Buddhist teachings.

The noncanonical literature consists of commentaries on the canonical texts and a number of original works in Pāli and Sanskrit. The Hīnayāna Buddhists hold to the Pāli canons, the Mahāyāna Buddhists to the Sanskrit works, but recognize the authenticity of the Pāli canons. The earliest known Mahāyāna text is *Prajñā-pāramitā-sūtra* (circa first century B.C.), which was translated into Chinese in the first century A.D. Other early Sanskrit works are *Saddharma-puṇḍarīka-sūtra, Daśabhūmika-sūtra, Aṣṭasāhasrikā-prajñā-pāramitā,* etc. Later Pāli and Sanskrit writings are numerous. Many of these Buddhist texts have been translated into Chinese, or Tibetan, or both.

9. *The decline of Buddhism; its external and internal causes.*

With the extension of Buddhism its intensity decreased. It had to accommodate itself more or less to the local conditions wherever it went. Thus, many new elements were incorporated into the original system. This contributed more to its weakness than to its strength. As Buddhism spread, its centralization became a serious problem, particularly because of the difficulty of communication in those days. In India multitudes of foreign settlers with their divergent customs, racial characteristics and cultural standards found access into the fold of Buddhism, which had no caste restriction as did Hinduism. Some foreign rulers of Indian territories, who inhabited the country, embraced the new religion. At the early stages of its development Buddhism flourished under their patronage, particularly under the Greek King Menander (Milinda, c. first century B.C.) and the Kushan King Kaṇiṣka (c. first century A.D.). But about five hundred years later it suffered incalculable loss of lives and property from the fanatical barbarities of the Huns and other invaders of India. And this hastened its decay. The death blow came from the Turks (c. twelfth century A.D.), who wiped out its remnants. Other than the external, there were internal causes that led to the gradual break-up, decadence, and final disappearance of Buddhism from the land of its birth. It is also to be noted that to a great extent it was reabsorbed by the mother-religion Hinduism.

The successful working of a principle or a plan depends not solely on its soundness or sublimity, but on the competence of its adherents as well. From the very beginning Buddhism emphasized the monastic life and had within the order many Brāhman converts of high intellectual and moral calibre, who constituted its strength to a considerable extent. But at the same time hosts of recruits, without previous training and disciplinary habits, were enlisted indiscriminately. After the Buddha's death there was no supreme authority to control the order, which did not even adhere to the Pāli canons as a body. Nearly a century later a second council was held at Vaisali. There the main issue was the enforcement of discipline, on which the order was split into two parties — conservatives and liberals, known respectively as the Sthaviravādins (or Theravādins) and the Mahāsaṅghikas. Both the parties became further divided and subdivided in the next three centuries. From the Sthaviravādins emerged the Hīnayāna sect, from the Mahāsaṅghikas the Mahāyāna sect — the two main branches of later Buddhism. Today the Hīnayāna prevails in the southern Asiatic countries such as Ceylon, Burma, Thailand, Cambodia, and the Mahāyāna in the Northern countries such as Tibet, China, Japan, Korea.

There was also a cause of dissension in Buddhism itself. Shortly after the death of the Buddha controversies arose on those vital questions to which he gave no categorical answers. To give an illustration, the priest Yamaka expressed the view that the person who attained nirvāṇa was annihilated. Many considered it heretical. The matter was referred to the venerable Sāriputta, who approached the venerable Yamaka and explained to him the unreality of the ego. The implication was, what is unreal is destroyed, but not the reality underlying it.[35] Try howsoever we may, we cannot evade metaphysical questions. The reason is that we cannot explain the facts known — physical or psychical — without reference to what is beyond.

The final solution of sociological and psychological problems rests on metaphysical truths. Neither the objective manifold nor an individual being as perceived by us is self-explanatory. The explanation of the multiplicity is in the unity; of the changeful in the changeless; of the material existence in the conscious spirit that manifests it. The soundness of a religious doctrine, or an ethical code, or a psychological theory depends on the soundness of its metaphysical ground. The Buddha's silence on the subjects of great import, such as the fundamental Reality, the real self of man and his ultimate goal, left ample room for conflicting views with regard to them and consequent disunity in the order.

Another cause of the decline of Buddhism is that it was ill suited to the average man. It could appeal only to those who were disillusioned of the charms of life and sought release from all bondages. Its promise of complete deliverance from sufferings had little meaning for the generality of human beings, whose main concern was the fulfillment of their immediate needs and desires for pleasure. The Vedic religion, on the contrary, took into account not only the seekers of the Supreme Good, but also the seekers of wealth and happiness. It enjoined social duties, ethical conduct, and even the performance of rites and ceremonies for the fulfillment of man's desires for temporal values here and hereafter. It is to be noted that an unrighteous person was not qualified for the performance of sacrificial rites. The search for the temporal good regulated by the ethical ideal was intended to prepare the seeker's mind for the spiritual pursuit; that is, for the direct approach to eternal good. But the Buddha prescribed no rites and

[35]See Henry Clarke Warren, *Buddhism in Translations,* (Cambridge, Mass.: Harvard University Press, 1953), pp.138-145. "There is no ego . . ."

ceremonies. He offered only an austere course of ethical conduct and mental discipline leading to nirvāṇa.

Further, the Buddha did not even acknowledge the Personal God. There was no room in his religion for prayer, worship, or divine grace. He wanted his disciples to rely on themselves and attain nirvāṇa by self-effort. But how many are capable of following the course? As long as death is inevitable and distress inescapable, and as long as there are mishaps and catastrophes beyond human control, man cannot but turn to an almighty, all-knowing, all-merciful Being for His protection, help, and grace.

The strongholds of Buddhism were its monasteries, on which its development depended. The lay community was not a dominant force in it as it was in the Brāhmaṇical religion. From the time of Aśōka the Great (273-232 B.C.) who made Buddhism the state religion, its monasteries had thrived for about six hundred years supported by the munificence of the monarchs and the benefactions of the classes. This was the most glorious period of Buddhism. Then in the fourth century A.D. the Gupta dynasty came into power (320-740 A.D.) and championed the Brāhmaṇical religion. Being deprived of the royal patronage, the Buddhist monasteries languished. This was the beginning of the decline of Buddhism and the rise of Hinduism.

10. *The development of image-worship in Buddhism. Its adoption by Hinduism. The mutual influence of the two religions.*

Since the Buddha did not avow God, ironically, he himself had to fill the place of God in his religion. In less than three hundred years after his disappearance his followers deified him, installed his images in huge and gorgeous temples, and carried on ceremonial worship. Other deities were also introduced liberally and relic-worship started in magnificent stupas. Architecture and sculpture developed immensely. Such a step was necessary to popularize the religion; but this at the same time lowered its high intellectual standard. From a predominantly ethical course, Buddhism turned into a ritualistic religion evidently under the influence of Hinduism. The change was more evident in the Mahāyāna than in the Hīnayāna sect. It was from Buddhism that image-worship entered into Hinduism. The Vedas prescribed the use of concrete symbols, but not the use of images. The Hindu Tantras fully adapted the use of images to the worship of Viṣṇu, Śiva, Śakti and other deities and elaborated on the rituals. At the same time the Hindu deities found access to Buddhism. Both the religions gained from the mutual influence.

Though there was no persecution on either side, both religions had a critical attitude towards the other. This too had a salutary effect on both. Each tried to maintain its moral, intellectual, and social standards as high as possible. In Hindu social life there was a slackening of the rigors of the caste-system determined by parentage. As is evident from the Purāṇas, a tendency to follow the original ideal of the social order based on guṇa and karma (merit and duty) prevailed. Though the principle of universal love and service to all beings was enunciated by the Upaniṣads, its practical application in the lives of the spiritual aspirants in general was not much emphasized before the Buddha. The Hindu Purāṇas took up the ideal and promulgated it. The story of King Ranti Deva in the *Bhāgavatam* is indicative of this (see p. 109). Thus the two religions were getting closer to each other. In many respects Mahāyāna Buddhism resembled Hinduism. On the metaphysical side its Mādhyamika school was tending towards monistic Vedanta.

11. *The four Buddhist schools of philosophy. The advent of Śaṅkara. His distinctiveness.*

In ancient India there were rivalries among different schools of thought. Each school had to maintain its position against the criticism of its opponents. The Buddhist teachers had to meet the challenge of the non-Buddhist philosophers. This led to the development of speculative philosophy in Buddhism. Thus arose four major schools of Buddhist philosophy — (1) Vaibhāṣika, (2) Sautrāntika, (3) Yōgācāra, and (4) Mādhyamika. The first two belonged to the Hīnayāna and the last two to the Mahāyāna branch. The Vaibhāṣikas and the Sautrāntikas are realists. They hold the view that the external objects exist independently of the perceiver's mind and are therefore real. According to the Vaibhāṣikas they are directly perceived; according to the Sautrāntikas they are known indirectly by inference. So the difference between these two schools is evidenced by the way the external objects are cognized. The Yōgācāras maintain subjective idealism. In their view the external objects are but the projections of the mental ideas and therefore unreal. But the Mādhyamikas deny the reality of both physical objects and mental ideas. Their theory is called *śūnya-vāda,* the theory of vacuity or voidness. It is to be noted that according to both Yōgācāra and Mādhyamika schools there can be an illusory appearance without a substratum.

None of these schools recognize any abiding entity or a permanent principle either in the objective manifold or in an individual being. They all uphold the doctrine of momentariness, *kṣaṇa-bhaṅga-vāda.* According to this theory nothing lasts more than an instant. An external object is a continuous conformation of momentary physical elements; similarly, the knowing subject, the ego, is a continuous conformation of psychical elements. As a configuration, either can be of a short or long duration. The view that there is no changeless self beyond the psychophysical flux we call an individual, is known as the doctrine of no-self, *nairātmya-vāda.* The purport of the theories seems to be this: neither the things perceived nor the percipient are real in the way they are assumed to be; being convinced of their falsity, a person can be free from all attachment to them; he who is devoid of "I-ness" and "thy-ness" attains nirvāṇa.

The great Buddhist philosophers and logicians, e.g., Nāgārjuna and Āryadeva of the Mādhyamika school; Asaṅga, Vasubandhu, Diṅgnāga, Dharmakīrti of the Yōgācāra school — maintained by subtle dialectics the doctrines of momentariness and no-self. The Vedic schools, particularly Nyāya, Sāṁkhya, Mīmāṁsā, sharply reacted to their arguments and repudiated their epistemological views in order to overthrow their doctrines. It is said that the great Mīmāṁsā philosopher, Kumārila Bhaṭṭa, defeated Dharmapāla, the celebrated Buddhist teacher of the university of Nalanda, in an open debate (see sec. 15). This discredited Buddhism considerably. It was under Dharmapāla that Kumārila had studied Buddhism. He travelled all over India and had debates with Buddhist and Jaina philosophers, who acknowledged defeat. Thus he made the Mīmāṁsā school predominant. It was at this stage that Śaṅkarācārya appeared on the scene and challenged the Mīmāṁsā school, which was not true to the intent of the Vedas. He established Advaita Vedanta on a rational foundation after having refuted all contrary views, the Vedic as well as the non-Vedic. He consummated the work that Gauḍapāda, the teacher of his teacher (parama guru), had initiated.

The six Vedic schools and the non-Vedic Jainism have explained the Buddhist śūnya-vāda, lit. the theory of voidness or vacuity, as nihilism, as the denial of all existences. According to the great Pāli commentator and author, Buddhaghōṣa (400 A.D.), nirvāṇa is *śūnyatā,* absolute nonexistence. There is no doubt as to the original meaning of the term. But as used by Nāgārjuna (2nd century A.D.), the greatest exponent of the Mādhyamika school, the term *śūnyatā* implies on the one hand, the nonexistence of all that is dependent on causes and conditions, and, on the other, the nonrelational absolute existence, undiversified, incomprehensible, and indescribable. In this sense Nāgārjuna's view can be said to be the precursor of the monistic philosophy, which attains its culmination in the Advaita Vedanta of Śaṅkara.

However, there is a vast difference between the way of Nāgārjuna and the way of Śaṅkara. Whatever may be the implication of the term śūnyatā or śūnya, the trend of śūnya-vāda is to disprove the phenomenal existence rather than to establish the transcendental Reality. But, on the contrary, one can see that the sole purpose of Śaṅkara in disproving the objective manifold has been to establish Nondual Brahman. Unlike the Mādhyamikas, he affirms that there cannot be an illusion without a substratum. By instituting the theory of māyā he has clarified the Advaita position with regard to the empirical order and the transcendental Reality. The cornerstone of his philosophy is man's changeless, indubitable self transcending the ego, which none of the Buddhist schools recognize. According to Śaṅkara, it is by realizing the identity of the individual self with the Supreme Self that one attains Liberation and not by comprehending the falsity of the world of phenomena. Rarely does one find in Nāgārjuna's philosophy any such positive statement on the nature of the ultimate Reality as Śaṅkara has frequently drawn from the Upaniṣads in support of the Advaita view. To quote a few instances:

> Brahman is Truth, Knowledge and Infinite.[36]
>
> This self is Brahman.[37]
>
> Verily all this is Brahman.[38]
>
> He shining all this shines. Through His radiance all this is manifest.[39]

The nondualism of Śaṅkara is based on the rational exposition of the Upaniṣads, the *Brahma-sūtras*, and the *Bhagavad-gītā*. It is not a development of Buddhist religion and philosophy, but their

[36]Tai.U. II:1.3. [37]Ma.U. II. [38]Ch.U. III:14.1. [39]Ka.U. II:2.15.

fulfillment. He was by no means "a veiled Buddhist (pracchanna Bauddha)", as some philosophers presume. Rather the Buddha can be appropriately considered, as indicated by an eminent contemporary scholar, a veiled Advaitist.

12. *The deficiencies of Buddhism. The task before Śaṅkara.*

Though derived from the Upaniṣads, Buddhism was but a partial presentation of their tenets. What metaphysical truths of the source were implicit in the teachings of the Buddha were later repudiated by a majority of his followers. The strength of Buddhism lay in the exemplary life of its founder, its message of lofty ethical conduct, its ideal of self-dedication to the service of all living beings, and its promise of complete deliverance from all sufferings. Notwithstanding its excellences Buddhism had shortcomings, as we have indicated above. Unlike other religions, it recognized no scriptural authority as the authentic source of man's suprasensuous knowledge. It denied the changeless, immortal self beyond the ego, the "sheet anchor" of every other religion. Buddhism acknowledged no Personal God, despite the fact that the belief in Him is indispensable in the lives of a vast majority of human beings. It gave no precise positive view of nirvāṇa, the ultimate Goal of man. Nor did it point to any metaphysical ground of man's disinterested love for all living beings.

In short, Buddhism lacked comprehensiveness. It was especially intended for the life of renunciation. It made no adequate provision for the fulfillment of man's desires for temporal good. One distinctive characteristic of the Vedic religion is that it takes into full consideration different grades of men and prescribes disciplinary courses according to their stages of development with the object of leading them all to the highest goal. It has due regard for the seekers of temporal good as well as for the seekers of the supreme good. This principle of recommending courses in view of the individuals' competence is known as Adhikāri-bheda-vāda, the doctrine of differentiating the aspirants according to their capacities. But Buddhism did not observe this as a tenet. In admitting persons to the holy orders it hardly considered the prerequisites for the monastic life, which were stressed by the Vedic religion. Śaṅkarācārya addressed himself to the supreme task of establishing a religio-philosophical system free from all the deficiencies of Buddhism.

13. *The early life of Śaṅkara. His mission.*

The seer-philosopher Śaṅkarācārya came of a well-known orthodox Brāhmaṇa family of Malabar in southwest India. He was thoroughly steeped in the Vedic lore. While the Buddha denied the authority of the Vedas, Śaṅkara was fully loyal to them. Yet he cannot be charged with dogmatism. In his interpretation of the Vedic mystical truths and religious tenets, he was rational throughout. His arguments are remarkable for their cogency. His religio-philosophical system is well-known for its consistency. In his view there cannot be any illogical authority. An authentic source of knowledge must be rational. So the acceptance of authority does not necessarily mean the rejection of reason. It is not unreasonable to rely on the reliable. The transcendental truths, though supramental and suprarational, are not irrational. They admit of rational exposition. They explain the facts of life we experience and do not counteract them.

Even as a boy Śaṅkara was calm and contemplative. His intellect and memory were prodigious. By the time he was seven years old he had finished the entire course of the Vedic studies under an able teacher, who was astounded by the pupil's genius. The boy's profound scholarship and wisdom won the admiration of one and all. His fame extended far and wide. Students gathered around him. The King of Kerala sent him presents and paid his respects. But learning and fame, wealth and position, meant little to young Śaṅkara, whose mind yearned for the experience of the supreme Truth, the sole reality of Brahman. He decided to leave home and approach the great teacher Gōvindapāda, a perfect knower of Brahman, for instruction and initiation into the monastic life (sannyāsa). He had lost his father at the age of five. Now he was eight. The widowed mother naturally wanted to keep her only child to herself. But Śaṅkara's earnestness prevailed upon her to give permission to leave on the condition that wherever he might be, he would come to her at the time of death and perform her funeral rites. Later in life, an ordained sannyāsī as he was, Śaṅkara kept his word.

At Onkarnath on the river Narmada, Śaṅkara lived at the feet of his guru about three years and realized Nondual Brahman in nirvikalpa samādhi. As a result of this experience his heart was filled with spontaneous love for one and all, compelling him to enlighten their minds and guide them on the way to supreme peace and blessedness. He was told by Guru Gōvindapāda that he had come to this world to fulfill a divine mission: to reinstate the Vedic religion in its pristine purity and glory after its decline during the rise of Buddhism. To accomplish this purpose he was to write a commentary on Bādarāyaṇa Vyāsa's *Brahma-sūtras* (a resumé of the Upaniṣadic teachings and the basis of the Vedanta philosophy) and establish Advaita Vedanta as the meeting ground of all monotheistic and dualistic views, contradictory though they might appear to be. According to an Advaitist, one and the same fundamental Reality is viewed differently from different standpoints by the founders of different systems.

14. *Śaṅkara as a teacher. Lays the foundation of Advaita philosophy by writing commentaries on the triple basis of Vedanta.*

At the instruction of the guru, Śaṅkara, a young boy of twelve, came to Varanasi (Banaras), an ancient seat of the Vedic religion and culture, and started teaching in public. Here his first monastic disciple, Sanandana (afterwards known as Padmapāda), one of the chosen four, joined him.[40] As a personal attendant he was closest to Śaṅkara. Gradually many more disciples came. Śaṅkara's charming personality, his lucid and cogent exposition of the scriptural texts, and his marvelous presentation of the sublime truths drew around him many a scholar and seeker of Self-knowledge, who were invariably older than the teacher himself. As an illumined personage ever established in the knowledge of the identity of the self with Brahman, he worked for the good of humanity only with a semblance of the ego.

After staying in Varanasi for some time, Śaṅkara travelled on foot with his disciples all the way to Hardwar and from Hardwar to Badarikashrama, a place of pilgrimage near the source of the Alakananda[41] in the high Himalayan altitudes. A temple of Viṣṇu stands there. Pilgrims from all parts of India come and worship there every year during the summer. On his way from Varanasi Śaṅkara visited every notable sacred place and worshipped the Deity in the temple, setting an example for the followers of the path of devotion and demonstrating at the same time that a knower of Nirguṇa Brahman (the Impersonal Absolute) is not devoid of devotion to Saguṇa Brahman, the Personal God. It is said in the *Bhāgavatam:* "Such is the excellence of the Lord Hari (the Remover of all distress) that even the sages whose delight is in the Supreme Self and who are free from all bondages offer the

[40]Padmapāda's sub-commentary on Śaṅkara's commentary on the first four Sūtras (aphorisms) of the *Brahma-sūtras* is well-known as Pañcapādikā. It laid the foundation of the Vivaraṇa school, one of the two main schools of Advaita Vedanta of Śaṅkara. The other is the Vācaspati school.

[41]The Ganges is formed of three streams in the Himalayas — the Bhagirathi, the Mandakini, and the Alakananda. The Bhagirathi is the main stream. The two others are tributaries.

Supreme Lord spontaneous devotion."[42] According to Advaita Vedanta, only highly qualified spiritual aspirants can follow the path of knowledge, the direct approach to Nirguṇa Brahman. Others have to realize Saguṇa Brahman along the path of devotion before they can reach the Nirguṇa.

Wherever the old temples were found dilapidated, neglected, or even deserted, Śaṅkara had them rehabilitated. At every place crowds of people came to see him and hear his words of wisdom. It is said that the illumined souls sanctify sacred places, which have a tendency to degenerate in course of time. This may be one of the reasons why he made it a point to visit holy places as he travelled on foot throughout the length and breadth of India 'well-nigh twice.'

While staying at Badarikashrama he wrote his most important works — the commentaries on the ten principal Upaniṣads, the *Brahma-sūtras,* and the *Bhagavad-gītā,* the triple basis of Vedanta philosophy. And he taught his disciples what he wrote. It took about three years. He then visited other holy places in the Himalayas, e.g., Kedarnath (the temple of Śiva, near the source of the Mandakini), Gangotri and Gomukhi (the source of the Bhagirathi), and Yamunotri (close to the source of the Yamuna). Even today these places are not easily accessible.

15. *Śaṅkara meets Kumārila Bhaṭṭa. Debates with Maṇḍana Miśra, the great Mīmāṁsā philosopher, who acknowledges defeat and follows him as a disciple.*

After resting for some time at Uttarakashi (a well-established Himalayan retreat of the ascetics for the quiet life of study, contemplation and meditation), Śaṅkara came down to the plains and walked as far as Prayag (Allahabad), an ancient seat of Hindu culture, at the confluence of the Ganges and the Yamuna. His

[42]SB I:7.10.

purpose was to hold a debate with Kumārila Bhaṭṭa, the greatest advocate of the Mīmāṁsā system, which upheld the Vedic ritualism in opposition to the way of Self-knowledge and the monastic ideal. As the Mīmāṁsā school was predominant at the time, the defeat of Kumārila would prove the invalidity of his system and the validity of Advaita Vedanta. It so happened that just at that time Kumārila was getting ready to immolate himself on a funeral pyre of corn husks in expiation of his sin against his teacher Dharmapāla of Nalanda. He had studied Buddhism under Dharmapāla disguised as a Buddhist sramaṇa (itinerant ascetic) with the secret object of challenging him in a debate on behalf of the Mīmāṁsā school (see sec. 11).

Kumārila directed Śaṅkara to hold the debate with his pupil, Maṇḍana Miśra, whom he considered even greater than himself and who was living at the time at Mahishmati (a small city not far from Onkarnath where Śaṅkara met his guru Gōvindapāda). Followed by his disciples Śaṅkara went there. Though at first annoyed at the sight of the shaven head of the young sannyāsī, Maṇḍana Miśra agreed to the debate. Now the question arose, who was to be the arbiter? Something unprecedented in history happened. Both the parties agreed to the arbitration by Maṇḍana's very wife, Ubhayabhāratī, who was well reputed for her erudition and keen understanding. It was a very delicate situation for her; for, according to the custom of those days, the stake at the debate was that the losing contestant would embrace the winner's view and way of life. Sharp disputation went on for about eighteen days. Finally, Ubhayabhāratī conceded that Śaṅkara had won. Maṇḍana Miśra left his hearth and home and followed Śaṅkara as a disciple. In monastic life he became known as Sureśvarācārya, the celebrated author of a number of valuable works on Advaita Vedanta. Of the chosen four disciples of Śaṅkarācārya — Padmapāda, Sureśvara, Hastāmalaka, and Tōtakācārya — the last two came later.

16. *Śaṅkara travels all over India, propagates the teachings, and works for the restoration of the Vedic religion unto the last hour of his life.* (See Appendix B, "The Vedic Scriptures.")

Śaṅkara was by now past sixteen. After completing his tour in South India as far as the temple of Rāmeśvara Śiva, near the southernmost point of India, he turned northwards and travelled throughout the length and breadth of the country, revisiting many of the holy places. At every notable place he explained the Advaita position and invited its opponents of the Vedic as well as of the non-Vedic schools, to open debate. But not many accepted the challenge. There were a number of debates, mostly with the supporters of the Vedic systems, but none as momentous as the one with Maṇḍana Miśra. In most places people came to him for enlightenment and guidance, for the solution of their problems and for the discussion of their views. He did not reject any religious doctrine or system of thought altogether, not even the Buddhist or the Jaina; but he pointed out its deficiencies, its misconceptions, its incongruities with the Vedic teachings, rectifying its errors and drawbacks, and striving to make it harmonious with the Advaita view. He prescribed religious courses according to the worshipper's inner development and situation in life. He stressed the performance of duties according to the social status (varṇa) and the stage of life (āśrama). He wanted to reform the social order by reforming the lives of individuals without any revolutionary attempt.

In accordance with the Vedic social ideal Śaṅkara enjoined on every householder the performance of a daily fivefold duty: (1) the worship of God or the deity representing some aspect of God, (2) the cultivation of scriptural knowledge, (3) the preservation and development of the ancestral heritage, (4) service to humanity, and (5) service to other living creatures. This was intended for the discharge of a man's fivefold debt, viz.: (1) debt to God or the deities controlling the cosmic phenomena, (2) debt to the seers and sages for their legacy of spiritual knowledge, (3) debt to the forebears for their cultural bequest, (4) debt to human beings for the services received knowingly or unknowingly, and (5) debt to other living creatures for helping us in countless ways. Here the individual life is conceived as an integral part of the cosmic life. An individual is related not only to his family, community, nation, the human race, the animal world, but to the cosmos as a whole. Man is considered a born debtor. He has more debts to pay than the right to claim. Indeed, he owes to the world much more than the world owes him. For each morsel of his food millions of hands have to work; so also for each piece of cloth he wears. Even tiny creatures render him great service, being ever engaged in cleaning the air, water, and soil.

In many places Śaṅkara established not only monasteries and temples, but also Sanskrit academies for the Vedic culture. Besides the commentaries on the Upaniṣads, the *Brahma-sūtras,* and the *Bhagavad-gītā,* he wrote a number of valuable guide-books, both in prose and poetry, for the seekers of Self-knowledge. He composed many poems and hymns in praise of Śiva, Viṣṇu and Śakti. He stressed the worship of the Personal God especially in these three aspects. His poetry is remarkable for the sublimity of thought and devotional fervor. He was as great a poet as a prose-writer. His style is fluent and rhythmical. His language is marked by profundity and clarity. About twenty-two commentaries, seventy-five hymns and poems, and fifty-four guide-books and primers are ascribed to him. Several of them were not his composition in the opinion of many. Śaṅkara was a versatile genius: a mystic, a saint, a philosopher, a polemist, an indefatigable reformer, and a literary man of the highest order.

After twenty years intense work for the revival of the Vedic religion throughout India, Śaṅkara came to Kedarnath for the second and last time. He was now in his thirty-second year. He knew that the term of his life was going to expire. But something was yet to be done for the continuity of the work. For the cultivation and the dissemination of spiritual knowledge under monastic guidance he had planned the foundation of four principal monasteries (maths) at four cardinal points of India — at Śṛṅgerī in the south, at Purī in the east, at Dwārkā in the west, and at Yōśī in the north. Each monastery, under the leadership of one of his four chief disciples, was meant to be the custodian of one of the four Vedas. India was to be divided into four sections — southern, eastern, western and northern — each under the jurisdiction of one of the four monasteries. Being aware of his approaching end Śaṅkara called his disciples to his side and told them about his plan.

The monastery at Śṛṅgerī had already been established by him with Sureśvarācārya as its head. Now he assigned to Padmapāda the leadership of the Gōvardhan Math at Purī, Hastāmalaka the leadership of the Sāradā Math at Dwārkā, and Tōtakācārya the leadership of the Jyōtirmath at Yōśī in the Himalayas. He also decided that *Yajur-Veda* was to be taken care of by Śṛṅgerī Math, *Ṛg-Veda* by Gōvardhan Math, *Sāma-Veda* by Sāradā Math, and *Atharva-Veda* by Jyōtirmath. The head of each monastery was to promote both by example and precept the spiritual well-being of the laity as well as the monastics within his jurisdiction. There should be no ill-will towards any religious community. Śaṅkara organized the Vedantic order of sannyāsins under ten main heads. Of these ten groups, three were made over to Śṛṅgerī Math, two to Gōvardhan Math, two to Sāradā Math, and three to Jyōtirmath. Further, he drew up certain regulations for the guidance of the monasteries.

As he got ready to leave the body in mahāsamādhi he asked the disciples if they had any question to ask. The disciples said, "Through thy grace, O thou divine master, the purpose of our life is fulfilled. What else shall we ask for? Thou hast given us all that we need. Now it remains with us to follow thy example and carry out thy orders." "I bless with all my heart that you be fully established in the knowledge of Brahman, and dedicate yourself to the propagation of the same," spoke Śaṅkara as he closed his eyes. Perfect stillness prevailed over the mountaintop sacred to Śiva, well guarded by snow-clad peaks!

17. *Śaṅkara's special contribution: a complete religio-philosophical system.*

Śaṅkara's special contribution to world-culture is the presentation of the most comprehensive and coherent religio-philosophical system, which is intended not to antagonize, but to fulfill, other systems of thought and culture. Its method is to appraise them in the light of the universal truths, to which they are expected to conform, and not to categorically deny them. By a rational exposition of the three standard works on Vedanta — the Upaniṣads, the *Brahma-sūtras,* and the *Bhagavad-gītā* — he has held before man a complete perspective of life, in which mysticism, philosophy, religion, psychology, logic, ethics, and aesthetics have their appropriate places.

In his view the same Impersonal Absolute has various aspects in relation to the manifold. The one and the same Supreme Being can be approached in many different ways. There is no contradiction in his system between faith and reason, between knowledge and devotion, between action and contemplation. The relative importance of different aspects of life — spiritual, moral, intellectual, aesthetic, and physical — have been determined and their coordination indicated. The path of pleasure and the path of perfection are harmonized. Being well regulated the one leads to the other, which is the direct way to the supreme Goal.

Śaṅkara has maintained by reason, as well as on the authority of the scriptures, the reality of Nondual Brahman and disproved all contrary views, the Vedic and the non-Vedic. By cogent arguments he has refuted the ritualism of the Mīmāṁsā school, the dualism of Sāṁkhya and Yōga, the pluralism of Nyāya and Vaiśeṣika, the realism, the idealism, and the nihilism of the Buddhist schools as well as their theory of momentariness. Further, he has repudiated the Jaina plurality of souls and the incongruity in their nature. The absolute unity of Reality as Pure Being-Consciousness-Bliss affirmed by Śaṅkara is the ultimate ground of all metaphysical conceptions, of all religious doctrines, of all scientific truths, and of all ethical ideals. There is the culmination of human knowledge.

18. *The influence of Śaṅkara's Nondualism on other Vedanta schools. It has created a monistic trend in all of them.*

Śaṅkara's Advaita has changed the tone of Hindu religion and philosophy. Since his time the monism of Vedanta has dominated the religious life and thought of India. All dualistic and pluralistic doctrines have paled into insignificance. Atheism has all but disappeared. The Vedic religion has flowed in two main channels: (1) nondualism, and (2) monotheism. The two schools based on Śaṅkara's commentary on the *Brahma-sūtras* — known as the Vivaraṇa school and the Vācaspati school — are nondualistic. The five Vaiṣṇava schools — the Viśiṣṭādvaita of Rāmānuja, the Dvaitādvaita of Nimbārka, the Dvaita of Madhvācārya, the Śuddhādvaita of Vallabhācārya, and the Acintyabhedābheda of Śrī Caitanya,[43] are monotheistic. All these five strictly come under Vedanta, being founded on its triple basis — the Upaniṣads, the *Brahma-sūtras,* and the *Bhagavad-gītā.* They are all monistic in the sense that none of them recognize two ultimate principles but a

[43]Actually founded by Śrī Jīva Gōswāmī on the teachings of Śrī Caitanya and later corroborated by Valadeva Vidyābhūṣaṇa by a commentary on the *Brahma-sūtras.*

single fundamental reality, one Supreme Being that holds the entire manifold. God is the sole reality according to all of them.

Not only is there no other God, but there is nothing else beyond Him. He is the One Self of all that exists. There is no absolute dualism in Vedanta. Even the system of Madhva, though usually designated as dualism (dvaita), is not dualistic in the sense in which the Sāṁkhya system of Kapila is. As regards Madhva's dualism Prof. Hiriyanna remarks:

> If the Advaita explains the prevailingly absolutistic standpoint of Upaniṣadic teachings by postulating only one reality and explaining the rest of the universe as its appearance, the Dvaita does the same by postulating God as the supreme entity and explaining the rest as altogether dependent upon him.[44]

Besides the schools of Vaiṣṇavism there are in Hinduism other monotheistic schools, e.g., those of Śaivism and Śāktism. The same Supreme Being is worshipped in three different aspects: as Viṣṇu (the Omnipresent Preserver) by the Vaiṣṇavas, as Śiva (the All-good and transcendent Being) by the Śaivas, and as Śakti (Śiva's power, the Mother of the Universe) by the Śāktas. The monotheistic systems of the Śaivas and the Śāktas, though in many respects similar to those of the Vaiṣṇava schools, are not usually included in the Vedanta philosophy, since they are not directly based on the *Brahma-sūtras* in the way Advaitism and Vaiṣṇavism are. Nevertheless, they recognize the authority of, and are sustained by, the triple Vedanta — the Upaniṣads, the *Brahma-sūtras,* and the *Bhagavad-gītā.* The same Upaniṣadic Brahman is conceived by the Vaiṣṇavas as Sat-cid-ānanda Viṣṇu, by the Śaivas as Sat-cid-ānanda Śiva. It is the dynamic aspect of Śiva that the Śāktas worship as Śakti (power). Thus in a wide sense the Śaiva and the Śākta schools are Vedantic. None of them is

[44]M. Hiriyanna, *The Essentials of Indian Philosophy,* (London: George Allen and Unwin, 1949) p.195.

dualistic. Kāśmīra-Śaivism and Śāktism are even closer to Advaita Vedanta in their metaphysical conceptions than Vaiṣṇavism.

It may be noted in this context that present-day Hinduism is, truly speaking, the religion and philosophy of Vedanta. Hinduism is a misnomer.[45] Its original names are *Vaidika-dharma* (the Vedic religion) and *Sanātana-dharma* (the Eternal religion). None of the six Vedic systems but Vedanta has a religious following in Modern India. There are, however, solitary instances of spiritual aspirants who follow the purely Sāṁkhya or the Yōgic method of self-realization. Buddhism in its decadence has been assimilated by Hinduism. It did not die out in India. Finally, by declaring the Buddha an Incarnation of God the Hindu sages turned the Buddha into a Hindu god and his religion into a part and parcel of Hinduism. In three Sanskrit hymns on the Ten Incarnations of Viṣṇu (Daśāvatāra-stōtra), one of which is ascribed to Śaṅkara, the Buddha is paid tribute as an Incarnation. Living Hindu religion is mainly monotheistic Vedanta in different forms. Its prevailing monistic tone is due to the influence of Śaṅkara's Advaita Vedanta.

19. *The sum and substance of Śaṅkara's Advaita philosophy. The meaning of "Brahman is real; the world is unreal."*

As stated by Śaṅkara, the gist of the Vedantic texts, numerous as they are, is this: "Brahman is real; the world is unreal. The jīva is verily Brahman and no other."

[45]The word *Hinduism* is derived from *Sindhu*, the Sanskrit name of the river Indus, which the ancient Persians misspelt as *Hindu*. Gradually the term *Hindu* was applied to the inhabitants of ancient India, and their religion became known as Hinduism. Similarly, *India* is a foreign appelation, derived from the same word *Sindhu*, which the Greeks mispronounced as *Indus* and called the adjoining country *India* and her people "the Indians." The original name of the country is *Bhārata* or *Bhārata-varṣa*.

In declaring the reality of Brahman and the unreality of the world, Advaita Vedanta repudiates the ultimate reality of the world of experience, but not its empirical existence. When the jīva attains illumination and realizes Brahman the Absolute, the relative order disappears altogether. So from his standpoint the world is utterly false. But an unillumined person invariably perceives the phenomenal world and not Brahman. To him the diversified universe is a fact of experience; it is not false in the sense that the son of a barren woman is false. Nobody ever perceives the son of a barren woman either in reality or in illusion. As long as a person dreams, the dream-world is real to him; dream-water allays his dream-thirst. He knows the dream-world to be unreal only when he wakes up. So says Śaṅkara: "Empirical experiences are valid until the identity of the self with Brahman is realized, as are dream-experiences until awaking."[46]

To be explicit, the world, as characterized by Advaita Vedanta, is neither real nor unreal. It is not real, because it is sublated by the knowledge of Nondual Brahman. Yet it is not unreal, because it is a fact of experience for the unillumined. Thus, the world-order can be viewed from the standpoint of the illumined and also from the standpoint of the unillumined. On this twofold world-view Śaṅkara observes:

> This phenomenal world, caused by diversification and deceptive, is a fact for those who hold that things are different from Brahman and also for those who do not.
>
> The adherents of the supreme Truth, however, while investigating, in accord with the Śruti, the true nature of things, whether they really exist or not, arrive at the conclusion that Brahman alone *is,* the One without a second, beyond all relativity. So there is no contradiction between the two views.
>
> We do not maintain the existence of anything but Brahman in the state in which the Supreme Truth is attained; as the Śrutis say, "One

[46]BS II:1.14, S.com.

only without a second" and "Without interior or exterior." Nor do we deny in the relative plane of name and form the validity for the ignorant of the empirical facts comprising action, its agent, its instrument, its result, and so forth.

Therefore, the scriptural and the empirical outlooks rest on knowledge and ignorance. So there is no fear of contradiction between them. No school can deny that the existence and the nonexistence of the phenomenal world depend on the relative and the absolute standpoint.[47]

Sense-perception and the Śruti may appear to be mutually contradictory. But they are not. According to Śaṅkara, both are sources of valid knowledge in their respective spheres. The province of sense-perception is the world of appearance. The province of the Śruti is the transcendental reality, which is beyond sense-perception. The suprasensuous cannot be reached even by inference. The reason is that inferential knowledge depends on the knowledge of the invariable concomitance between the thing perceived and the thing inferred, and such knowledge is lacking in the case in point. Nor can any other means of knowledge dependent on sense-perception acquaint us with the nature of the suprasensuous. Therefore, the Śruti is the only valid source of knowledge with regard to the transcendental reality.

Most philosophers and scientists recognize the inherent incapability of perception to probe into the fundamental reality. Its province is the world of appearance.[48] It is with regard to the transcendental reality that the Śruti declares: "There is no diversity whatsoever in this [Brahman]."[49] So it does not contradict sense-knowledge. When one person says, "The sun moves," and another with his astronomical knowledge says, "The

[47]Br.U. III:5.1, S. com.

[48]Cf. Sir James Jeans, *Physics and Philosophy* (New York: The McMillan Co., 1943), p.15. "Our studies can never put us into contact with reality; we can never penetrate beyond the impressions that reality implants in our minds."

[49]Br.U. IV:4.19.

sun does not move," the two statements do not contradict each other, but represent two different viewpoints regarding the sun. Similarly, the two statements "Man is mortal" and "Man is immortal," mutually contradictory though they appear to be, are true from two different viewpoints, physical and spiritual. There is no conflict between them. But the value of either depends on the merit of its standpoint. This is so in all such cases.

The following remarks of Madhusūdana Sarasvatī in his *Advaita-siddhiḥ* are to the point: "Only the empirical validity of perception and other allied means of knowledge is a proven fact; that is not controverted by the scriptures (āgama). What is controverted is its ultimateness, which is by no means a proven fact. Therefore there is no conflict between perception and the scriptures (āgama)."[50]

The fundamental Reality is the substratum of the world-appearance. In fact, it is Nondual Brahman that appears as the manifold. The world, as it appears, is unreal; but in its essential nature as Brahman the world is absolutely real. So the Upaniṣad says: "Verily all this is Brahman."[51] As the supreme principle immanent in the universe, Brahman is its very basis and being. "From Him all things originate, into Him do they dissolve and by Him are they sustained."[52] The same nonrelational, Nondual Brahman is in relation to the world its originator, sustainer, and absorber. Transcendentally Pure Being-Consciousness-Bliss, Brahman as immanent in the universe is its All-pervading, All-knowing, All-powerful, All-merciful Lord. So says Śaṅkara, "Two kinds of Brahman are stated [in the Upaniṣads]: the one having as its adjuncts the diversities of the universe, the modifications of name and form; the other, its contrary, completely free from all adjuncts."[53] The one is called *apara* (the

[50]M.Sarasvatī, *Advaita-siddhiḥ* (Bombay: Nirnaya Sagar Press, xxxx), ch. I, sec. 18, pp.373-74.

[51]Ch.U. III:14.1. [52]*Ibid.* [53]BS I:1.11, S. com.

lower), the other *para* (the higher). The one is saguṇa (with attributes), the other is nirguṇa (without attributes).

20. *The identity of the jīva and Brahman explained.*

From the position of the jīva, the individual experiencer, the world of experience is real, and so is their supreme Ruler. The existence of the individual soul and the universe presupposes the existence of the Supreme Lord, because neither of the two is self-existent or self-sufficient. These three are coexistent and interrelated, but are not on the same grade as manifestations of Brahman. None of the three has a beginning. As pointed out by Śaṅkara, their beginning is untenable.[54] The Supreme Lord is the one Self of all. He holds the universe comprising the living and the nonliving. So says Śaṅkara: "To the contemplative nothing other than the Supreme Lord exists. He is manifest in the eightfold form of the unmoving and the moving, viz. earth, water, fire, air, ether, the sun, the moon, and the individual soul."[55] In the inanimate, He, who is intrinsically Pure Being-Consciousness-Bliss, is manifest only as being, in the animate He is manifest as consciousness as well. It is He who shines as the conscious self in every individual.

One may pertinently ask, how does the undifferentiated One become differentiated, the Unlimited limited, the Changeless changeful? The question is possible only from the standpoint of the unillumined, who view the world-appearance as real. The point is, all differentiations, limitations, and changes belong to the realm of appearance. The transcendental Reality only *appears* to be different from what It is, but does not *become* so. The cause of this appearance, according to Advaita Vedanta is māyā (lit. that which measures), a mysterious principle that apparently measures

[54]See BS II:1.36, S. com.
[55]Dakṣiṇāmūrti-stōtram (Hymn to the Benign Lord in the form of the guru).

the Immeasurable, diversifies the Undiversified, mutates the Immutable. All transformations are in māyā, but are superimposed on Brahman. As is the effect, so is the cause. Just as the world-appearance is neither real nor unreal, so is māyā. It rests on Brahman without affecting Him in the least. Brahman associated with māyā is the Supreme Lord of the universe, its originator, preserver and absorber. He is also the All-gracious Savior of souls. He is the Adorable One. Māyā serves Him as His power.

According to Advaita Vedanta māyā is true so far as the world-appearance is concerned. It does not inhere in Brahman as an ultimate principle. According to all monotheistic systems, māyā, the creative energy of God, inheres in Him. It is inseparably connected with His being. Nevertheless, Advaita Vedanta argues that in that case any changes in māyā must mean changes in God Himself and the seed of imperfection of the world must be within Him; so this position is not tenable.

The phenomenal world is real to the individual soul (the jīva), but cannot be reckoned as his creation. The existence of māyā, its origin, is a fact from his position. With individual ajñāna (ignorance) there must be cosmic māyā, associated with the Supreme Lord (Īśvara). The one betokens the other as the fruit betokens the tree. This does not mean, of course, that cosmic māyā exists because of individual ajñāna. It is individual ajñāna that derives from cosmic māyā and not cosmic māyā from individual ajñāna. Brahman is apparently the locus of both. Brahman with the adjunct of cosmic māyā is Īśvara, the Supreme Lord; Brahman with the adjunct of individual ajñāna is the jīva, the individual soul. Thus the jīva is identical in essence with Īśvara. But with their respective adjuncts, they are ever different from one another. By realizing the essential identity with Īśvara the jīva becomes Brahman, what he really is. Verily, the knower of Brahman attains Brahman.

Īśvarahood is invariably linked with jīvahood. Both are

manifestations of Brahman through māyā in its cosmic and individual aspects. Īśvara is ever related to the jīva as Ruler to the ruled. The one is the supreme object of worship, the other is the worshipper. The jīva can never be Īśvara.[56] They are coexistent and without beginning. But neither is ultimate. As observed by Śaṅkara:

> And He (Īśvara) stands in the empirical realm in the relation of the Ruler to the cognizing souls called the jīvas, which are really one with His own Self (just as portions of ether inside jars are one with the universal ether), but are limited by the aggregates of the body and the senses made of names and forms brought forth by ajñāna. Therefore, the Lordship of Īśvara, His omniscience, omnipotence, are relative to the finite selves due to limiting adjuncts derived from ajñāna, while in reality such expressions as the ruler, the ruled, omniscience, and so forth, do not apply to the Self from whose being all adjuncts are wiped out by right knowledge.[57]

Further he says:

> Moreover, when the consciousness of the identity [of the individual soul with the supreme Being] is aroused by such instruction of their identity as "That thou art," then the finiteness of the individual soul and the creatorship of Brahman vanish at once, because all experience of difference proceeding from wrong knowledge is annihilated by perfect knowledge.[58]

Beyond both jīvahood and Īśvarahood is undifferentiated Pure Consciousness that Brahman is. The truth that the Śruti reveals by the terse formula, "That thou art," is confirmed by reason and verified by the seer's experiences.

21. *In Swami Vivekananda the Buddha and Śaṅkara meet.*

Though well-grounded in the Vedantic texts and Western thought Swami Vivekananda did not formulate a new

[56]See BS IV:4.17. [57]BS II:1.14, S. com. [58]BS II:1.22, S. com.

philosophical system. It is Śaṅkara's Advaita philosophy that he accepted and expounded in modern terms and found its widest application in modern life. So far as the basic ideas of Advaita Vedanta are concerned he does not differ from Śaṅkara, but there are some differences in his way of presentation and the emphasis laid by him on its practical aspects. He lived about twelve centuries after Śaṅkara under altogether different circumstances. He has aligned the spiritual outlook of Śaṅkara with the modern outlook upon life and the world. He has explained from the Advaita position how to spiritualize the modern view and way of life. His aim has been the reconstruction of humanity on a spiritual foundation.

Śaṅkara reinstated the Vedic religion in its pristine purity and glory after a long period of decadence; so did Swami Vivekananda in the present age. While the Buddha did not acknowledge the authority of the Vedas, both Śaṅkara and Vivekananda accepted the Vedic texts as the authentic source of suprasensuous knowledge and found them amenable to reason. If the Buddha can be called "the rebel child of Hinduism," both Śaṅkara and Vivekananda can be regarded its most loyal scions. Both were proud of India's spiritual heritage, and not without reason.

Being a born lover of humanity Swami Vivekananda was naturally drawn more to the Compassionate Buddha as a person than even to Śaṅkara. He united the spiritual idealism of Śaṅkara with the dynamic spirit of the Buddha. In him we find a delightful combination of Śaṅkara's intellect and the Buddha's heart. He impregnated Hinduism with the ideal of complete self-dedication to the service of humanity. He also enkindled in Hinduism the zeal for the dissemination of the gospel of universal truths for the welfare of many, for the happiness of many. Approximately fifteen hundred years after the decadence of Buddhism, Swami Vivekananda was the first spiritual messenger of India to the Western world.

Just as the Buddha's heart cried for the alleviation of the sufferings of one and all without any distinction of caste or creed, race or nationality, age or sex, so did Swami Vivekananda's. With the ideal of renunciation, he has emphasized the ideal of service: "The national ideals of India are renunciation and service. Intensify her in those two channels and the rest will take care of itself."[59] A seeker of Liberation is urged to render service to humanity as a mode of worship. *Ātmanō mōkṣārtham jagaddhitāya ca* ("For one's own Liberation and for the good of the world") is his watchword for the Ramakrishna Order. How earnestly he wants those who are ready to join the banner of service to carry the universal, uplifting message of Vedanta to one and all without any distinction whatsoever!

> Aye, let every man and woman and child, without respect of caste or birth, weakness or strength, hear and learn that behind the strong and the weak, behind the high and the low, behind everyone, there is that Infinite Soul, ensuring the infinite possibility and infinite capacity of all to become great and good. Let us proclaim to every soul — "Arise, awake, and stop not till the goal is reached."[60]

22. *Swami Vivekananda in his youth. His spiritual genius recognized by Sri Ramakrishna at the first meeting.*

It is said that the leaders of men are born and not created. It cannot but be so especially in the case of those perfected souls who do not merge in Brahman but retain their individuality and are reborn, when necessity arises, under Divine dispensation, for the enlightenment and guidance of humanity. Nevertheless, circumstances help to bring out their inborn genius for leadership and prepare the stage for their specific role. Young Naren (Swami Vivekananda's family name was Narendranath Datta, he was nicknamed "Naren"), a lad of eighteen, was recognized as such a

[59]CW V:157. [60]CW III:192.

free soul by Sri Ramakrishna, the great Hindu saint and mystic (1836-1886 A.D.), at their first meeting at Dakshineswar in December, 1881. A sophomore of the General Assembly's Institute[61] in Calcutta, Naren came there accompanied by two of his relatives, who were staunch devotees of Sri Ramakrishna. Naren was a talented singer and expert in instrumental music, and he used to sing at the services of the Brāhma Samāj. That day at the request of the devotees he sang two devotional songs. Sri Ramakrishna went into ecstasy as he heard him sing. Sri Ramakrishna treated Naren with special care and affection and asked him to come again. Naren felt mysteriously drawn to the God-intoxicated saint, and this meeting was a turning point in his life.

Over short intervals, he repeated his visits without any companions. Much bewildered by the saint's loving care and regard for him despite preoccupation with God, one day Naren asked point-blank, "Sir, have you seen God?" "I see Him more intensely than I see you" was the prompt reply. "You can also see Him, if you want," added Sri Ramakrishna. For the first time Naren found a person who could give an affirmative answer to the question on which he had been pondering for a number of years and with which he had already approached several notables without receiving a satisfactory reply.

Born with a deep spiritual disposition and brought up in a religious atmosphere in an age of intellectual ferment, Narendranath was torn between faith and reason. He had come to the conclusion that his problem could not be solved unless God was a fact of experience. Direct perception of God must be the only solvent for all doubts with regard to His existence. The life of Sri Ramakrishna, being a complete demonstration of God-realization, had deep meaning for him, yet he could not readily

[61]Founded by the Scottish General Missionary Board and later known as the Scottish Church College.

accept Sri Ramakrishna's spiritual visions, ecstasies, and experiences.

This was the time when religion was carrying on a last ditch fight, as it were, with materialistic and rationalistic philosophy. Theism, materialism, atheism, agnosticism, and scepticism were vying with one another for a hold on human thought and life. Since the introduction of English education in India about the middle of the eighteenth century, Western ideas had been infiltrating Hindu minds. In his thirst for the knowledge of Truth Narendranath zealously read Western science, history, and philosophy. Being possessed of extraordinary intellect and memory, he did not require much time to prepare his college courses. The rest of the time he could devote to extensive study. For the time being he seemed to be influenced more or less by Hume and Bentham's atheism, Spinoza's pantheism, Darwin's doctrine of evolution, Comte and Spencer's positivism and agnosticism, and other theories of Western philosophy and science.

Even before he met Sri Ramakrishna Narendranath used to live the austere life of a spiritual aspirant and daily practiced meditation on God. His physical valor, moral courage, generous disposition, and self-sacrificing love for others were remarkable. Many more qualities of head and heart betokened his future greatness. Principal Hastie of the General Assembly's Institute marked him as one of the rare geniuses among students. It was from him that Narendranath first heard about the mystical experiences of Sri Ramakrishna, which the professor referred to in the course of explaining the poetic trances of Wordsworth. Urged by spiritual tendencies Narendranath joined the Brāhma Samāj under its third great leader, Keshab Chandra Sen, and regularly attended its services.

It was in 1875 that Keshab met Sri Ramakrishna for the first time and since then had been much drawn to him. The Brāhma

Samāj was a socio-religious movement considerably influenced by Western thought and culture. It was primarily based on reason and ethics and not on the seers' suprasensuous experiences. It served as a check against English-educated youths becoming converts under the influence of the Christian missionaries. But it could not satisfy Narendranath's yearning for direct knowledge of God. The Samāj was opposed to Hindu image-worship, caste-distinction, and child-marriage, and unlike Hinduism supported widow-marriage. Young Naren was in favor of its ideas of reform, but its conventionality lacking in true devotion to God had little charm for him.

23. *India at the time of Sri Ramakrishna; his contribution.*

During the seven hundred years of Mohammedan rule in India, Hinduism had a hard struggle for self-preservation. A number of Hindu saints arose and started reform movements for harmonious relations between the two communities. Since the decline of the Moghul sovereignty in the beginning of the eighteenth century, the country had been in a state of political and social chaos. With the establishment of the British rule, English education was introduced as peace and order were restored. Modern civilization with all its accessories — manners, customs, machinery, steam-boat, locomotive, telegraph — was advancing over the country, while its thoughts and views were encroaching on the minds of the people.

At the same time the Christian missionaries were decrying Hindu social customs and religious beliefs and practices. The loss of political freedom had already dealt a severe blow to the national self-esteem of the Indians. Dazed by the glare and self-assurance of the Western civilization, they began to doubt the efficacy of their traditional ideals and ways of life. Under these circumstances, English-educated Indians often lost faith in their ancient culture and religion and wanted to adopt Western ideals and methods for the salvation of their country. Not a few brilliant Indians actually deserted their time-honored faith and turned atheists or Christian converts.

But the national spirit of India soon reacted to the impact of Western thought and culture. A number of religious and social movements sprang up to stem the tide of the Western cultural aggression. The most important of them all were the Brāhma Samāj of Bengal and the Ārya Samāj of the Punjab. But none of these movements, whether progressive or reactionary, liberal or conservative, were able to call forth the national genius of India. None could point out to India's children the true import of their voluminous scriptures, the universal character of their religion, the inner harmony of their multifarious beliefs, the fundamental unity of their national life despite divergencies of sect, creed, caste, color, custom, and language. None could restore their faith in their ancient heritage and indicate how to accept the new on the basis of the old and apply the eternal religious principles to modern conditions.

It was at this juncture that Sri Ramakrishna appeared. His life and message threw light on all these points. In them Narendranath found the key to the soul of India and the way to arouse her slumbering self-consciousness and engage her in the twofold task of national regeneration and spiritual awakening of humanity at large. Sri Ramakrishna's life was a beacon in an age of spiritual darkness. He spoke from his own experience and not from book-learning or speculative knowledge. His statements corroborated the scriptural truths. His life demonstrated the reality of God.

Sri Ramakrishna realized God not in one particular aspect but in many different aspects and forms. He practiced one after another the different modes of worship and spiritual disciplines of various Hindu cults and systems and reached God through each one of them. Then he followed the Islamic course with a similar result. Later in life he turned to Christianity and had a vision of Jesus Christ and was convinced of His Divine Sonship. As a result of his spiritual realizations his mind was able to dwell on different levels of God-consciousness. It could move up and down the whole gamut of spiritual experience from devotional ecstasy to complete absorption in Nondual Brahman as undivided, undiversified Pure Being-Consciousness-Bliss. The realization of God is the keynote of his teachings. His message can be summed up as follows:

To realize God is the goal of human life.

The methods of God-realization differ according to the seekers' capacities and conditions of life.

By following a progressive course of discipline an individual can proceed towards God from any sphere or level of life.

Every religion is a pathway to God-realization.

There should be harmony among the followers of different religions.

God dwells within man as the inmost self.

Man is to be served in the spirit of worshipping God.

In Sri Ramakrishna's life and message Narendranath found the full meaning of religion.

24. *The training of Swami Vivekananda under Sri Ramakrishna, the Divine Master.*

Since their first meeting towards the end of 1881 Narendranath was in close contact with Sri Ramakrishna until his passing away on August 16, 1886. It was during this period that most of Sri Ramakrishna's lay and other disciples (the would-be monks) gathered around him. Rakhal (later Swami Brahmananda), an intimate friend of Naren, had already met Sri Ramakrishna. Naren used to come to Dakshineswar once or twice almost every week, and sometimes stayed there at night. Other disciples also visited Sri Ramakrishna as often as they could.

One day when Sri Ramakrishna asked him if he saw any light before sleep, Narendranath replied that every night as he closed his eyes to sleep, he saw a ball of light between his eye-brows; it changed colors, gradually expanded and enveloped his whole body with white radiance; while watching this light he fell asleep. Since this was a daily occurrence from his childhood, he thought everybody had a similar experience before sleep, until he spoke about it to a friend. On hearing this Sri Ramakrishna remarked that it indicated his past spiritual greatness, his inborn capacity for meditation on the transcendental Self, and the tendency of his mind to rest on that involuntarily.

Sri Ramakrishna recognized Naren's special aptitude for the attainment of Nirguṇa Brahman, whereas his other disciples had a natural bent of mind for Saguṇa Brahman. He had in his room a copy of *Aṣṭāvakra-Saṁhitā,* a treatise on Advaita Vedanta. He encouraged only Naren to read this. But Naren was not yet ready to comprehend the Advaita (Nondualistic) view, according to which Brahman is the sole Reality. One day, being asked by Sri Ramakrishna, he began reading the book to him. But as soon as he came across the statement that all this is Brahman, he closed the book and going into the adjoining verandah was ridiculing the idea in the presence of a co-villager of Sri Ramakrishna. "Is it not a blasphemy to say that this earthen jar is Brahman, this brick-wall is Brahman, this tree is Brahman?" Sri Ramakrishna at once went out of the room and gently touched him.

The vision of Narendranath was immediately changed. Everything surrounding him seemed shadowy. The solid, tangible, concrete objects appeared as ever-changing forms in the one formless, intangible, all-pervading Reality. For the first time Naren had the foretaste of the Supreme Being, immanent and all-transcendent, to whom the Upaniṣadic seers make obeisance as they say: "To that self-effulgent Being who is in fire, who is in water, who is in plants, who is in trees, who has entered into the whole world, we bow down, we bow down."[62]

Early in 1884 Naren's father, Viśvanātha Datta, who was an attorney-at-law of the High Court in Calcutta, suddenly died of heart-failure. He had a good income, but, being too generous, he liberally helped his relatives and friends, and often lived beyond his means. On his unexpected death the widowed mother of five children found herself in dire pecuniary distress. She was reputed to be an intelligent, pious, and sober woman and faced the situation bravely. But the family was on the verge of starvation. Naren had just graduated from college. Being the eldest son he had to bear the burden of the bereaved family. After a long search he secured temporary employment as a high school teacher. As soon as the school term was over he looked for other employment day in and day out, but without success. Having lived so long in affluent circumstances, Naren came to know from actual experience the sufferings of the poverty-stricken. The family was too proud to beg even the relatives for help.

Greatly distressed in mind Naren came to Dakshineswar and implored Sri Ramakrishna to pray to the Divine Mother for the removal of the distress of the Datta family. "The Mother will not listen to my prayer, since you do not believe in Her," said Sri Ramakrishna, "You better go to the temple yourself and pray to Her. She will listen to your prayer." Putting full trust in Sri Ramakrishna's words, Naren, who hardly believed in image-worship, went to the temple. The vesper service was over. It was about nine o'clock on a Tuesday evening. As soon as Naren stood before the stone image of Kālī, he felt an abiding living presence all around, the image appeared as the embodiment of the all-pervading Conscious Energy that controls the universe. Deeply

[62]Sv.U. II:17.

impressed, he was transported to a different level of consciousness and forgot all about his material needs, all about the distress at home. His only prayer was for true devotion to Her feet, true knowledge, and complete freedom from all bondages.

When he came back to Sri Ramakrishna, he was asked whether he had prayed to the Divine Mother for the fulfillment of the needs of the family. Naren related to him what had happened. Sri Ramakrishna sent him back to the temple urging him to pray for the removal of their material wants. But the same thing happened again. At Sri Ramakrishna's request Naren went to the temple a third time, but with the same result. When he came back, Sri Ramakrishna was highly pleased and said, "Naren, you are not meant for worldly pleasures. Through the Mother's grace your family will be provided with the essential needs of life." It was the first time that Naren fully grasped the deep meaning of the Motherhood of God and of His worship in images and other symbols.

One day in the year 1884, while talking about the Vaiṣṇava tenet of practicing kindness to living beings, Sri Ramakrishna passed into an ecstatic mood and observed, "Oh, no, why kindness! Who are you to be kind? Not kindness to living beings, but service to them in the spirit of worshipping God. Not kindness to the jīva, but serving the jīva as Śiva." Narendranath, who was present at the time, remarked as he came out of the room, "I have found wonderful light in these few words of the Master. It has been the general tendency all these years to practice Vedanta in seclusion. But Vedanta can be practiced in work-a-day life as well. The Vedantic knowledge of the divinity of the soul can be harmonized with a man's common duties. Work and worship can go together. If God grants me the opportunity I will proclaim this message to one and all in course of time."[63]

[63]See Swami Saradananda's *Sri Ramakrishna, the Great Master,* 4th edn. (Madras: Sri Ramakrishna Math, 1952), pp. 817-18.

25. *Sri Ramakrishna's last illness. The inception of the Ramakrishna Order. The attainment of nirvikalpa samādhi by Narendranath.*

In the summer of 1885 Sri Ramakrishna had a throat ailment, which developed into cancer and terminated his life in a year. In spite of illness he did not stop teaching. As usual, visitors came without any previous notice from a long distance and he spoke to them incessantly. This continued till the last day of his life. So his condition grew worse despite the best medical care. For the facilities of medical treatment and attendance he was finally removed to a commodious garden house in Cossipore, a suburb of Calcutta. Here twelve of the young disciples banded together under the leadership of Narendranath and attended on the Master day and night by turn. Their whole-souled devotion and service to the Master united them into a brotherhood, which led to the foundation of the monastic institution known as the Ramakrishna Order. One day the Master presented to each of them a piece of ochre cloth, the symbol of the monastic life.

Sri Ramakrishna's virgin wife, Sri Sarada Devi, whom he looked upon as the earthly image of the Divine Mother, lived in a tiny room on the topmost floor and prepared Sri Ramakrishna's diet. She is venerated by all his followers as the Holy Mother.

Having understood that Sri Ramakrishna would not be with them long, the young disciples became still more eager for the realization of God and intensely carried on their spiritual practice in addition to serving the Master. Naren's mind yearned for nirvikalpa samādhi. From time to time he begged the Master to grant him the same. One summer evening in 1886 — a few months before Sri Ramakrishna's passing away — as Naren was meditating in a room downstairs, he lost all external consciousness, his body became stiff and perfectly still, as if life had passed out of it. His brother-disciple, Gopal Senior, who was in the room, was alarmed and hurried upstairs to report to the Master that something tragic had happened.

Sri Ramakrishna, who knew the truth, smiled and remarked, "Now he has what he was so eager for. Let him stay there for a while." On regaining the usual consciousness Narendranath hastened to see the Master, who spoke to him thus: "Now the Divine Mother has opened unto you the whole truth. But the key will remain with me. You will have to work for the fulfillment of the Divine Mission for which you have been chosen. When the work will be over, this treasure will again be opened unto you."

On another occasion Naren expressed a strong desire to remain immersed in nirvikalpa samādhi. At this the Master said, "You are not meant for this. You are to see God in one and all and serve Him in them. To realize God in nirvikalpa samādhi is knowledge (jñāna). A few blessed souls come down from that stage and see God dwelling in all: this is supra-knowledge (vijñāna)." It may be noted that this is the state in which Sri Ramakrishna constantly lived. And this he set as an ideal before his monastic disciples. Later on we shall find this level of God-consciousness to be Swami Vivekananda's forte.

A few days before his passing away on August 16, 1886, Sri Ramakrishna told the young disciples to look upon Naren as their leader, and then turning to Naren he said, "I leave the boys to your care. Hold them by your love. See that they devote their lives to the spiritual ideal and do not go back to the world." He also transmitted his powers to Naren saying, "By these powers you will accomplish great things in the world. Until then you will not go back where you have come from." Next to Naren in the brotherhood was Rakhal, afterwards Swami Brahmananda, who was chosen by the Divine Mother as the spiritual son of Sri Ramakrishna and whom Naren regarded as the Master's successor and called "Rajah (king)" with his approval and told the other brother-disciples to do the same. Afterwards, Rakhal became known to the followers of Sri Ramakrishna as the Maharaj (the king of kings) and Naren as Swamiji.

26. *Founding of the new monastery and the Ramakrishna Order after the Master's departure. Swami Vivekananda as the itinerant monk. His arrival in America.*

Shortly after the Master's disappearance the young disciples[64] rallied and started, with the help of the lay disciples, a monastery in a rented house at Baranagore close to Dakshineswar. There in January, 1886, at Naren's suggestion, they all took sannyāsa (the monastic vow) according to the Vedic rite. There were fifteen of them. Each had a new name. Naren became known as Swami Vivekananda and Rakhal as Swami Brahmananda. Another disciple of Sri Ramakrishna joined the monastic order a few years later. Thus the nucleus of the Ramakrishna Order of monks was formed with sixteen immediate disciples of the Master. Under the guidance of Swami Vivekananda the monastery became an animated center of intense spiritual practice, devotional worship, scriptural study and discussion. The monastics lived a very austere life. But most of them did not live in the monastery very long. Their minds soon became eager for the itinerant life of renunciation, for contemplation and meditation in solitude. Many of them went out on pilgrimages to the Himalayas and other parts of India.

For about six years Swami Vivekananda travelled as an itinerant monk all over India from the Himalayas to Cape Comorin. He came in close touch with the people of all classes and ranks, from the mahārājas to the peasants, from the learned Brāhmaṇas to the pariahs. His heart bled at the sight of the abject poverty, misery, and ignorance of the Indian masses. He

[64]Excepting one, Gopal Senior, who was even older than Sri Ramakrishna by six years, the rest were in their twenties or younger.

concluded that for the regeneration of India he must shoulder a twofold arduous task: the upliftment of the people in general and the improvement of the condition of women.

Filled with the deepest compassion for the suffering millions of India, as Swami Vivekananda awaited an opportunity to start work for the reconstruction of the country, there arose an occasion for his coming to America. He was asked by some of his devoted admirers of southern India to represent Hinduism at the Parliament of Religions to be held at the World's Fair in Chicago in September, 1893. This he hailed as an opening for his contemplated mission. He conceived the idea that he could convey to America India's spiritual wisdom, and in return America could provide India with scientific knowledge and technology for the improvement of her material conditions. On May 31, 1893, he sailed from Bombay and arrived in Vancouver, British Columbia on the steamer Empress of India on July 25, via Colombo, Singapore, Canton and Yokohama (see frontispiece). From Vancouver he came to Chicago by train.

27. *Swami Vivekananda's message at the Parliament of Religions in Chicago. Stabilizing the Vedanta work in America.*

All obstacles to his admission to the World's Parliament of Religions being providentially removed, Swami Vivekananda was finally accepted as a delegate of Hinduism. His message of the divinity of man and the harmony of religions delivered from the depth of his inner experience made a profound impression on the audience at the Parliament of Religions and paved the way for the propagation of the universal gospel of Vedanta in the Western world. While delivering his address at the opening session of the august assembly on September 11, 1893, he recited the following Sanskrit verse rendered into English, illustrating the Vedantic attitude towards the different religions of the world:

As the different streams having their sources in different places all mingle their water in the sea, so O Lord, the different paths which men take through different tendencies, various though they appear, crooked or straight, all lead to Thee.[65]

In his paper on Hinduism read at the Parliament on September 19, he echoed the Vedic sage declaring the divinity of the soul and the way to immortality:

"Hear, ye children of immortal bliss! Even ye that reside in higher spheres! I have found the Ancient One, who is beyond all darkness, all delusion: knowing Him alone you shall be saved from death over again." "Children of immortal bliss" — what a sweet, what a hopeful name! Allow me to call you, brethren, by that sweet name — heirs of immortal bliss — yea, the Hindu refuses to call you sinners. Ye are the Children of God, the sharers of immortal bliss, holy and perfect beings. Ye divinities on earth — sinners? It is a sin to call a man so; it is a standing libel on human nature.[66]

In his concluding address at the final session of the Parliament of Religions on September 27, 1893, he proclaimed with a prophetic voice:

The Christian is not to become a Hindu or a Buddhist, nor a Hindu or a Buddhist to become a Christian. But each must assimilate the spirit of the others and yet preserve his individuality and grow according to his own law of growth.

If the Parliament of Religions had shown anything to the world it is this: It has proved to the world that holiness, purity, and charity are not the exclusive possessions of any church in the world and that every system has produced men and women of the most exalted character. In the face of this evidence, if anybody dreams of the exclusive survival of his own religion and the destruction of the others, I pity him from the bottom of my heart, and point out to him that upon the banner of every religion will soon be written, in spite of resistance: "Help and not Fight," "Assimilation and not Destruction," "Harmony and Peace and not Dissension."[67]

[65] *Hymn on the Greatness of Śiva,* 7.
[66] CW I:9. See Sv.U. II:5 and III:8.
[67] CW I:22.

Vivekananda as a Delegate to the Parliament of Religions

For nearly three years he stayed in different places from the Atlantic Coast to the Mississippi River, lecturing before popular and learned audiences, holding classes and conversations in drawing rooms and clubs, giving interviews to people of various ranks, and gaining admirers, friends, and followers by his all-comprehensive teachings and forceful, radiant personality.

Closely allied with his message of the divinity of the soul and the harmony of religions was his teaching of the realization of God as the goal of life. Man must realize his divine nature. This is the supreme purpose of life. This is the one end of every religion. Though the goal is the same, the ways differ to suit men and women of different tendencies and capacities. Hinduism emphasizes the ideal of God-realization above all. "This is the very center, the very vital conception of Hinduism," said he at the Parliament of Religions. This is the theme that he often reverted to. We quote from two of his addresses delivered in America:

> The end of all religions is the realizing of God in the soul. This is the one universal religion. If there is one universal truth in all religions, I place it here, in realizing God. Ideals and methods may differ, but this is the central point. There may be a thousand different radii, but they all converge to the one center, and that is the realization of God.[68]

> Religion is realization, not talk, nor doctrines, nor theories, however beautiful they may be. It is being and becoming, not hearing or acknowledging; it is the whole soul becoming changed into what it believes. That is religion.[69]

Before leaving America he was able to consolidate his work by establishing the Vedanta Society of New York and facilitating the publication of three of his books, *Rāja-yōga, Karma-yōga,* and *Bhakti-yōga.*

About the arduousness of his task of teaching the Hindu

[68]CW I:322-23.

[69]CW II:394. (The lecture on "The Ideal of a Universal Religion" delivered in New York, January 12, 1896.)

religion to the Western world Swami Vivekananda wrote in a letter to Alasinga Perumal on February 17, 1896:

> To put the Hindu ideas into English and then make out of dry philosophy and intricate mythology and queer startling psychology, a religion which shall be easy, simple, popular, and at the same time meet the requirements of the highest minds — is a task only those can understand who have attempted it.
>
> The abstract Advaita must become living — poetic — in everyday life; out of hopelessly intricate mythology must come concrete moral forms; and out of bewildering yōgī-ism must come the most scientific and practical psychology — and all this must be put in a form so that a child may grasp it. That is my life's work. The Lord only knows how far I shall succeed. "To work we have the right, and not to the fruits thereof" [BG II:47].[70]

28. *Lectures on Vedanta in England. Refers to Buddha and Śaṅkara as teachers of Advaita Vedanta. Stresses its need in the present age. Returns to India. The twofold significance of his mission: national and universal.*

In April, 1896, Swami Vivekananda went to London. From there he planned to return to India. This was his second visit to England. During his stay in London in 1896, Swami Vivekananda lectured mostly on Jñāna-yōga. As in America, so in England his spiritual greatness, breadth of vision, dignified bearing and saintly purity impressed many minds and attracted to him very talented and devoted disciples. Chief among them were Miss Margaret E. Noble and Mr. & Mrs. Sevier. Miss Noble (afterwards known as Sister Nivedita) dedicated her life to the education of Indian girls and founded a school in Calcutta, which became known as "The Ramakrishna Mission Sister Nivedita Girls' School."[71] Mr. and Mrs. Sevier took up the cause of Advaita Vedanta, followed

[70] *Letters of Swami Vivekananda,* 3rd ed. (Calcutta: Advaita Ashrama, 1970), no.121, p.284.

[71] Later, "The Ramakrishna Sarada Mission Sister Nivedita Girls' School."

Swami Vivekananda to India, and established the Himalayan center at Mayavati, Almora, known as Advaita Ashrama, which was dedicated to the Nondualistic ideal and became the principal publication center of the Ramakrishna Order.

Both in England and America Swamiji expounded Śaṅkara's Advaita Vedanta. He held that Advaita twice saved India from materialism, once through the teachings of the Buddha, and the second time through the teachings of Śaṅkara. "By Buddha the moral side of the philosophy was laid stress upon and by Śaṅkarācārya, the intellectual side. He worked out, rationalized and placed before men the wonderful coherent system of Advaita."[72] Swami Vivekananda expressed the view that in the modern age again Advaita Vedanta will save the world from materialism; it alone can satisfy the modern skeptic. The spiritual oneness of all souls taught by Vedanta is the rational basis of ethics; the discoveries of modern science do not weaken, but strengthen the Advaita position. "The salvation of Europe depends," said he, "on a rationalistic religion, and Advaita — the nonduality, the Oneness, the idea of the Impersonal God — is the only religion that can have any hold on any intellectual people. It comes whenever religion seems to disappear, and irreligion seems to prevail, and that is why it has taken ground in Europe and America."[73]

During his stay in England Swamiji visited the great Orientalist, Professor Max Müller of Oxford University, who had already written for *The Nineteenth Century* an article on Sri Ramakrishna, entitled "A Real Mahātman," and who wanted to know more about the saint. The facts supplied by Swami Vivekananda as well as Swami Saradananda (who at Swamiji's call had arrived in London on his way to New York) helped the

[72] CW II:139. (Lecture on "The Absolute and Manifestation" delivered in London, 1896.)

[73] *Ibid.*

professor substantially to bring out his book *Ramakrishna, His Life and Sayings.*

After a tour of the continent, during which he met Professor Paul Duessen at Kiel, Swamiji returned to India in January, 1897, accompanied by Mr. and Mrs. Sevier and Mr. J. J. Goodwin, another English disciple, who joined him in America, and to whose tireless labor and faithful transcripts we are indebted for many of the Swamiji's recorded lectures.

Swamiji's experiences in the East and the West convinced him that spirituality was the distinctive characteristic of India's national existence and that she had maintained it under the most trying circumstances. He observed that while the West, for strengthening its civilization and culture, needed the spiritual wisdom, inner strength, calmness, patience, and contentment of India's life, India, for her national reconstruction on the existing spiritual foundation, needed the technical efficiency, the scientific knowledge, the power of coordination and organization of the West. The Swami's historical knowledge and insight unveiled to him the fact that India's special gift to the world throughout the ages had been the profound truths of spiritual life and that on her regeneration depended the regeneration of the world.

Thus Swami Vivekananda's mission has a twofold significance, national and universal, and the two aspects are closely allied. On the one hand, it calls for the consolidation of the spiritual consciousness of India, setting her to the task of national reconstruction on that basis; on the other hand, it calls for the spiritual awakening of the world at large by sending out from India special messengers trained for the purpose, and the fellowship based on mutual appreciation and acceptance of the various world religions.

29. *Awakening India. Delivers his message throughout the country. Founds religious and philanthropic institutions for*

the reconstruction of India and the spiritual enlightenment of man.

Throughout his stay in the West Swami Vivekananda, by letters and writings, was urging his brother-disciples, friends, and students all over India to prepare themselves for the noble mission. He wrote to his disciples in Madras on January 24, 1894:

> My whole ambition in life is to set in motion a machinery which will bring noble ideas to the door of everybody, and then let men and women settle their own fate. Let them know what our forefathers as well as other nations have thought on the most momentous questions of life. Let them see specially what others are doing now, and then decide. We are to put the chemicals together, the crystallization will be done by nature according to her laws. Work hard, be steady and have faith in the Lord. Set to work, I am coming sooner or later. Keep the motto before you — "Elevation of the masses without injuring their religion."
>
> Remember that the nation lives in the cottage. But alas! Nobody ever did anything for them. Our modern reformers are very busy about widow remarriage. Of course I am a sympathizer in every reform, but the fate of a nation does not depend upon the number of husbands their widows get, but upon the *condition of the masses.* Can you raise them? Can you give them back their lost individuality without making them lose their innate spiritual nature. Can you become an occidental of occidentals in your spirit of equality, freedom, work, and energy and at the same time a Hindu to the very backbone in religious culture and instincts? This is to be done and *we will do it.*[74]

An unprecedented welcome was accorded Swami Vivekananda on his return to the motherland; everywhere he received ovations. As the nation's hero he proceeded from Colombo to Calcutta, awakening India by his soul-stirring addresses. Again and again he reminded his country-men of their glorious spiritual heritage and their special role in the modern world. But they must set their house in order to get ready for the work outside.

[74]*Letters of Swami Vivekananda,* no. 27, p. 64.

Reconstruction of India must be based on the bed-rock of her spiritual resources, the Upaniṣads, the mine of infinite strength. What but faith in the ātman — ever-free, pure, immortal, self-luminous, as declared by the Upaniṣads, can give man strength? This is what India needed most. Swami Vivekananda stressed the need of the Upaniṣadic teachings on ātman for the regeneration of India and the world at large:

> Therefore, my friends, as one of your blood, as one that lives and dies with you, let me tell you that we want strength, strength, and every time strength. And the Upaniṣads are the great mine of strength. Therein lies strength enough to invigorate the whole world; the whole world can be vivified, made strong, energized through them. They will call with trumpet voice upon the weak, the miserable, and the downtrodden of all races, all creeds, and all sects, to stand on their feet and be free. Freedom, physical freedom, mental freedom, and spiritual freedom are the watch-words of the Upaniṣads.[75]

Swami Vivekananda has emphasized a twofold application of Vedanta in practical life — (1) arousing man's faith in himself, as noted above, and (2) serving man in the spirit of serving God. Says he:

> Look upon every man, woman and everyone as God. You cannot help anyone, you can only serve; serve the children of the Lord, serve the Lord Himself, if you have the privilege. If the Lord grants that you can help anyone of His children, blessed you are; do not think too much of yourselves. Blessed you are that that privilege was granted you, while others had it not. Do it only as a worship.[76]

> You may invent an image through which to worship God, but a better image already exists, the living man. You may build a temple in which to worship God, and that may be good, but a better one, a much higher one, already exists, the human body.[77]

[75]CW III:238.

[76]CW III:246.

[77]CW II:311. (Lecture on "Practical Vedanta" delivered in London on November 12, 1896.) Cf. "Know ye not that ye are the temple of God, and that the spirit of God dwelleth in you?" St. Paul's Epistle, I. Cor. 3:16.

After arousing India by public addresses delivered from one end of the country to the other, Swami Vivekananda set to work immediately. With the help of his brother disciples (most of whom had already returned to the monastery at his request from their pilgrimages and solitary living) and the young probationers, who, inspired by his message, had joined the Order, as well as the lay devotees, all of whom were at his beck and call, Swamiji organized the twin institutions: the Ramakrishna Math and the Ramakrishna Mission. The one is a monastic institution, the principal purpose of which is to develop its members and lay devotees spiritually by means of religious practices, such as worship, prayer, meditation, study, and also to train the monks to be fit teachers of religion. The other is a philanthropic body composed of both monastic and lay members. It is devoted to public service in all forms, such as religious, cultural, educational, and medical. Centers were started in Calcutta and Madras for regular activities and also for temporary relief operations in times of famine, epidemic, flood, earthquake, tornado, and so forth.

To direct the growing activities of the Math and Mission, Swami Saradananda was called back from America in 1898. Swami Abhedananda went from London to New York to take charge of the Vedanta Society there. The present site of the Ramakrishna Math and Mission headquarters at Belur Math was occupied in January, 1899. The next year Swami Vivekananda formed the Board of Trustees of the Belur Math, but did not include himself on it. Swami Brahmananda was elected President of the Board and therefore of the Math and the Mission, which position he filled till the end of his life on April 11, 1922. Swami Saradananda became the Secretary and conducted the work until he passed away on August 19, 1927.

At this time an important part of Swamiji's work was the training of the Western disciples, who came to India for the education of Indian girls. With the blessings of the Holy Mother, the Sister Nivedita Girls' School was started in November, 1898. Visitors poured in to discuss various problems of the country with him. A biweekly journal in English, *Brahmavadin,* was started in Madras on September 14, 1895, and the next year another journal in English, *Prabuddha Bharata* (The Awakened India). The second journal was transferred from Madras to Almora in the Himalayas in 1898 and later to Mayavati. The first Himalayan issue (August, 1898) appeared with Swamiji's apostrophic poem, "To the Awakened India." The Bengali magazine *Udbodhan* was published in January, 1899, with an introduction by Swamiji dwelling on "The Problem of Modern India and Its Solution." He contributed a number of articles to both the magazines.

30. *Second visit to America. Starts work on the West Coast. The growth of Indian work. His mahāsamādhi.*

On June 20, 1899, Swami Vivekananda sailed from Calcutta for a second visit to America. He was accompanied by his brother-disciple Swami Turiyananda. Sister Nivedita accompanied them as far as London. An illuminating account of Swamiji's personality during the voyage has been given by the Sister in her book *The Master as I Saw Him.* The two Swamis arrived in New York on August 16. After a short stay in the East, where the work of the Vedanta Society was being ably conducted by Swami Abhedananda, they went to California. From December to May of the next year Swami Vivekananda gave several courses of lectures in Los Angeles, San Francisco, and adjoining places. To stabilize the work the Vedanta Society of San Francisco was organized and placed in the charge of Swami Turiyananda.

Meanwhile, the work in India was ardently conducted, during Swamiji's absence, by Swami Brahmananda (President) and Swami Saradananda (Secretary). Swami Brahmananda took special care to mould the spiritual lives of the young monks and the novices, who gradually increased in number. He enjoined on them the regular practice of meditation along with other essentials for their spiritual development. It was his conviction that unless they developed spiritually they could not be truly helpful to themselves and to others.

After attending the Congress of the History of Religions in Paris, before which he spoke twice, Swamiji travelled in Europe and then returned to India. Without any previous notice he arrived unexpectedly at Belur monastery in the evening of December 9, 1900. Towards the end of the month he made a trip to Advaita Ashrama at Mayavati in the Himalayas. This was his first and last visit there. Its special purpose was to console Mrs. Sevier, who had lately lost her husband. Talking about the late Mr. Sevier Swamiji remarked that he had died as a martyr to the cause of Advaita Vedanta. The journey through the snowbound Himalayan range in deep winter was an arduous enterprise and Swamiji's health had already declined under the strain of ceaseless activities. Yet during his two week's stay at Mayavati he wrote three articles for *Prabuddha Bharata.*

He returned to Belur Math on January 24, 1901. The next spring he made a trip to Dacca and other notable places in East Bengal and Assam, where he gave public lectures. Afterwards two more centers were started, one in Banaras and the other in Kankhal. But Swamiji's health was fast declining; everyone was deeply concerned. He was asked to take complete rest. His attention was now directed especially to the training of the young monks and the novices by holding study classes and giving spiritual instructions. Even on the last day of his life, Friday, July the fourth, 1902, he meditated three hours in the morning; in the afternoon he conducted a Sanskrit class for nearly three hours, and then took a walk for about two miles with his brother disciple, Swami Premananda, the abbot of Belur monastery.

In the evening he sat for meditation. An hour later he lay down on the bed and with his eyes fixed in the center of his eye-brows entered into mahāsamādhi (the highest state of Divine Communion from which there is no return). A heavenly lustre shone upon his face. The shocking news of the sudden departure of the mighty leader cast a gloom upon countless human hearts the world over.

31. *A distinctive character of Swamiji's message is its comprehensiveness. It is meant for all grades of men.*

In conformity with the Vedic teachings, both Śaṅkara and Vivekananda recognize a twofold way to the Supreme Good — the path of secular desires (pravṛtti-mārga) and the path of renunciation or desirelessness (nivṛtti-mārga); in other words, the search for the temporal and the search for the eternal. As we have already noted, the path of secular desires being regulated by the moral ideal (dharma) leads to the path of renunciation, or desirelessness, which is the direct way to the Supreme Good. Śaṅkara aptly remarks in the beginning of his commentary on the *Bhagavad-gītā:* "The religion of the Vedas is a twofold way: the way of desire and the way of renunciation. This twofold religion, in which one of the ways is the direct means to prosperity and the other to the Supreme Good, is the basis of world order and security." Nevertheless, his message is intended primarily for the followers of the path of renunciation.

The followers of the path of secular desires are expected to be ready for the path of renunciation in due course. Śaṅkara's attention has not been directed to them. The same is true with regard to other great spiritual leaders. Their teachings apply specifically to the spiritually inclined rather than the worldly-minded. Śrī Kṛṣṇa's message, called the *Bhagavad-gītā,* is definitely a mōkṣa-śāstra, the scripture that dwells on Liberation and its means. It prescribes Karma-yōga (performance of work without any secular desire) as the stepping stone to spiritual life proper. How few can follow this course! The Buddha has in his view men and women who are eager to go beyond all sufferings. Not many face this problem. The direct appeal of Jesus Christ is to the seekers of the Kingdom of Heaven and not to the seekers of the earthly kingdom. The burden of Sri Ramakrishna's teachings is the renunciation of lust and greed. Though the great spiritual leaders were interested in the welfare of all, yet it is the seekers of Supreme Good that have engaged their special attention.

But Swami Vivekananda's all-encompassing vision has included the seekers of temporal values as well as the seekers of the Supreme Good. He sees humanity as a whole and feels equally concerned about all grades of people. His aim is to lead every individual at whatever level, or in whatever sphere of life, to the highest Goal along his own line of development. This, indeed, is the intent of the Vedic religion. To quote Swami Vivekananda:

> Take man where he stands, and from there give him a lift.[78]
>
> All the men and women in any society are not of the same mind, capacity, or of the same power to do things; they must have different ideals, and we have no right to sneer at any ideal.[79]
>
> Our duty is to encourage everyone in his struggle to live up to his own highest ideal, and strive at the same time to make the ideal as near as possible to the truth.[80]
>
> Unless a man passes through *rajas* [right activity with desire] can he ever attain to that perfect *sāttvika* state [serenity of mind conducive to self-knowledge]? How can one expect *yōga,* or union with God, unless one has previously finished with his thirst for *bhōga* or enjoyment? How can renunciation come where there is no vairāgyam or dispassion for all the charms of enjoyment?[81]

32. *His divergences from the traditional way of Vedanta do not mean deviation from its true spirit.*

[78]CW II:382.
[79]CW I:39.
[80]*Ibid.*
[81]CW IV:338.

From the earliest days the Upaniṣadic seers have imparted the cardinal Vedic teaching of the divinity of the soul exclusively to the seekers of Self-knowledge. Their sole purpose has been the spiritual development of the aspirant. Śaṅkara and other classical teachers of the Advaita school have followed this time-honored course. But Swami Vivekananda has deviated from the traditional way. As we have noted above (sec. 21 and 29), he proclaimed this message of the divine nature of man to one and all, to the seekers of temporal values as well as to the seekers of Self-knowledge. He recommends its application not only for spiritual development but for material and intellectual development as well. Says he:

> This infinite power of the spirit brought to bear upon matter evolves material development, made to act upon thought evolves intellectuality, and made to act upon Itself, makes of man a God. . . . Manifest the divinity within you, and everything will be harmoniously arranged around it.[82]

However, Swamiji's method is not inconsistent with the way of the Vedic religion, which recommends lower as well as higher forms of worship of God — the one with secular desire and the other without secular desire — according to the worshipper's inner development. The truth is, the worship of God with desire (sakāma upāsanā) gradually leads to the worship of God without desire (niṣkāma upāsanā). By continuing to worship God even for temporal values, the worshipper develops the disposition to worship God for God's sake, as he becomes convinced of His loving grace. Similarly, by trying to hold to the spiritual self beyond the ego even for the sake of secular interests, a person gradually becomes awakened to the innate glory of the self and turns to the ideal of Self-realization.

The awareness of the divinity of the self is the secret of man's development both in individual and collective life, secular as well

[82]CW IV:297-98.

as spiritual. It finds expression in two distinct ways: "I am divine" and "Thou art divine." As a man becomes aware of his own divinity he becomes aware at the same time of the divinity of his fellow-beings. Consequently, along with the development of his faith in himself his regard for others grows. His potentialities develop as his self-faith is intensified. His desire and capacity for serving his fellow-creatures necessarily increase, and pave the way for his spiritual enlightenment through inner purification.

Another instance of Swami Vivekananda's divergence from the classical Vedanta may be noted here. Traditionally, the Vedantic teachers instruct the seekers of Liberation to devote themselves to solitary spiritual practice for the cultivation of Self-knowledge as a means to Liberation. But Swami Vivekananda enjoins on them a twofold duty — the cultivation of Self-knowledge by solitary spiritual practice and also rendering service to humanity as a part of the discipline for Self-realization. So his watchword for the Ramakrishna Order — *Ātmanō mōkṣārtham jagaddhitāya ca* ("while striving for his own liberation the seeker should work for the good of the world as well").

Further, in Swami Vivekananda's view the great exponents of the different systems of Vedanta, such as Dvaita, Viśiṣṭādvaita, and Advaita, have been in a sense one-sided in their interpretation of the Upaniṣadic texts. Though the main theme of the Upaniṣads is the identity of the jīva and Brahman and the ultimate reality of nonrelational, nondual Brahman, yet they contain passages representing viewpoints other than Advaita to suit different grades of spiritual aspirants. But the founder of every system, Śaṅkara not excepted, has tried to explain the Upaniṣadic passages, one and all, from his particular position. As observed by Swami Vivekananda: "We find that an Advaitist teacher keeps intact those texts [of the Upaniṣads] which especially teach Advaitism, and tries to interpret the Dualistic or Qualified-nondualistic texts into his own meaning. Similarly we find Dualistic teachers trying to read their Dualistic meaning into Advaitic texts."[83]

True to the Advaita standpoint, Swami Vivekananda does not repudiate the monotheistic systems of Vedanta, but looks upon them as gradations of metaphysical views that culminate in Advaita. Says he:

> I want you to note that these three systems [Dvaita, Viśiṣṭādvaita, and Advaita] have been current in India almost from time immemorial — for you must not believe that Śaṅkara was the inventor of the Advaita system. It had existed ages before Śaṅkara was born; he was one of its last representatives. So with the Viśiṣṭādvaita system; it had existed ages before Rāmānuja appeared, as we already know from the commentaries he has written; so with the dualistic systems that have existed side by side with the others. And with my little knowledge, I have come to the conclusion that they do not contradict each other.
>
> Just as in the case of the six darśanas [the six Vedic philosophical systems], we find they are a gradual unfolding of the grand principles, whose music beginning far back in the soft low notes, ends in the triumphant blast of Advaita, so also in these three systems we find the gradual working of the human mind towards higher and higher ideals, till everything is merged in that wonderful unity which is reached in the Advaita system.[84]

Advaita Vedanta does not repudiate even the unqualified dualism of Sāṁkhya and Yōga and the pluralism of Nyāya and Vaiśeṣika, not to mention the Vedantic monotheism. The six Vedic systems do not contradict each other, but serve as grades of philosophic knowledge leading to the highest. Gauḍapāda remarks on the harmonizing outlook of Advaita Vedanta:

> The dualists, cocksure of their respective methods leading to their conclusions, contradict one another, whereas the Advaitin finds no conflict with them. Since nonduality is the ultimate Reality, duality is said to be its apparent variation. But for the dualists there is duality either way [in the unconditioned as well as in the conditioned]. Hence nondualism does not conflict with dualism [which holds to the apparent variation].[85]

[83]CW III:397. [84]CW III:396-97. [85]*Māṇḍūkya-kārikā* III:17,18.

33. *The difference between Śaṅkara's and Swami Vivekananda's view of karma does not involve any contradiction between them.*

Sankara admits no conjunction (samuccaya) of jñāna (knowledge) and karma (work). According to him the two are contradictory. They cannot be practiced together. Jñāna is the sole means to Liberation. There is no alternative way to this Goal. Thus he refutes the alternation (vikalpa) of jñāna and karma as well as their conjunction (samuccaya) in the attainment of Liberation.

But Swami Vivekananda obviously supports both vikalpa (alternation) and samuccaya (conjunction) of karma and jñāna as means to Liberation. Says he:

> Each one of our yōgas is fitted to make man perfect even without the help of the others, because they have all the same goal in view. The yōgas of work, of wisdom, and of devotion are all capable of serving as direct and independent means for the attainment of Mōkṣa.[86]
>
> But you must, at the same time, remember that these divisions are not very marked and quite exclusive of each other. Each blends into the other. But according to the type which prevails we name the divisions. It is not that you can find men who have no other faculty than that of work, nor that you can find men who are no more than devoted worshippers only, nor that there are men who have no more than mere knowledge.[87]

Yet the contradiction between Śaṅkara and Vivekananda is only apparent. The truth is, they have used the term *karma* from two different points of view. Consequently, their verbal statements regarding karma differ, but present truths from two different angles. For instance, when one person says, "Man is mortal," and another says, "Man is immortal," their statements do not actually

[86]CW I:91.
[87]CW I:106.

contradict each other, but declare truths regarding man from two different viewpoints, physical and spiritual.

Swami Vivekananda has used the term *karma* in a wider sense than Śaṅkara. As long as the work is done with the ego-idea, such as "I do the work," "I must enjoy its fruits," it creates a bondage for the worker. In such a case the work is regarded as *karma* by both Śaṅkara and Vivekananda. But when the worker overcomes the ego-idea by developing an insight into the true nature of the self, his activities no longer create a bondage for him, and his work, in Śaṅkara's view, is only a semblance of karma, but actually a form of jñāna (knowledge). But even then the work is counted *karma* by Swami Vivekananda. The difference between Śaṅkara and Vivekananda is evidently due to the fact that in considering karma the one has been inclined to the subjective and the other to the objective viewpoint.

The Vedantic teachers agree on the point that when a spiritual aspirant by the practice of Karma-yōga gains the competence for the practice of the yōga of knowledge (jñāna), or devotion (bhakti), or meditation (dhyāna), through the purification of the mind (cittaśuddhi), he can still continue the performance of his duties, domestic or social, even though work is no longer necessary for his inner development. But although working, he is no longer a Karma-yōgī according to Śaṅkara; but Swami Vivekananda chooses to call him a Karma-yōgī. Thus, in Vivekananda's view Karma-yōga reaches as near the goal as any of the other three yōgas; it can lead a person to Liberation singly or conjointly with the other yōgas.

It is worthy of note in this context that both Śaṅkara and Swami Vivekananda hold that the immediate cause of Liberation (mōkṣa) is the knowledge of the identity of the self with Brahman, which rends the veil of primal ignorance that hides Reality from the aspirant. That none of the yōgas can lead to Liberation (mōkṣa) but through the knowledge of the identity of the self with

Brahman, has been thus indicated by Swami Vivekananda in the course of a conversation:

> The various methods of spiritual practice that have been laid down in the scriptures are all for the attainment of the knowledge of Ātman. Of course these practices vary according to the qualifications of different aspirants. But they also are a kind of work, and so long as there is work, the Ātman is not discovered. The obstacles to the manifestation of the Ātman are overcome by practices as laid down in the scriptures, but work has no power of directly manifesting the Ātman; it is only effective in removing some veils that cover knowledge. Then the Ātman manifests by Its own effulgence. Do you see? Therefore does your commentator (Śaṅkara) say — "In the knowledge of Brahman there is not the least touch of work."[88]

That a seeker of Self-knowledge, whose mind is purged of all secular desires, does not necessarily give up his duties towards his fellow-beings, Śaṅkara admits; but in no case does he consider him a Karma-yōgī, but a Jñāna-yōgī pure and simple. It is not even a case of Jñāna-yōga cum Karma-yōga in his view. This idea is thus expressed by him in his commentary on the *Bhagavad-gītā.*

> Now a person, who having been first engaged in work owing to ignorance and worldly attachment and other evil tendencies, and having once attained purity of mind by sacrificial rites, charity, austerity, etc., arrives at the knowledge of the grand truth that "all is one, the Brahman, the Absolute, the non-agent," may continue performing work in the same manner as before with a view to set an example to the masses, though neither work nor its result attracts him any longer. This semblance of active life on his part cannot constitute that course of action with which knowledge is sought to be conjoined as a means of attaining mōkṣa.[89]

Thus, according to Śaṅkara, the yōgas of jñāna (knowledge) and karma (work) are intended to be practiced by spiritual aspirants of two different grades. Or they can be practiced by the same spiritual aspirant at two different stages of development.

[88]CW VII:176. [89]BG II:11, S. com.

34. *Swami Vivekananda's view that karma attended with devotion to God can lead to Liberation has the support of both Śrī Kṛṣṇa and Śaṅkara.*

That karma associated with devotion to God can be effective of Liberation has been clearly stated by Śrī Kṛṣṇa in the *Bhāgavatam:*

> He who worships Me constantly and exclusively, through the performance of his duties, knowing My presence in all beings, soon attains to a steadfast devotion to Me. O Uddhava, through his undying devotion he comes to Me, the great Lord of all beings, the originator and destroyer of all, their Cause, the Brahman.
>
> Having his mind thus purified by the performance of his duties, knowing My Divinity, he becomes endowed with knowledge and realization and soon attains to Me. All his duty consisting of specific rites, of those belonging to the castes and orders of life, if attended with devotion to Me, become supreme and conducive to Liberation.[90]

That the yōga of devotion, even though attended with karma, can be effective of Liberation through right knowledge (samyak-darśana) is also acknowledged by Śaṅkara. Says he in his commentary on the *Bhagavad-gītā:*

> A sannyāsin, or even a man of work (karmī), who serves Me — the Īśvara, Nārāyaṇa dwelling in the heart of all beings, with a never-failing Bhakti-yōga, crosses beyond the three guṇas (sattva, rajas and tamas) . . . and is fit to become Brahman, i.e., for mōkṣa (Liberation).[91]

On this Ānandagiri remarks:

> Bhakti-yōga is the supreme love (parama-prema) which leads to communion with the Supreme. To serve God in Bhakti-yōga means to constantly contemplate Him by completely withdrawing the mind from all external objects, from the not-self. By virtue of the Divine Grace he is imbued with right knowledge. Thus enlightened, he becomes Brahman while still alive.

[90]SB XI:18.44-47.

[91]BG XIV:26, S. com.

35. *The reason why Śaṅkara has taken a restricted and Swami Vivekananda a wide view of karma. Vivekananda has also recognized the Buddhist ideal of selfless work as a means to nirvāṇa.*

In order to establish the reality of Nondual Brahmaṇ as declared by the Upaniṣads, Śaṅkara had to repudiate the Mīmāṁsā doctrine of the supremacy of karma and advocate the supremacy of jñāna. This is perhaps the reason why he emphasized jñāna and used *karma* in a restricted sense. While refuting the Mīmāṁsā view that the purpose of the entire Vedas, comprising karma-kāṇḍa (work-section) and jñāna-kāṇḍa (knowledge-section) is to advocate action and not knowledge, Śaṅkara maintains that the work-section of the Vedas prescribes karma for the unillumined as preparatory to Self-knowledge, which is the direct means to Liberation and the purport of both the sections.[92] He stresses the inner spirit of renunciation resulting from knowledge rather than the actual performance of work.

But Swami Vivekananda had to face a different situation. He lived in the modern age. He had to deal with the present active, busy complex life of intellectual triumph and material achievements — a life which cannot be readily turned into primitive simplicity or meditative quietude. The age therefore demanded of him some spiritualizing principle of karma, which would serve as a pivot for its maddening course of activity. Then, there were others, particularly in India, who betook themselves to inaction under the pretense of contemplative passiveness. They had to be roused to action with a fresh and sublime vision of the active life. Consequently Swami Vivekananda had to present Karma-yōga with a broad and elevated outlook. In fact, he laid greater stress on renunciation *in* work than renunciation *of* work. It should not, however, be supposed that the Swami did not find

[92]See BS I:1.4, S. com.

any necessity of karma-sannyāsa (complete renunciation of work) for this age. The bliss and glory of the reposeful life of a recluse had a peculiar charm for him. It had to him a value all its own. But rare individuals are entitled to this. "The highest kind of men," says he, "silently collect true and noble ideas, and others — the Buddhas and the Christs — go from place to place preaching them and working for them."[93]

Swami Vivekananda has further widened the scope of Karma-yōga by allowing it a position independent of theistic faith and metaphysical doctrines. As observed by him:

> The Karma-yōgī need not believe in any doctrine whatsoever. He may not believe even in God, may not ask what his soul is, nor think of any metaphysical speculation. He has got his own special aim of realizing selflessness; and he has to work it out himself. Every moment of his life must be realization because he has to solve by mere work, without the help of doctrine or theory, the very same problem to which the jñānī [the seeker of Self-knowledge] applies his reason and inspiration and the bhakta [the devotee of God] his love.[94]

Here Swami Vivekananda has in his view the Buddhist discipline of selfless work as a means to nirvāṇa. The practice of nonattachment means self-denial, the abnegation of the ego, the empirical self. Complete self-abnegation ends in Self-realization. By nirvāṇa the Buddha means the extinction of the apparent self associated with the psychophysical flux and the consequent manifestation of the transcendental Self. It is the same as the Vedantic ideal of attaining mōkṣa by the realization of the nondual Ātman beyond the relativity of the subject and the object. Negatively, it is the elimination of all superimposed adjuncts, and positively, it is the attainment of the real Self, the ground of all knowledge and experience.

[93]CW I:103.
[94]CW I:109.

36. *By introducing work as worship into every sphere of life, Swami Vivekananda has welded together the ethical and the spiritual ideal. This is his special contribution to the present age.*

In one respect Swami Vivekananda has made a distinct contribution to the ideal and practice of Karma-yōga. To do one's duties surrendering the fruits of actions to God is, of course, an indirect way of worshipping Him. God is the inmost Self dwelling in the hearts of all. As we have noted (sec.29), Swami Vivekananda exhorts man to see God in his fellow-beings and worship Him directly through service to them. Further, he says:

> We have to cover everything with the Lord Himself, not by a false sort of optimism, not by blinding our eyes to the evil, but by really seeing God in everything. Thus we have to give up the world, and when the world is given up, what remains? God. What is meant? You can have your wife; it does not mean that you are to abandon her, but that you are to see God in the wife. . . . So in everything. In life and in death, in happiness and in misery, the Lord is equally present. The whole world is full of the Lord. Open your eyes and see Him. This is what Vedanta teaches.[95]
>
> He who sees Śiva in the poor, in the weak, and in the diseased, really worships Śiva; and if he sees Śiva only in the image, his worship is but preliminary.
>
> He who has served and helped one poor man seeing Śiva in him, without thinking of his caste, or creed, or race, or anything, with him Śiva is more pleased than with the man who sees Him only in temples.[96]

In Swami Vivekananda's view, all domestic and social duties as well as humanitarian deeds, can be performed in the spirit of worshipping God in man. His message is the logical conclusion of the teachings of the Upaniṣads and the *Bhagavad-gītā*. Truly

[95]CW II:146. (Lecture on "God in Everything" delivered in London on October 27, 1896.)

[96]CW III:141-42.

speaking, it is not altogether a new message. But its practical application in every sphere of human life has not been tried before. In the *Śrīmad-bhāgavatam* Śrī Kṛṣṇa urges Uddhava to see God in all beings and regard them as such:

> With a pure mind one should observe in all beings as well as in oneself only Me, the Ātman, who am both inside and out, and all-pervading like space.
>
> This looking upon all beings as Myself in thought, word, and deed, is to My mind, the best of all methods of worship.[97]

As declared by the Upaniṣads and other Vedantic texts this mode of seeing and worshipping God in all beings is natural with the seers and the lovers of God who attain illumination. It is the spontaneous expression of their inner experience. Rare individuals, highly advanced in spiritual life, have also carried this ideal into actual practice. But its application in the lives of spiritual aspirants in general has not been tried before. As we have mentioned before (see page 79), such a course has been recommended by Sri Ramakrishna in the present age. "No, not kindness to living beings, but service to God dwelling in them," says he. Further, "If God can be worshiped through a clay image, then why not through a man?"

It was the genius of Swami Vivekananda to find new light in this precept of the Master and seek its practical application in the modern age for the amelioration of man's condition in every sphere of life. For this purpose he had founded the Ramakrishna Math and Mission — a religious and philanthropic institution that has developed into a world-wide organization — the monastic and the lay members of which strive to render service to the ignorant, the needy, the distressed and the diseased as the veritable worship of God dwelling in them. Herein the ethical and the spiritual ideal have been welded together.

[97]SB XI:29.12, 19.

37. *In the neo-Vedanta of Ramakrishna-Vivekananda, ethical and spiritual idealism blend — a significant note of distinction from the classical Vedanta of Śaṅkara.*

Finally, I shall dwell on a significant point of distinction between the neo-Vedanta of Ramakrishna-Vivekananda and the classical Vedanta of Śaṅkara. Both the sections hold that a person can realize Brahman and attain Liberation while dwelling in the body and live in the world as a free soul until the term of life due to karma expires. But Śaṅkara and his school have emphasized the ideal of Liberation — the cessation of all sufferings and the attainment of supreme Bliss in complete absorption in Brahman; whereas Sri Ramakrishna and his disciples have emphasized the ideal of living in the world as a free soul for the well-being of humanity.

To come down to the realm of manifestation (the Līlā) after realizing the Absolute (the Nitya) and live with full consciousness of God ever-present in all things and beings, is declared by Sri Ramakrishna as the state of supra-knowledge and supra-devotion. In his own words: "A man should reach the Nitya, the Absolute, by following the trail of the Līlā, the Relative. It is like reaching the roof by the stairs. After realizing the Absolute, he should climb down to the Relative and live on that plane in the company of devotees, charging his mind with the love of God."[98]

Sri Ramakrishna himself lived on the border-line between the Absolute and the Relative; so he was able to move from one to the other with ease. He saw Nārāyaṇa (the Omnipresent Being) dwelling in all and dealt with them with that spirit. He urged his disciples to live in the world as free souls after the realization of Brahman, and render service to God dwelling in all beings instead of being merged in the Absolute. As we have noted above, one day the young disciple Naren begged Sri Ramakrishna to grant him

[98]GSR, p. 257.

the boon to remain immersed in the Bliss of Brahman. The Master rebuked the pupil for being so narrow-minded and said, "You see, Naren, there is a state even higher than this, you are meant for that. To see God alone without the world is knowledge (jñāna). After attaining this, one can see God dwelling in all and love and serve Him in them; this is supra-knowledge (vijñāna)."

How fully the disciple responded to this exhortation of the Master is evident from his own words written in a letter to an American admirer on July 9, 1897: "May I be born again and again, and suffer thousands of miseries so that I may worship the only God that exists, the only God I believe in, the sum-total of all souls — and above all, my God the wicked, my God the miserable, my God the poor of all races, of all species, is the special object of my worship."[99] This reminds us of Avalōkiteśvara, who, being animated by the Bōdhisattva ideal of mahākaruṇā (supreme compassion), sacrificed personal nirvāṇa within his reach in order to strive for the deliverance of all living creatures. He did not want to attain final emancipation until all others had been set free completely.

Sri Ramakrishna once chided another young disciple, Hari (Swami Turiyananda), for seeking Liberation by being merged in Brahman. Swami Turiyananda related to us the following incident, as we gathered in his room in Varanasi (Banaras) one morning in January, 1921 for his blessed company. In his words, "One day as I visited the Master he asked me, 'Well, Hari, what do you want?' 'Mōkṣa,' I forthwith replied. 'You are small-minded,' he rejoined. I looked at him in wonderment. I thought within myself, do not all Vedanta books proclaim mōkṣa to be the highest goal of life? 'You see,' continued the Master, 'the expert chess-players are so sure of winning the game that they deliberately turn down the pieces just before reaching the goal in order to continue the play. The illumined souls know that they are ever-free.

[99]*Letters of Swami Vivekananda,* no. 157, p. 350.

Whether they dwell in the body or not it makes no difference to them. So they are not afraid of being reborn time and again for helping the bound souls to attain Liberation. But the unillumined seekers are too eager to get free from the wheel of birth and rebirth!' "

Swami Turiyananda at the same time pointed out that only a select few among the liberated-in-life (jīvanmukta) are capable of dedicating themselves to the supreme ideal of helping all living creatures to attain Liberation without seeking final emancipation by merging into the Infinite Bliss of Brahman. Sri Ramakrishna called these blessed ones "ever-free (nitya-mukta)." He included some of his disciples, especially Swami Vivekananda and Swami Brahmananda, in this rank.

It is worthy of note in this context that the Mahāyāna Buddhism sets before every bōdhisattva (the aspirant after bōdhi or nirvāṇa) the ideal of mahākaruṇā (supreme compassion), being filled with which he should seek Buddhahood so that by becoming a Buddha he can work for the emancipation of all living beings before attaining final nirvāṇa himself.[100] That this ideal of mahākaruṇā had considerably influenced the Brāhmaṇical religion is evident from the following prayer of Ranti Deva in the *Śrīmad-bhāgavatam:*

> I desire not of the Lord the greatness which comes by the attainment of the eightfold miraculous powers, nor do I pray to Him that I may not be born again. My one prayer to Him is that I may feel the pain of others, as if I were residing within their bodies, and that I may have the power of relieving their pain and making them happy.[101]

Be that as it may, by emphasizing the ideal of service to humanity in the spiritual life before and after the attainment of Illumination, Swami Vivekananda has linked Vedantism with

[100]See Śānti Deva's *Bōdhicaryāvatāra.*
[101]*Śrīmad-bhāgavatam* IX:21.12.

Buddhism in modern times. In his life and message we find a happy union of the ethical idealism of the Buddha and the spiritual idealism of Śaṅkara. In his view ethical life must be a natural expression of spiritual consciousness; one is incomplete without the other.

CHAPTER III

THE RAMAKRISHNA-VIVEKANANDA VEDANTA MOVEMENT

1. *Its two wings: The Ramakrishna Math and the Ramakrishna Mission.*

The Ramakrishna-Vivekananda Vedanta Movement is the revival in the present age of the universal religious spirit of Vedanta. It has found expression in twin institutions: the Ramakrishna Math and the Ramakrishna Mission. The Ramakrishna Math is a monastic institution, the principal purpose of which is to develop its members and lay devotees by means of spiritual practices, such as worship, prayer, meditation and study, and to train monks to be competent teachers of religion. The Ramakrishna Mission is a philanthropic body composed of both monastic and lay members. It is devoted to public service in various forms, such as religious, cultural, educational and social. Both the Math and the Mission have affiliated centers in different places in India and abroad.

Though distinct, the two organizations are interconnected. Both have their headquarters at Belur Math, District Howrah, situated five miles to the northwest of Calcutta, across the Ganges. The Board of Trustees of the Math is the governing body of the Mission under the same President, and the resident workers of the Mission Centers are mostly the monks of the Order. It is to be

Revised and enlarged edition of "The Ramakrishna Movement" contributed by the author to *Religion in the Twentieth Century*, edited by Virgilius Ferm (New York: The Philosophical Library, 1948), pp. 393-413.

noted that the funds of each Center of the Math and the Mission are kept separate.

2. *Vedanta and Hinduism.*

Vedanta (literally, the end of the Veda, which comprises the Upaniṣads) is the culmination of the religion and philosophy of the Veda. There are four Vedas, i.e., *Ṛk, Yajuḥ, Sāma, Atharva,* which are the original and the most authoritative scriptures of the Hindus and the world's oldest records of religious experience. They do not advocate any dogmatic faith, but enunciate the spiritual truths underlying all religious doctrines, practices, and experiences. Strictly speaking, Vedanta is not a particular religion but the common basis of all religions.

Being derived from Vedanta, Hinduism is identified with it. In fact, Hinduism, consisting of various religious doctrines, methods, and metaphysical truths, rests basically on universal principles and not on the authority of any person. The original name of Hinduism is the Vaidika-dharma (the Vedic religion). It is also called Sanātana-dharma (the Eternal religion), inasmuch as it affirms eternal truths and finds their application in life.

Broadly speaking, there are two main schools of Vedanta, monistic and monotheistic. According to the monistic school, known as Advaita (nondualistic) Vedanta, Nirguṇa Brahman (the Supreme Being possessed of no attributes) is the ultimate Reality. It is the impersonal, absolute Being, formless, featureless, beyond the distinction of attributes and substance. According to the monotheistic school, Saguṇa Brahman (the Supreme Being possessed of attributes) is the fundamental Reality. He is the Personal God, the repository of all blessed qualities, the omnipotent, omniscient, omnipresent, all-gracious Ruler of the universe.

The Advaita (nondualistic) school recognizes the monotheistic position, but does not consider it ultimate. According to both schools the finite self within every individual is intrinsically pure, illumined, and free. The monotheistic school holds that the finite self is akin to Brahman (Saguṇa), but maintains an inherent distinction between the two in some form or other. To realize the unity of the individual self with the Supreme Self is the goal of life. According to the nondualistic school, to realize the identity of the finite self with the Supreme Self is the ultimate goal of life; it is possible to realize the identity after realizing the unity.

3. *The principal tenets of the Advaita (nondualistic) school which we consider as Vedanta proper, may be summed up as follows:*

   a. Nirguṇa Brahman, Pure Being-Consciousness-Bliss (Satcit-ānanda), is the ultimate Reality.
   b. Transcendentally, One without a second, Brahman is immanent in the phenomenal world as its all-pervading Self. It is the Creator, Preserver, and Destroyer of the manifold (Destruction means dissolution into the causal state). The same Supreme Being is the God of love, goodness and grace worshipped by the devotees, and also the indwelling spirit in all living beings. Thus the One absolute being has different aspects, Nirguṇa is manifest as Saguṇa in relation to the universe.
   c. Man's real self is essentially identical with Brahman, the Supreme Self.
   d. To realize the unity or the identity of the individual self with Brahman, the Supreme Self, is the goal of human life. All life-values must subserve man's spiritual interest.
   e. Methods of realization vary according to the aspirant's tendencies, capacities and conditions of life, within the framework of the fundamental principles.

f. Different religions are basically so many ways leading to the realization of Brahman, Saguṇa or Nirguṇa.

The essence of spiritual knowledge has been expressed by Vedanta in the terse formula, "That Thou Art." Resolved into the two factors "Thou Art He" and "Thou Art His," it comprehends the approaches to Nirguṇa and Saguṇa Brahman, Impersonal and Personal God, the Supreme Being. It thus embraces the entire spiritual life of mankind.

4. *The distinctness of the Ramakrishna-Vivekananda Movement from the traditional Vedanta.*

That the real self of man is ever pure, self-luminous, free, is universally true. The present movement declares this truth as central to all religions, although it is more or less explicit in some and in others more or less implicit. By arousing man's faith in himself it can serve as the key to his edification and advancement. The practical application of this truth in modern times by the movement is in some respects an innovation on the traditional methods of Vedanta. The general tendency of classical Vedanta is to impart this knowledge to earnest seekers of Truth and to apply it to their spiritual development particularly. On the other hand, the neo-Vedanta movement aims to teach it to men and women in various levels of life, thereby awakening their faith in themselves and others, so that they can achieve physical, mental, and moral growth individually and collectively with a spiritual outlook on life and proceed toward the Supreme Goal from their present level of development, whatever that may be.

Moreover, traditional Vedanta stresses the need for the secluded life for spiritual aspirants and exhorts them to carry on their own Liberation by Self-knowledge. But this Movement enjoins on them a twofold duty: striving after Liberation by solitary practice, and also doing good to the world as a part of spiritual discipline for Self-realization.

There are sharp differences among Vedanta schools, monistic (nondualistic) as well as monotheistic. The monotheistic school includes no less than five distinct systems. The different systems of Vedanta have often been considered contradictory, while the Ramakrishna Order views them as complementary, as so many ways of comprehension, or stages of realization, of Brahman.

A distinct contribution of the Ramakrishna-Vivekananda Vedanta Movement to the modern world is its message that all help given to men by individuals or by society should be based on the recognition of man's innate divinity regardless of man's differences. The only way to mutual regard, love and unity among mankind, on which rest peace and progress in life, is to find an all-embracing ground of human relationship that transcends all distinctions of race, nationality, color, creed, rank, and merit. That this precept can actually be carried into practice has been exemplified by the Movement's various institutions, framed for the service of God in man. The Movement calls on its followers to see God in the needy, the distressed, and the diseased, and to serve them as if one were serving God. Work done in this spirit is veritable worship.

5. *Sri Ramakrishna, an exemplar of the universal truths of Vedanta. His Divine Mission. The formation of the Ramakrishna Order.*

The Ramakrishna-Vivekananda Vedanta Movement has its origin in, and draws its inspiration from, the life of the great Hindu saint and seer, Sri Ramakrishna, whose name it is associated with. Born of devout Brāhmin parents in an idyllic village of Bengal in the year 1836, he had ecstatic experiences in boyhood, which intensified his inborn love of God. At the age of seventeen he went to Calcutta to live with his brother, who conducted a Sanskrit academy. There he occupied himself mostly with religious duties. Though possessed of extraordinary memory, keen intellect, and artistic aptitudes, he refused to acquire secular knowledge. His brother tried in vain to give him a Sanskrit education, but his heart yearned for the spiritual enlightenment that would remove all darkness forever.

Three years later he was appointed priest for the worship of Kālī, the Divine Mother of the universe, in a newly founded temple situated on the Ganges at Dakshineswar four miles north of Calcutta. As soon as he began worshipping the Divine Mother in the image installed in the temple, an all-consuming longing for her vision grew within him. He was unable to think even of food or rest. Sleep forsook him. No longer could he perform the prescribed rituals of worshipping the Deity. In the intense hunger of his soul, he practiced hard disciplines, prayed to the Divine Mother day and night, intently meditated on Her, poured out his devotion at Her feet in song, and cried bitterly like a child to see Her. At last one day he entered into a state of beatitude in which She revealed Herself to him. Yet he could not rest satisfied. His heart craved a continuous vision of Her. He prayed more and more and before long was able to see Her not only in ecstasy but in the normal state of consciousness, with open eyes.

He was in constant divine inebriation, yet even so he yearned for the realization of God in different aspects and forms. With superhuman energy, ardour, and devotion he practiced, one after another, various spiritual disciplines prevalent in Hinduism — from the intricate ritualism of the Tantras to the abstruse meditation of Yōga, from the ecstatic devotional practices of Vaiṣṇavism to the transcendental Self-realization of nondualistic Vedanta — and he attained the Supreme Being through each of them. Afterward he turned to Islam, with the same result; and later in life, to Christianity. In regard to the latter, he had a vision of

Jesus Christ and was convinced of His Divine Sonship.

His tremendous struggle for God-realization extended over twelve years. During this period and the remaining eighteen years of his life he had varied mystical experiences and realizations repeatedly. He saw myriads of spiritual visions, and dwelt in sublime ecstatic moods. In his spiritual practices he was guided by adepts, who came to him at the hour of need, directed as it were by the Divine Will.

He attained to the pinnacle of spiritual realization — the transcendental experience of Nirguṇa Brahman, the One without a second, free from all distinctions. Once he stayed in that state continuously for six months. Indeed, so accustomed did he become to its sublime height that the natural tendency of his mind was to soar beyond time and space, name and form, to the Limitless One. However, at the Divine Call, he gradually trained his mind to occupy a unique position in the spiritual realm. His mind usually stayed on the borderline of the Absolute and the relative, so that it could turn to either at any time. As a result, in the normal state of consciousness he always perceived the One in the many and the many in the One, and he was able to shift from the manifold experience to the Unitary Consciousness with ease.

Though the aspirant is very rare who can rightly practice even a single spiritual method and reach the goal after lifelong struggle, yet it was the genius of Sri Ramakrishna to finish the whole course of the world's spiritual lessons, so to speak, within a few years. Thus he demonstrated the truth that the Goal is the same, though the paths vary, that the Divine Being is both transcendental and immanent, and that It has many aspects and forms. In dealing with people he always looked upon them as Nārāyaṇas, the veritable manifestations of God.

It was revealed to Sri Ramakrishna by his spiritual experiences that he had a Divine Mission to fulfill; that his practices and realizations were intended not for his personal benefit but for the good of humanity. He was to establish a new religious order for the regeneration of India, for the spiritual awakening of mankind, and for the establishment of harmony among the different religions of the world. He foresaw that earnest seekers of various sects, communities, and ranks of society would come to him for solace, inspiration, guidance, and enlightenment. During the last twelve years of his life just such a stream of people constantly flowed into his room. He also had the vision that his message would spread far beyond the seas among devotees who spoke a language which he himself did not know.

Sri Ramakrishna had visions of his intimate disciples and devotees, lay and monastic, even before they came to him. Some of them, he knew, would be young — they were the potential monks especially chosen by the Divine Mother to carry out Her mission. They arrived one by one during the last six years of his life (1881-1886) — most of them were indeed very young — and he recognized each of them at first sight. It was during his last illness in 1886 that the entire band of his intimate disciples rallied around him. The would-be monks altogether numbered sixteen.

Twelve of them, who constantly attended on him, organized themselves under the leadership of Narendranath (afterward Swami Vivekananda) and served the Master with utmost care, love, and veneration. Their whole-hearted love of God and devotion to the Master and his ideals led to the formation of the brotherhood, which soon after his death was to develop into the Ramakrishna Order.

The Master himself took decisive steps to lay its foundation. He often exhorted the young disciples to follow the path of renunciation for the realization of God and for the service of God in man. On a certain occasion, charging Narendranath not to let his ideas die out after his death, he said to him, "I leave these boys in your charge. See that they dedicate themselves to the Divine Mission and do not enter into the world." As preparatory to monastic life he once asked the young disciples to beg their food from door to door, regardless of caste. A few days later he gave each of them a piece of ochre cloth, the emblem of the life of renunciation. Shortly before his passing away on August 16, 1886, he transmitted his powers to Narendranath, saying to him, "By virtue of this gift you will do immense good to the world, and not until then will you gain release."

6. *The import of Sri Ramakrishna's life and teachings in a critical period of India.* (See also chap. 2, sec. 23.)

At the time of Sri Ramakrishna's advent India was emerging from a state of torpor. The decline of the Mogul sovereignty, dating from the beginning of the eighteenth century, had produced political and social chaos in the country. Then, in the latter part of the eighteenth century, the British power had begun to rise. With the establishment of British supremacy, as law and order had been restored, English education was introduced, evangelism of the Christian missionaries started, and Western customs and manners were transmitted on as vast a scale as was Western merchandise.

The political subjugation of the country by Britain had dealt a severe blow to the national self-esteem of the Indian people. With the spread of English education the materialistic views of Western science and philosophy infiltrated their minds. Dazzled by the glare and self-assurance of Western civilization, they began to doubt the efficacy of their traditional ideals and ways of life. The Christian missionaries were severely critical of the social and religious beliefs and practices of the Hindus. It is not strange that under the circumstances English-educated Indians often lost faith in their own culture and religion and were ready to adopt Western ideals and methods for the salvation of their country. Not a few brilliant Indians deserted their time-honored faith. Some became Christian converts. Some turned atheists. It seemed that the barge of Indian national life was going to be cut adrift from its ancient moorings.

But this was not to be. The inner spirit of India soon reacted to the cultural impact of the West. Of the religious and social movements that sprang up to counteract the foreign influence, the most important were the Brāhma Samāj of Bengal and the Ārya Samāj of the Punjab. But whether such movements were progressive or reactionary, liberal or conservative, none of them proved able to call forth the national genius of India. None pointed out to India's children the import of their voluminous scriptures, the universal character of their religion, the inner harmony of their diverse beliefs, and the fundamental unity of their national life despite divergencies of sect, creed, caste, color, custom, and language. None could restore their faith in their ancient heritage and indicate how to accept the new on the basis of the old and apply the eternal religious principles to modern conditions. The life and teachings of Sri Ramakrishna furnished a clue to the fulfillment of all these needs and stimulated the slumbering self-consciousness of India. In him India found herself.

7. *The message of Sri Ramakrishna and its significance for the present age.*

The spiritual realizations of Sri Ramakrishna verified the truths affirmed by Vedanta. Without studying the scriptures, he discovered them. His extraordinary purity, blissfulness, wisdom, compassion, and power to transform the lives of others, nay, to transmit spirituality by a mere touch, word, glance, or wish, testified to the validity of his inner experiences. His message, a restatement of the Vedantic truths, can be summed up as follows:

a. God alone is real.

b. To realize God is the goal of human life; man must live with that end in view.
c. God is one, but various are His names, forms, and aspects. He is also without names and forms.
d. A person can choose for worship any name, form, or aspect of God that appeals to him most, and thereby he can realize Him if he has real longing, steadfastness, purity, and devotion.
e. Different religions are but varied ways to God-realization.
f. Religions in their essentials are entirely harmonious. The adherents of different religions should live in perfect amity. There is no place for dogmatism or intolerance in religion.
g. God is manifest in human beings more than anywhere else. See Him in man and serve Him there.

The four cardinal points of Sri Ramakrishna's message are thus found to be that God is real, that He can be realized, that religions are essentially harmonious, and that man is to be served in the spirit of serving God. These truths have deep significance for the modern age. Each of them has an important bearing on our life and thought. Sri Ramakrishna's life was a beacon in an age of spiritual darkness. At the very time when religion was being classified as a relic of barbarism, as the last surviving superstition that humanity must outgrow in consequence of scientific knowledge; when "enlightened" people the world over were discarding all ideas of the suprasensuous, such as God, soul, heaven, and so forth, and holding to the material universe as the sole reality — at that very time Sri Ramakrishna, turning his back upon the sensible universe, plunged into the unseen in search for the Real and came out with the discovery that God alone exists in the true sense.

His experience was a challenge to materialism and its concomitants, such as skepticism, naturalism, agnosticism, and atheism, which dominated human thought with the progress of the physical sciences during the nineteenth century. By declaring the Ultimate Reality to be Pure Consciousness he rendered inestimable service to the cause of human knowledge. His experience corroborates the logical truth that the fundamental concept cannot be inert matter, energy, life-force, or blind will, that it can be nothing but Absolute Consciousness. Every existence presupposes Consciousness, which alone is self-existent, self-intelligent. Every branch of knowledge, in order to come to right conclusions, must conform to the basic Reality. No philosophic or scientific view, if contrary to It, can be acceptable.

Sri Ramakrishna placed before humanity one supreme ideal — God-realization. Not only is it indispensable to ultimate freedom and eternal bliss, but also to worldly peace, security, happiness, and prosperity. Man cannot be great and glorious even here unless he directs his life to that Goal; unless he cultivates his physical, mental, and moral powers and establishes social, economic, and political systems with that end in view. As long as earthly power and prosperity are the ideals of life, man's intellectual, aesthetic, and ethical natures must subserve material interests and tend to degenerate. There can be little possibility of peace and harmony in individual or collective life in such a case.

On the contrary, when man turns to the spiritual ideal and regulates his entire existence accordingly, he raises himself physically, mentally and morally. Only better men and women can make a better world. Laws and institutions do not make men; it is men who make them. The peace and progress of the world depend primarily on human individuals. In rendering service to the world the Ramakrishna-Vivekananda Vedanta Movement gives first consideration to the human factors and directs its primary attention to the development of man's inner life.

Religious bigotry, fanaticism, and feuds have caused untold misery to human beings. As long as these persist men can never live in peace and amity. Before there can be peace in any other field there must be peace in the domain of religion, because peace is the special object of religious life. For unity and harmony among the followers of different religions mutual understanding and regard are essential. Mere tolerance is not adequate for the purpose. Sri Ramakrishna teaches us to accept every religion worth the name as an approach to the Supreme Being. His harmony of religions is based on the recognition of the fundamental unity underlying their divergences. It views them as so many methods of God-realization intended for men and women of diverse capacities and conditions of life.

But fellowship of faiths cannot be achieved by mere eclecticism or by syncretism. Eclecticism seeks unity of religions by combining into a single system their choice features. The religious synthesis achieved by the eclectic method is comely but not natural, like a bouquet of flowers. It has no root in the soil of life. It does not spring from the living experience of God-men. It cannot, therefore, serve as a spiritual force. Syncretism stresses the similarities and disregards the differences. Sri Ramakrishna seeks harmony not in spite of, but with the differences, because in his view differences have a deep significance; they fulfill the spiritual needs of different types of worshippers.

Sri Ramakrishna's idea of serving God in man is the keynote of the Movement. One day in 1884, in the course of a conversation with Narendranath and other devotees, the Master said, "Kindness to living beings! Who are you to be *kind* to them? Serve them as manifestations of God. Does not God exist in all?" These words went straight into the heart of Narendranath. He found in them the answer to how he would channel the knowledge of Vedanta into practical life.

Sri Ramakrishna himself was the living example of this teaching. He saw God in all and treated all as such. He looked upon all women, including the fallen, as the Divine Mother in disguise. One day (the twenty-fifth of May, 1873), he formally worshipped his own wife as the veritable image of the Divine Mother, when at the age of 18, nearly 13 years after their marriage, she came to Dakshineswar to live with him; and he always looked upon her as the manifestation of the Divine Mother. She in her turn behaved as his wife and disciple, and always looked upon him as the "Divine Master" and served him devotedly. She was, at one and the same time, virgin and wife. Younger than Sri Ramakrishna by 17 years, she outlived him by 33 years and played an important role in strengthening the foundation of the movement by her exemplary life. Her motherly love, her simplicity and humility, her self-denying service, her extraordinarypiety, her boundless compassion, and her profound wisdom have been a source of inspiration for all. She is held in high reverence by the followers of Sri Ramakrishna. Because of her spiritual eminence she is adored as the earthly image of the Divine Mother and called "the Holy Mother."

8. *Swami Vivekananda, the foremost disciple of Sri Ramakrishna. His plan for the regeneration of India.*

Shortly after the passing of the Master on August 16, 1886, the young disciples banded themselves into the Ramakrishna Order, which was in line with the Vedantic Order of sannyāsins (monks) to which Sri Ramakrishna and his Advaitist (nondualistic) teacher, Tōtāpurī, had belonged. The young monks were joined by an elderly monastic disciple who was older than the Master. The total number of monastic disciples was sixteen. Foremost among them was Swami Vivekananda, their leader, and second only to him, Swami Brahmananda, the spiritual son of Sri Ramakrishna. With the help of Sri Ramakrishna's lay disciples a monastery was started in a rented house at Baranagore near Dakshineswar. This was the nucleus of the Ramakrishna Math.

But most of the young disciples did not stay in the monastery very long. Though they had experienced communion with God at the touch or blessing of Sri Ramakrishna, they were eager to make Divine Communion their permanent possession. Several of them went out as itinerant monks on pilgrimages to the Himalayas and other parts of India, lived austere solitary lives and practiced meditation. Only one of them, Swami Ramakrishnananda, remained in the monastery all along as its pivot. With rare devotion and steadfastness he performed the daily worship and other duties of the monastery for ten long years, until Swami Vivekananda returned from the West and sent him to Madras to establish a new monastery there.

As we have already noted, before leaving for America Swami Vivekananda traveled all over India as an itinerant monk for about six years — from the Himalayas to Cape Comorin. In the course of his wanderings he came in close touch with people of all classes and ranks, from the Princes to the peasants, from the learned Brāhmins to the pariahs. His heart bled at the sight of the abject poverty, misery, and ignorance of the Indian masses. He concluded that he must shoulder two arduous tasks for the regeneration of India, the upliftment of the people in general and the improvement of the condition of women.

He observed the weaknesses as well as the strength of India. He studied her various problems — economic, political, social, educational, and religious, and he decided what was necessary for their solution. Underlying all diversities of doctrines, rites, and customs, he discerned the spiritual unity of Indian life. He found that spirituality was the very lifeblood of India; that her national regeneration must be on a spiritual basis.

9. *Beginning work in the West; its twofold significance.*

As Swami Vivekananda, filled with deepest compassion for the suffering millions of India, awaited an opportunity to start his work, an occasion arose for his coming to America. He was to represent Hinduism at the Parliament of Religions held at the World's Fair in Chicago in September, 1893.

His message of the divinity of man and the harmony of religions, delivered from the depth of his realizations, made a profound impression on the audiences at the Parliament of Religions. It paved the way for his preaching the universal gospel of Vedanta in the Western world. For nearly three years he stayed in the United States lecturing before popular and learned audiences, holding classes and conversations in drawing rooms and clubs, giving interviews to people of various ranks, and gaining admirers, friends, and followers by his all-comprehensive teachings and forceful, luminous personality in many places from the Atlantic to the Mississippi. Before leaving the country in April, 1896, he placed his work on a permanent basis by founding the Vedanta Society of New York and by summoning his brother-disciple, Swami Saradananda, from India to take charge. His books on *Rāja-Yōga, Karma-Yōga,* and *Bhakti-Yōga,* containing many of his collected addresses as well as his original writings, were published or were ready for publication.

During his stay in London in 1896, the Swami lectured mostly on Jñāna-Yōga. His spiritual fervor, dignified bearing, and saintly purity deeply impressed many minds and attracted some very talented and devoted disciples to him. Chief among them were Miss Margaret E. Noble and Mr. and Mrs. J. H. Sevier. Later Miss Noble dedicated her life to the education of Indian girls. She became known as Sister Nivedita (the consecrated one). The Ramakrishna Mission (now Sri Sarada Mission) Sister Nivedita Girls' School in Calcutta, named after her, owes its origin to her tireless and self-sacrificing efforts. Mr. and Mrs. J. H. Sevier took up the cause of Vedanta, followed Swami Vivekananda to India, and established the monastery known as the *Advaita Ashrama* at

Mayavati (near Almora) in the Himalayas. It was dedicated primarily to the culture of nondualistic Vedanta and became the principal publication center of the Ramakrishna Order.

While in England Swami Vivekananda met the great Orientalist, Professor Max Müller of Oxford University, who had already written an article on Sri Ramakrishna for the *Nineteenth Century* under the caption "A Real Mahātman," and who wanted to know more about the saint. The facts supplied by Swami Vivekananda and his brother disciple, Swami Saradananda (who came to London from New York at his request), helped the Professor substantially in completing his book, *Ramakrishna, His Life and Sayings.*

After a tour of the continent, during which he met Professor Paul Duessen at Kiel, Swami Vivekananda returned to India in January, 1897, accompanied by Mr. and Mrs. Sevier and Mr. J. J. Goodwin, another English disciple, who joined him in America. We are indebted to Mr. Goodwin's tireless labor and faithful transcripts for many of the Swami's recorded lectures.

From the time of his arrival in America the Swami had been struck by the material achievements, the technical efficiency, the scientific knowledge, the capacity for organized work, and the orderliness of the Western people. Simultaneously there arose in his mind the dismal picture of misery and suffering in India, which by contrast made him feel India's distress the more keenly. At the same time he perceived the lack of spiritual understanding in the Western world. Beneath its activities and enjoyments, its pomp and power, were sense attachment, disquietude, confusion, and despair.

As we have noted in the previous chapter, the Swami's experiences in the Orient and the Occident confirmed his view that spirituality was the chief characteristic of India's national existence and that she had maintained it under the most adverse conditions. He saw that while the West for strengthening its civilization and culture needed the spiritual wisdom, inner strength, calmness, patience, and contentment of Indian life; India for her national reconstruction on the existing spiritual foundation needed the technical efficiency, the scientific knowledge, the power of coordination and organization of the West. The Swami's historical knowledge and insight revealed to him that India's special gift to the world throughout the ages had been the profound truths of spiritual life, and that on her regeneration depended the regeneration of the world.

Thus Swami Vivekananda's Mission has a twofold significance, national and universal, and the two aspects are closely allied. On the one hand, it calls for the consolidation of the spiritual consciousness of India, setting her to the task of national reconstruction on fundamental principles underlying her religion. On the other hand, it calls for the spiritual awakening of the world at large by sending out special messengers trained for the purpose from India, and for the fellowship based on mutual appreciation and acceptance of the universal truths common to all humanity.

10. *Organizing manifold activities for the reconstruction of India.*

Throughout his stay in the West Swami Vivekananda, by letters and writings, urged his brother-disciples, friends, and students all over India to prepare themselves for the noble mission. As a result, the Vedantic tribune, *The Brahmavadin* — and afterward another journal, *Prabuddha Bharata* — was started in Madras as early as 1895. One of his brother-disciples undertook educational work for the masses in Rajputana early in 1894. Others, renouncing their pilgrimages and solitary living, went back to the monastery near Calcutta, and novices began to join it.

An unprecedented welcome was accorded Swami Vivekananda on his return to the motherland. Everywhere he received ovations. As the nation's hero he proceeded from Colombo to

Calcutta, awakening India by his soul-stirring addresses. He set to work immediately. With the help of his brother-monks and the novices who, inspired by his message were drawn to the monastic life, he started Math Centers in Bengal and Madras and also Mission Centers for humanitarian service. Visitors poured in to discuss with him various problems of the country. On May 1, 1897, with the monastic and lay disciples of Sri Ramakrishna, he formally organized the Ramakrishna Mission. Then he undertook a lecture tour in Northern India, carrying his message and explaining his plan of work to all from the Maharajas to the common people. The response his message evoked from his countrymen was gratifying.

In July, 1897, he wrote to a friend in America:

> Only one idea was burning in my brain — to start the machine for elevating the Indian masses — and that I have succeeded in doing to a certain extent. It would have made your heart glad to see how my boys are working in the midst of famine and disease and misery — nursing by the mat-bed of the cholera-stricken pariah and feeding the starving chāṇḍāla, and the Lord sends help to me and to them all. . . .
>
> I must see my machine in strong working order, and then knowing sure that I have put in a lever for the good of humanity, in India at least, which no power can drive back, I will sleep without caring what will be next; and may I be born again and again, and suffer thousands of miseries, so that I may worship the only God that exists, the only God I believe in, the sum-total of all souls. And above all, my God the wicked, my God the miserable, my God the poor of all races, of all species, is the special object of my worship.[1]

To organize the growing activities of the Math and the Mission, Swami Saradananda was called back from America in 1898. Swami Abhedananda went from London to New York to take charge of the Vedanta Society there. The present site of the Ramakrishna Math and the Ramakrishna Mission headquarters

[1] *Letters of Swami Vivekananda*, no. 157, pp. 349-350.

at Belur was occupied in January, 1899. From the very beginning Swami Brahmananda, whom Swami Vivekananda looked upon as the spiritual son and successor of Sri Ramakrishna, was placed in charge of the Math and the Mission affairs.

The next year Swami Vivekananda formed the Board of Trustees of the Belur Math, and did not include himself in it. Swami Brahmananda was chosen President of the Board and therefore of the Math and the Mission. Swami Saradananda became the Secretary.

Swami Akhandananda founded an orphanage at Sargachi in the district of Murshidabad and Swami Trigunatita started the Bengali review *Udbodhan* in Calcutta early in 1899. At this time, an important part of Swami Vivekananda's work was the training of Western disciples who came to India for the education of Indian girls. With the blessings of the Holy Mother the Sister Nivedita Girls' School was started in November, 1898.

In the latter part of 1899, Swami Vivekananda, visiting America for the second time, was accompanied by Swami Turiyananda, a brother-monk whose spiritual fervor and ascetic habits were remarkable. In taking Swami Turiyananda with him, Swami Vivekananda's object was to present to America an ideal spiritual personality, rather than a preacher. After a short stay in New York State, where the work was being ably conducted by Swami Abhedananda, the two Swamis went to California. From December to May, Swami Vivekananda gave several courses of lectures in Los Angeles, San Francisco, and adjoining places. This created a stir in intellectual circles, and several groups of students were formed in both northern and southern California. To stabilize the work, the Vedanta Society of San Francisco was organized. Swami Vivekananda received a gift of about 160 acres of land in the valley of San Antonio, twelve miles from Lick Observatory on Mt. Hamilton, where Swami Turiyananda founded Shanti Ashrama (Peace Retreat) with a group of earnest students. Swami Vivekananda did not have a chance to visit this place.

Meanwhile, the work Swami Vivekananda had started and organized in India was continued with unabated zeal under the guidance of Swami Brahmananda. Besides religious, educational, and other regular activities, the Mission conducted relief operations in different parts of India, for helping in times of famine, epidemics, floods, landslides, and the like. Swami Brahmananda, in accordance with the rules laid down by Swami Vivekananda, devoted great care to moulding the lives of the young monks and the novices, who gradually increased in number. He enjoined on them the regular practice of meditation along with other essentials for their spiritual development. Without spiritual assets they could not be truly helpful to themselves and to others.

After attending the Congress of the History of Religions in Paris, where he spoke twice, Swami Vivekananda returned to India in December, 1900. Shortly after his arrival he made a trip to the Advaita Ashrama at Mayavati in the Himalayas, where his beloved disciple, Mr. Sevier, had recently passed away. His main object was to see and console Mrs. Sevier. The journey was very strenuous — it was winter, the whole region was snowbound, and the Swami was indisposed.

After coming down from Mayavati he visited several places in East Bengal and Assam and gave public lectures. Along with Math Centers (monasteries), Sevāshramas (homes of service) were started to serve the diseased and the destitute in Banaras and Kankhal. But the Swami's health was fast declining. Everyone was deeply concerned about him. He was asked to take complete rest. His attention at this time was directed especially to the training of the young monks and the novices at the Headquarters. He held study classes and gave them spiritual instructions. Even on the last day of his life, the fourth of July, 1902, he conducted a class on Sanskrit Grammar (Pāṇini) for about three hours in the afternoon. In the evening he sat for meditation, and calmly withdrawing from his body, entered into Mahāsamādhi (the highest state of Divine Communion) and left the body.

11. *The continuous growth of the work in India and abroad. Its far-reaching influence.*

The sudden passing of the mighty leader at the early age of thirty-nine was a tremendous shock to the whole Movement. Though the loss was irreparable, the work continued to grow in all directions under the able guidance of Swami Brahmananda, Swami Saradananda, Swami Premananda, and other great disciples of Sri Ramakrishna. Swami Brahmananda especially emphasized the spiritual side of the Movement, serving as its President till the end of his life — April 10, 1922. Most of the administrative work was taken care of by Swami Saradananda, who was the Secretary of the Math and the Mission until his death on August 19, 1927, that is, for a period of about thirty years.

Since the time of Ramakrishna and Vivekananda there has been a resurgence of new life in India. The national consciousness has manifested itself not only in the religious but also in the social, cultural, economic, and political life of the country. The political movement for the Independence of India was only a phase of a deeper national awakening. While rousing the spiritual consciousness of India, the Ramakrishna-Vivekananda Vedanta Movement has created a spirit of self-sacrifice among the people in general and an urge to serve others. As a result, the country is dotted with various educational, medical, and religious organizations owing allegiance to Sri Ramakrishna and Swami Vivekananda, some of which, however, do not belong to the Ramakrishna Order. The selfless activities of these organizations have tended to create a cordial relation between the classes and the masses, between the literate and the illiterate.

There has been a continuous demand for the Swamis of the Order in and outside India since Swami Vivekananda inaugurated the work over eighty years ago. There are at present about ninety centers in India, fifteen in other Asiatic countries, three in Europe, twelve in the United States, one in South America (Buenos Aires), belonging to the Ramakrishna Order. Swamis are sent to the West by the Headquarters at Belur Math, India, at the invitation of groups interested in Vedanta. They are like guest teachers rather than missionaries. They do not seek converts in the ordinary sense. Their ministration is twofold: to help the seekers to develop spiritually and to promote mutual understanding and appreciation among the followers of different religions.

Persons belonging to any religion can receive the Swamis' help without changing their faith. By explaining the universal spiritual principles Vedanta gives them a better understanding of their own religion and intensifies their devotion to God. It widens their religious outlook and seeks to make them free from bigotry and intolerance. Thus Vedanta helps a Christian to be a better Christian, a Jew to be a better Jew, a Mohammedan a better Mohammedan, a Hindu a better Hindu.

In fact, there is no vital difference between a true Christian and a true Hindu, so far as the spiritual life is concerned. One can be as near God as the other. If we approach the sun along different radii we come closer to one another as we near it. The Vedantic teaching that man can attain complete self-fulfillment by realizing God provides all with the meaning of life. It infuses hope in the nonbelievers, as it confirms the believers. Vedanta stresses the need of moral values for both material and spiritual well-being, and points out that man's moral life is not secure without a spiritual foundation. Thus while developing man's spiritual nature, Vedanta promotes peace, progress, and security in individual and collective life.

Sri Ramakrishna is worshipped today by millions in India and abroad as a God-man, one in line with Kṛṣṇa, the Buddha, and Christ. Swami Vivekananda was the first Hindu to carry the spiritual message of India to the Western Hemisphere. He interpreted in modern terms the ancient wisdom of India, as illustrated in the life of Sri Ramakrishna, a wisdom which he himself had realized. The lives lived by Sri Ramakrishna and Swami Vivekananda and the message they delivered have been a source of inspiration to millions of human beings in different parts of the world; and millions more have been directly or indirectly influenced by them. The Movement initiated by them and carried on by dedicated workers has contributed immensely to a new spiritual awakening in the present age. The world is witnessing a spiritual rebirth. Materialistic ideas have been losing ground, and men and women are veering to spiritual idealism. Religions are crying for rapprochement. It is true that the situation in social, economic, political and ethical fields is disheartening. These are, however, the after-effects of skeptical secularism. In the spiritual realm the situation is promising.

CHAPTER IV

SWAMI VIVEKANANDA'S UNIVERSALITY

A distinctive characteristic of Swami Vivekananda is the comprehensiveness of his vision. He is remarkably universal. His thought is universal, his love universal, his message universal, his life-work universal. He stands up for mankind in general, without distinction of race or nationality, creed or culture, sex or age. He has in his view all types and grades of human beings, takes into account the various aspects of human life, and dwells on the basic problems of human existence. He sees the divine self of man and looks upon the human form as the very symbol of the Divinity. In Vivekananda the universal spirit has found a loving, dynamic, and all-encompassing expression, which is rarely to be found elsewhere. In his scheme of life there is no inherent conflict between faith and reason, between science and religion, between poetry and philosophy, between action and meditation, between social and monastic ideals. His plan is to lead each and every individual at whatever level, or in whatever sphere of life, to the highest goal, to the realization of his innate perfection, along his own line of development. As expressed by Swami Vivekananda:

> Take man where he stands and from there give him a lift.[1]
>
> Our duty is to encourage everyone in his struggle to live up to his own highest ideal, and strive at the same time to make the ideal as near as possible to the truth.[2]

First published in *Swami Vivekananda in East and West* (London: Ramakrishna Vedanta Centre, 1968).

[1]CW II:382.

[2]CW I:39.

> All the men and the women in any society are not of the same mind, capacity, or of the same power to do things; they must have different ideals, and we have no right to sneer at any ideal.[3]

Like all other great teachers of religion Swami Vivekananda has a special interest in man's spiritual life, which leads to the highest Goal; yet he has included in his plan of human regeneration the seekers of the temporal values as well as the seekers of the supreme Good. The search for the temporal regulated by ethical principles leads to the search for the eternal regulated by spiritual idealism. The one is preparatory to the other. The Vedic religion consists of both the ways. They are called respectively *pravṛtti-mārga,* the path of activity characterized by desire and *nivṛtti-mārga,* "the path of detachment or renunciation." While stressing the second, which is the direct way to the ultimate Goal, Swami Vivekananda has shown due regard for the other way as well. Says he:

> What can be a greater giver of peace than renunciation? A little ephemeral worldly good is nothing in comparison with eternal Good; no doubt of that. What can bring greater strength than *sattva guṇa* [serenity of mind conducive to spiritual knowledge]? It is indeed true that all other kinds of knowledge are but 'non-knowledge' in comparison with Self-knowledge, but I ask — how many are there in the world fortunate enough to gain that *sattva guṇa*? . . .
>
> Unless a man passes through *rajas* [right activity with desire] can he ever attain to that perfect *sāttvika* state [serenity of mind]? How can one expect *yōga,* or union with God, unless one has previously finished with his thirst for *bhōga* or enjoyment? How can renunciation come where there is no *vairāgya* or dispassion for all the charms of enjoyment?[4]

As we have noted in Chapter II, this inclusiveness of Swami Vivekananda's message distinguishes it even from the messages of other great spiritual leaders of the world. Undoubtedly, they were

[3]CW I:39. [4]CW IV:337-38.

all interested in the welfare of humanity in general; yet they concerned themselves particularly with the spiritually inclined. Their messages are intended for the seekers of freedom from the bondage of life rather than the worldly-minded.

The *Bhagavad-gītā* embodying the teachings of Śrī Kṛṣṇa, is definitely a "mōkṣa-śāstra," a sacred book dwelling on Liberation and its means. Its starting point is Karma-yōga, the performance of duties with no secular desire. Only such as outgrow sense-desires and turn away from the search of the temporal to the search of the Eternal are capable of practicing Karma-yōga, with which the spiritual life begins.

Buddha's message of the four golden truths relating to human sufferings and the eightfold path to nirvāṇa can suit especially those who are awakened to the ideal of complete deliverance from every form of misery. Similarly, the teachings of Jesus Christ have direct appeal to the seekers of the Kingdom of Heaven rather than the seekers of the kingdom of the world. The burden of Sri Ramakrishna's teachings is the renunciation of lust and greed. How many are ready for this?

It should not be supposed, however, that the message of these great teachers has no universal appeal. Though not as inclusive as Swami Vivekananda's, their teachings are nevertheless universal. The universality of a message does not mean, as far as I can see, its applicability to every individual case anywhere. But it means that its appeal is not restricted to any particular section of humanity, to any religious community, nation, race, class, country, or age. An individual belonging to any of these is eligible for a universal message, that is to say, has the possibility of being qualified for it in due course, under due conditions.

Though working on the spiritual plane the religious leaders indirectly influence all other levels of life. They usually occupy themselves with the roots of life and hardly enter into its details. By taking care of the roots they mean to take care of the entire tree of life. It is man's spiritual self that supports his entire psychophysical constitution. With the development of spiritual consciousness, that is to say, with the growing awareness of the true nature of the self, an individual's moral and rational nature are bound to develop. And it is his moral and rational nature that make his cultural growth, his social relations, and his material well-being sound and secure. The exemplary lives lived by spiritual personages serve as guides for the men of the world. Their wisdom, their moral integrity, their lofty thoughts, and noble deeds even influence the masses. This is why in the wake of religious revival in a country there has been social, political, cultural, and material advancement as well, creating epochs in the history of human civilization. It was so in the past and it is so in the present.

Swami Vivekananda's universality is rooted in his experience of the spiritual oneness of existence. It is not due simply to his intellectual comprehension, extensive knowledge, keen interest in human values, and world-wide sympathy or fellow-feeling. It is different in character from humanism, humanitarianism, and universalism. All of these value man as man irrespective of creed, color, rank, or position. Their highest conception of man is from the empirical viewpoint. But Swami Vivekananda sees God dwelling in human forms. To his spiritual vision man's real self is ever pure, free, immortal, and divine. The same Supreme Being, Pure Consciousness, dwells within each psychophysical organism as the conscious self more or less manifest. In human individuals He shines distinctly as the knowing self.

The One Infinite Self is apparently divided into countless individual selves, even as the moon appears as myriad moons being reflected in innumerable ripples of water. Of all the living creatures man alone is capable of realizing his essential identity with the Divinity and his unity with all living creatures. He who attains this experience feels a spiritual relationship with one and all, the only relationship between man and his fellow-creatures that transcends all distinctions of the psychophysical adjuncts and develops universal love. So says Śrī Kṛṣṇa:

> The knowers of the Self look with an equal eye on a Brāhmaṇa endowed with learning and humility, a scavenger, a cow, an elephant, or a dog.[5]
>
> With imperfections exhausted, doubts dispelled, senses controlled, engaged in the good of all beings, the knowers of Truth attain complete freedom and blessedness [in this very life].[6]

We have already stated (see page 80) how one evening in the summer of 1886 Swami Vivekananda, a young man of twenty-three then known by the family name of Narendranath Datta, attained *nirvikalpa samādhi* in the garden-house of Cossipore in the suburb of Calcutta, where Sri Ramakrishna lived during his last illness and left the mortal body on August 16, 1886. In the *nirvikalpa samādhi* state, which is the acme of spiritual experience, the individual consciousness realizes its identity with the cosmic consciousness beyond all distinctions of the superimposed adjuncts, and then one undivided, undiversified, infinite Consciousness shines.

Swami Vivekananda's all-embracing love was the spontaneous expression of spiritual enlightenment in the highest sense. With regard to the illumined souls who work for the guidance and upliftment of humanity Śaṅkarācārya remarks:

> There are pure souls, calm and magnanimous, who do good to the world spontaneously as does the spring, and who, having themselves crossed the dreadful ocean of life, help others also to cross it, without any motive whatsoever.
>
> It is the very nature of the great-souled to move of their own accord towards removing others' troubles, even as the moon voluntarily soothes the earth parched by the flaming rays of the sun.[7]

[5]BG V:18. [6]BG V:25. [7]VC 37,38.

Swami Vivekananda is the standard-bearer of Sri Ramakrishna. Their divine mission is the reconstruction of humanity in the present age on a spiritual foundation, which means the recognition of four fundamental truths. Explicit or implicit, these basic principles underlie all religions. Not only do they sustain the religious life of man, but also uphold other human ideals. We may enunciate them as follows:

1. The ever-changing world of phenomena, marked by interdependence and consisting of pairs of opposites, is held by one eternal ideal Reality, usually called God, who is self-existent and self-manifest, and answers to man's conception of perfection in every way.
2. Every individual psychophysical system of ceaseless change is sustained by a central principle, which is constant, self-luminous, ever pure and free.
3. The central principle of the microcosm is not different from the central principle of the macrocosm, that is to say, there is kinship or unity between the soul of man and the soul of the universe. The truth is, what is innermost in the one is innermost in the other.
4. To realize this kinship or unity is the goal of life; all human concerns should be regulated with this end in view.

These universal truths have been declared primarily by the world's oldest religious literature, known as the Upaniṣads or the Vedanta. Swami Vivekananda has interpreted these in modern terms in view of modern problems. In so doing he has built a bridge between the ancient and the modern, between the East and the West. Today the world is in dire need of a universal message and a comprehensive view of life, both of which Swami Vivekananda has provided.

Swami Vivekananda perceived spiritual unity as the ultimate ground of all diversity. It is the goal of all human knowledge. It underlies all religious doctrines and experiences, all metaphysical conceptions, all ethical ideals, and scientific truths. It unites all forms of existence, penetrates all phases of life. Indeed, this imperfect world has perfection as its very basis and being. The same ideal existence has varied manifestations through divergent forms. The forms differ, but the substance is one and the same. He who finds this One Self of all abhors none. The following words of Swami Vivekananda remind us of his own experience:

> If you go below the surface, you find that Unity between man and man, between races and races, high and low, rich and poor, gods and men, and men and animals. If you go deep enough, all will be seen as only variations of the One, and he who has attained to this conception of Oneness has no more delusion. What can delude him? He knows the reality of everything, the secret of everything. Where is there any more misery for him? What does he desire? He has traced the reality of everything to the Lord, the Centre, the Unity of everything, and that is Eternal Existence, Eternal Knowledge, Eternal Bliss.[8]

Swami Vivekananda's penetrating insight finds no fundamental difference between one section of humanity and another; the Eastern and the Western form one human race struggling for the fulfillment of its highest destiny.

Romain Rolland aptly remarks:

> Far from feeling that there was a fundamental natural difference between Europe and Asia, he was convinced that deep contact between Europe and Asia would inevitably lead to a renaissance of Europe; for she would renew her vital stock of spiritual ideas from the East.[9]

Further,

> His intuition of unity of the human race did not stop at the arbitrary

[8]CW II:153-54.

[9]Romain Rolland, *The Life of Vivekananda and the Universal Gospel,* 4th impr. (Calcutta: Advaita Ashrama, 1953), p.154.

> divisions of races and nations. It made him say that he had seen in the West some of the best Hindu types, and in India the best Christians.[10]

On the method of uniting the East and the West Swami Vivekananda observes:

> India has to learn from Europe the conquest of external nature, and Europe has to learn from India the conquest of internal nature. Then there will be neither Hindus [Indians] nor Europeans — there will be the ideal humanity which has conquered both the natures, the external and the internal. We have developed one phase of humanity, and they another. It is the union of the two that is wanted. The word freedom which is the watchword of our religion means freedom physically, mentally, and spiritually.[11]

The special contribution of the Orient to world-culture is religion; the special contribution of the Occident to world-culture is science. In Swami Vivekananda's view the present age needs the union of the two; this will bring about a unique civilization. He has explained that there is no contradiction between science and religion; and that modern science has strengthened the position of religion rather than weakened it.

Without the recognition of the spiritual oneness of mankind the unification of the world cannot be accomplished. It is the only common ground where heterogenous human elements can meet despite racial, social, economic, political, and cultural differences. The various races and nations of the world cannot be any time at the same level economically, politically, socially, or culturally. Nor can their interests in all these fields ever be identical. Naturally, the developed nations will find themselves closer together and away from the under-developed. Races of similar cultural standards and tastes will come near to one another and away from the rest. The world-government, cultural unity, and

[10] *Ibid.*, p. 150, unnumbered footnote. [11] CW V:122.

world-organizations such as the United Nations will help considerably to unite the various sections of humanity, but at the same time will have a tendency to divide mankind into different blocks and groups with party interests.

Apart from the perception of the spiritual solidarity of the universe Swami Vivekananda's prophetic vision of a shrunken, compact world brought about today by marvelous facilities of transportation and communication was a contributive factor to his concept of mankind as a unity well integrated in all aspects of life. Humanity must move as one body in an orderly procession, in which every individual, every nation, will have a distinctive role to play. Unity in variety and not uniformity is the pattern for world-culture. There is no inherent conflict between one aspect of life and another. Physical, intellectual, aesthetic, moral, and spiritual development must continue hand in hand. Science and religion, arts and ethics, philosophy and mysticism will all have their respective places in human life. One expression of life does not contradict another as long as it contributes to the highest Good that man has to achieve. The goal of civilization cannot be different from the goal of religion. Said Swami Vivekananda before the dawn of the present century:

> One atom in this universe cannot move without dragging the whole world along with it. There cannot be any progress without the whole world following in the wake, and it is becoming every day clearer that the solution of any problem can never be attained on racial, or national, or narrow grounds. Every idea has to become broad till it covers the whole of this world, every aspiration must go on increasing till it has engulfed the whole of humanity, nay, the whole of life, within its scope.[12]

> We want today that bright sun of intellectuality, joined with the heart of Buddha, the wonderful, infinite heart of love and mercy. This union will give us the highest philosophy. Science and religion will meet and

[12]CW III:269.

> shake hands. Poetry and philosophy will become friends. This will be the religion of the future, and if we can work it out, we may be sure that it will be for all times and peoples.[13]

> Just as a physicist, when he has pushed his knowledge to its limits, finds it melting away into metaphysics, so a metaphysician will find what he calls mind and matter are but apparent distinctions, the reality being One.[14]

> The more advanced a society or nation is in spirituality, the more is that society or nation civilized. No nation can be said to have become civilized, only because it has succeeded in increasing the comforts of material life by bringing into use lots of machinery and things of that sort. . . . In this age as on the one hand people have to be intensely practical, so on the other hand they have to acquire deep spiritual knowledge.[15]

The message of Swami Vivekananda is, indeed, the gospel of universal truth. The religion and philosophy of Vedanta (wrongly called Hinduism), which he expounded, contains the essentials of all the religions of the world. Vedanta is not, truly speaking, one of the many faiths or religious systems, but the common basis of all of them, inasmuch as it dwells on the fundamental truths that underlie the different religious doctrines and practices. It is in a sense a system of religions. It teaches not one particular aspect or concept of God, but several; it prescribes not one particular spiritual discipline or method of worship, but several. It recommends different religious courses for the seekers of different capacities. The Goal is one and the same, but the ways differ according to the aspirants' aptitudes and conditions of life.

Vedanta looks upon the various religions of the world as so many approaches to one and the same Supreme Being. They are the varied expressions of one eternal, universal religion, man's search for God. "As the different streams having their sources in different places all mingle their water in the sea, so O Lord, the different paths which men take through different tendencies,

[13]CW II:140. [14]CW I:133. [15]CW VI:417-18.

various though they appear, crooked or straight, all lead to Thee."[16] This is the Sanskrit verse, rendered into English, which Swami Vivekananda recited while delivering his address at the opening session of the World's Parliament of Religions in Chicago, on September 11, 1893.

In his concluding address at the final session of the Parliament of Religions on September 27, 1893, he declared, as we have pointed out before:

> The Christian is not to become a Hindu or a Buddhist, nor a Hindu or a Buddhist to become a Christian. But each must assimilate the spirit of the others and yet preserve his individuality and grow according to his own law of growth.
>
> If the Parliament of Religions has shown anything to the world it is this: It has proved to the world that holiness, purity, and charity are not the exclusive possessions of any church in the world and that every system has produced men and women of the most exalted character. In the face of this evidence, if anybody dreams of the exclusive survival of his own religion and the destruction of the others, I pity him from the bottom of my heart, and point out to him that upon the banner of every religion will soon be written, in spite of their resistance: "Help and not Fight," "Assimilation and not Destruction," "Harmony and Peace and not Dissension."[17]

The universality of religion does not point to the existence of one religion the world over as the sole survivor of the rest, as the bigots imagine. It simply means the peaceful coexistence of all religions. It is to be achieved by mutual understanding and appreciation and a reverent attitude towards one another. Not even eclecticism nor syncretism can establish the harmony of religions that Swami Vivekananda envisions. Eclecticism aims to select the best out of every religion and combine them into a consistent whole. It may present something as attractive as a

[16] *The Hymn on the Greatness of Śiva,* 7.
[17] CW I:22. See also chap. 1, sec. 27.

bouquet of flowers. But this cannot grow, having no root in the soil of life. The eclectic method was tried in the past, but failed. Syncretism aims to reconcile the divergent religions by stressing the similarities among them and ignoring their differences. But in Swami Vivekananda's view the differences have deep meanings. They meet the requirements of the seekers of different capabilities and temperaments. With all their differences, religions should live together harmoniously. The only universal religion possible in the world is the amity of religions.

In his lecture on "The Way to the Realization of Universal Religion", delivered in the Universalist Church, Pasadena, California, on January 28, 1900, Swami Vivekananda observed:

> Our watchword, then, will be acceptance, and not exclusion. Not only toleration, for so-called toleration is often blasphemy, and I do not believe in it. I believe in acceptance. Why should I tolerate? Toleration means that I think that you are wrong and I am just allowing you to live. Is it not a blasphemy to think that you and I are allowing others to live? I accept all religions that were in the past, and worship with them all; I worship God with every one of them, in whatever form they worship Him. . . .
>
> The Bible, the Vedas, the Koran, and all other sacred books are but so many pages, and an infinite number of pages remain yet to be unfolded. I would leave it open for all of them. We stand in the present, but open ourselves to the infinite future. We take in all that has been in the past, enjoy the light of the present, and open every window of the heart for all that will come in the future. Salutation to all the prophets of the past, to all the great ones of the present, and to all that are to come in the future.[18]

Harmony of religions is the crying need of the day. It is essential to the peace and the progress of the world. No civilization can exist nor grow without this. All bigotry and intolerance, all narrowness and sectarianism must leave human minds. Instead there should be mutual regard, friendliness, and cooperation in all

[18]CW II:371-72.

spheres of life. Religion, which avowedly stands for love, charity, and peace, must take the lead. The time has come when religious ideas must broaden. The adherents of every religion must know the universal truths that underlie all religious doctrines and disciplines despite their differences. Without understanding them no follower of any religion can understand his own religion, or the religions of others. The lack of understanding means the lack of appreciation, the lack of appreciation the lack of sympathy and benevolence. The same spiritual principles that support religion support all other aspects of life. Spirituality is the key to life's development in all fields. Religious ideals in a broad sense must cover the entire life of man. Says Swami Vivekananda:

> No civilization can grow, unless fanaticism, bloodshed, and brutality stop. No civilization can begin to lift up its head until we look charitably upon one another, and the first step towards that much-needed charity is to look charitably and kindly upon the religious convictions of others. Nay more, to understand that not only should we be charitable, but positively helpful, to each other, however different our religious ideas and convictions may be.[19]

> Religion is the greatest motive power for realizing that infinite energy which is the birthright and nature of every man. In building up character, in making for everything that is good and great, in bringing peace to others, and peace to one's own self, religion is the highest motive power, and therefore, ought to be studied from that standpoint. Religion must be studied on a broader basis than formerly. . . .

> As the human mind broadens, its spiritual steps broaden too. The time has already come when a man cannot record a thought without its reaching to all corners of the earth; by merely physical means, we have come into touch with the whole world; so the future religions of the world have to become as universal, as wide.

> The religious ideals of the future must embrace all that exists in the world and is good and great, and, at the same time, have infinite scope for future development. . . .

[19]CW III:187-88.

> The power of religion, broadened and purified, is going to penetrate every part of human life. So long as religion was in the hands of a chosen few, or of a body of priests, it was in temples, churches, books, dogmas, ceremonials, forms and rituals. But when we come to the real, spiritual, universal concept, then, and then alone, religion will become real and living; it will come into our very nature, live in our every movement, penetrate every pore of our society, and be infinitely more a power for good than it has ever been before.[20]

The central truth of religion is the divinity of man. "The Kingdom of God is within you," says Jesus Christ.[21] To realize this divinity is the goal of spiritual life. As defined by Swami Vivekananda, "Religion is the manifestation of the divinity already in man."[22] The knowledge of this divinity is the secret of man's development both in individual and collective life, secular as well as spiritual. It finds expression in two distinct ways: "I am divine" and "Thou art divine." As a man becomes aware of his own divinity he becomes aware at the same time of the divinity of his fellow-beings. Along with the development of his faith in himself his regard for others develops. His potentialities grow as his self-faith is intensified. His capacity for serving his fellow-creatures necessarily increases. Says Swami Vivekananda:

> This infinite power of the Spirit, brought to bear upon matter evolves material development, made to act upon thought evolves intellectuality, and made to act upon Itself makes of man a God. . . . Manifest the divinity within you, and everything will be harmoniously arranged around it.[23]

In Vedantic culture this cardinal teaching of man's divinity has so far been imparted by the adepts to worthy pupils exclusively for their spiritual development. Swami Vivekananda's method is

[20]CW II:67-68.
[21]Luke 17:21.
[22]CW IV:304.
[23]CW IV:297-98.

evidently a departure from the traditional way. He has broadcast the supreme truth to one and all, the seekers of Self-knowledge and the seekers of secular values as well. Nevertheless his principle is not contradictory to the spirit of the Vedic religion, which recommends two kinds of worship of God — with secular desires and without secular desires — according to the worshipper's inner development. The truth is, the worship with desires (sakāma upāsanā) leads to the worship without desires (niṣkāma upāsanā). By worshipping God for temporal values, the seeker develops the tendency to worship God for God's sake. Similarly, by holding to the spiritual self for the sake of secular interests a person gradually becomes convinced of the innate glory of the self and turns to the ideal of Self-realization.

What led Swami Vivekananda thus to popularize the Vedantic truth was his unbounded compassion for one and all down to the lowest. His intense eagerness for the upliftment of man is evident from these impassioned words:

> Aye, let every man and woman and child, without respect of caste or birth, weakness or strength, hear and learn that behind the strong and the weak, behind the high and the low, behind every one, there is that Infinite Soul, insuring the infinite possibility and the infinite capacity of all to become great and good. Let us proclaim to every soul — "Arise, awake and stop not till the goal is reached." . . .
>
> Teach yourselves, teach everyone his real nature, call upon the sleeping soul and see how it awakes. Power will come, glory will come, goodness will come, purity will come, and everything that is excellent will come when this sleeping soul is roused to self-conscious activity.[24]

It is true that Swami Vivekananda had a very deep love for India. He has been called "The Patriot-saint of India." But it is to be noted that his love for India was a phase of his love for humanity in general. He was primarily a lover of man. His heart

[24]CW III:192,193.

bled for the poor, the ignorant, and the down-trodden everywhere. If he felt particularly for the suffering millions of India it was because he had witnessed their condition and because he knew that the spiritual regeneration of the world depended on the regeneration of India.

He was convinced that nothing but the supreme spiritual truths, which India had preserved from time immemorial, which had been verified by the mystical experiences of her sages and saints and interpreted in terms of reason by her seer-philosophers throughout the ages, could save the modern world from growing secularism, which threatened her civilization, nay, her very existence. Though the masses of India had been sunken in poverty, illiteracy, and passivity, yet she had her spiritual treasure intact. Never did she lose her soul. India has to learn from Europe the conquest of external nature, and Europe has to learn from India the conquest of internal nature: this was the outline of Swami Vivekananda's plan of the reconstruction of humanity. In raising India it was his aim to raise the world.

Swami Vivekananda's interest was neither national nor international, but universal. As an ideal sannyāsī (as a monk of the Nondualistic order) he ever knew in the depth of his heart that he was one with the Infinite; he did not belong to any particular country, nation or race. On September 9, 1895, he wrote from Paris, "I belong as much to India as to the world, no humbug about that . . . What country has any special claim on me? Am I any nation's slave?"[25] After starting the Ramakrishna Mission "for the good of many, for the happiness of many," he wrote from Almora, India, to an American admirer on July 9, 1897, as to his universality.[26]

Sister Nivedita testifies to Swami Vivekananda's love for man:

[25] *Letters of Swami Vivekananda,* no.105, p. 257.

[26] For the contents of the letter see the "Ramakrishna-Vivekananda Vedanta Movement," sec. 10.

> No institution, no environment, stood between him and any human heart. His confidence in that Divine-within-Man of which he talked, was as Perfect, and his appeal as direct, when he talked with the imperialist aristocrat or the American millionaire, as with the exploited and oppressed. But the outflow of his love and courtesy were always for the simple.
>
> When travelling in America, he had at first in certain southern towns been taken for a negro, and refused admission to the hotels, he had never said that he was not of African blood, but had as quietly and gratefully availed himself of the society of the colored race, when that was offered, as of that of the local magnates who hastened round him later, in mortified apology for what they deemed the insult put upon him. "What! rise at the expense of another!" he was heard to say to himself, long after, when someone referred with astonishment to this silence about his race, "Rise at the expense of another! I didn't come to earth for that!"[27]

Only the realization of spiritual oneness with all can develop such universal love. It is bliss and freedom at the same time. Says Swami Vivekananda from his own experience, no doubt:

> We have always heard it preached, "Love one another." What for? That doctrine was preached, but the explanation is here. Why should I love everyone? Because they and I are one. Why should I love my brother? Because he and I are one. There is this oneness, this solidarity of the whole universe. From the lowest worm that crawls under our feet to the highest beings that ever lived — all have various bodies, but are the one Soul. Through all mouths you eat; through all hands you work; through all eyes you see. You enjoy health in millions of bodies, you are suffering from disease in millions of bodies. When this idea comes and we realize it, see it, feel it, then will misery cease, and fear with it. How can I die? There is nothing beyond me. Fear ceases, and then alone come perfect happiness and perfect love. That universal sympathy, universal love, universal bliss that never changes, raises man above everything.[28]

[27]Sister Nivedita, *The Master as I Saw Him,* 10th edn. (Calcutta: Udbodhan Office, 1966), pp. 218-19.

[28]CW II:412-13.

The spiritual oneness of mankind is also the foundation of ethics. As stated by Swami Vivekananda:

> The infinite oneness of the Soul is the eternal sanction of all morality, that you and I are not only brothers — every literature voicing man's struggle towards freedom has preached that for you — but that you and I are really one. This is the dictate of Indian philosophy. This oneness is the rationale of all ethics and all spirituality.[29]

Swami Vivekananda has also introduced a universal form of worship. Since God dwells in man as the inmost Self, He can be directly worshipped by serving man. All social work and the teaching of religion as well should be carried on in the spirit of worshipping God in man. In this way humanitarian deeds turn into spiritual practice. The aspirants' inner development and the amelioration of the world condition can go together.

With this end in view Swami Vivekananda established the Ramakrishna Math and Mission — a religious and philanthropic institution that has developed into a world-wide organization — the monastic and the lay members of which strive to render service to the ignorant, the needy, the distressed, and the diseased as the veritable worship of God dwelling in them. "If God can be worshipped through a clay image, then why not through a man?" says Sri Ramakrishna.[30] Though this mode of worship was recommended by Śrī Kṛṣṇa in his message to Uddhava in the *Bhāgavatam,*[31] its practical application on a wide scale in the lives of the spiritual aspirants for the alleviation of human sufferings had never been tried before.

Thus exhorts Swami Vivekananda, as we have pointed out before:

> Look upon every man, woman, and everyone as God. You cannot help anyone; you can only serve; serve the children of the Lord, serve

[29]CW III:189. [30]GSR, p.407. [31]SB XI:29.12-22.

> the Lord Himself, if you have the privilege. If the Lord grants that you can help anyone of His children, blessed you are; do not think too much of yourselves. Blessed you are that that privilege was given to you, when others had it not. Do it only as a worship.[32]
>
> You may invent an image through which to worship God, but a better image already exists, the living man. You may build a temple in which to worship God, and that may be good, but a better one, a much higher one, already exists, the human body.[33]

All duties in domestic and social life can be performed with this worshipful attitude:

> We have to cover everything with the Lord Himself, not by a false sort of optimism, not by blinding our eyes to the evil, but by really seeing God in everything. Thus we have to give up the world, and when the world is given up, what remains? God. What is meant? You can have your wife; it does not mean that you are to abandon her, but you are to see God in the wife. Give up your children; what does that mean? To turn them out-of-doors, as some human brutes do in every country? Certainly not. That is diabolism; it is not religion. But see God in your children. So, in everything. In life and in death, in happiness and in misery, the Lord is equally present. The whole world is full of the Lord. Open your eyes and see Him. This is what Vedanta teaches.[34]

Swami Vivekananda stresses the importance of man above all. Man's inner nature is much more important than his outer resources. It is man that makes money; money does not make man. It is man that makes laws; laws do not make man. The final solution of world problems rests basically on the individuals'

[32]CW III:246.

[33]CW II:311. Cf. "Know ye not that ye are the temple of God and that the spirit of God dwelleth in you? If any man defile the temple of God, him shall God destroy; for the temple of God is holy which temple ye are." (St. Paul's First Epistle to the Corinthians 3:16,17.)

[34]CW II:146. Cf. "All this — whatsoever moves in the moving universe — should be covered by the Lord [the Immovable Self]. Save the Self by the spirit of renunciation. Covet not anyone's wealth [for there is no wealth but the Self]." (Is.U.I.)

moral and spiritual lives. If these be lacking nothing can save the human situation; no political or economic system, no social order, no world-organization, no advancement of scientific knowledge and technology, no development of arts, no defense measures, no subtle ideologies, can establish peace and security in the world. Even education without a sound outlook on life cannot help us in this respect. Whoever has the well-being of man in his heart will carefully weigh the following remarks of Swami Vivekananda:

> It is a change of the soul itself for the better, that alone will cure the evils of life. No amount of force, or government, or legislative cruelty will change the conditions of a race, but it is spiritual culture and ethical culture alone that can change wrong racial tendencies for the better.[35]

> But the basis of all systems, social or political, rests upon the goodness of men. No nation is great or good because Parliament enacts this or that, but because its men are great and good. . . . Religion goes to the root of the matter. If it is right, all is right.[36]

> Great indeed are the manifestations of muscular power, and marvelous the manifestations of intellect expressing themselves through machines by the appliances of science; yet, none of these are more potent than the influence which spirit exerts upon the world.[37]

> I direct my attention to the individual, to make him strong, to teach him that he himself is divine, and I call upon men to make themselves conscious of this divinity within. That is really the ideal — conscious or unconscious — of every religion.[38]

> It is a man-making religion that we want. It is man-making theories that we want. It is man-making education all round that we want. And here is the test of truth — anything that makes you weak physically, intellectually, and spiritually, reject as poison, there is no life in it, it cannot be true. Truth is strengthening. Truth is purity, truth is all-knowledge; truth must be strengthening, must be enlightening, must be invigorating.[39]

Swami Vivekananda was an apostle of strength. His words

[35]CW III:182.
[36]CW V:122.
[37]CW III:137.
[38]CW V:117.
[39]CW III:224.

infuse strength into the recipient immediately. He encouraged the cultivation of strength above all. If he was intolerant of anything, it was weakness. According to him all virtues can be summed up in one word *strength,* all vices in one word *weakness.* The secret of man's strength is faith in himself. It counteracts fear, which is paralyzing. What can give man greater faith than the consciousness of his own divine nature? It is the religion of strength that Swami Vivekananda taught. In his view strength is religion and weakness is irreligion. We quote some of his inspiring words on strength:

> What makes a man stand up and work? Strength. Strength is goodness; weakness is sin. If there is one word that you find coming out like a bomb from the Upaniṣads, bursting like a bomb-shell upon masses of ignorance, it is the word *fearlessness.* And the only religion that ought to be taught, is the religion of *fearlessness.* Either in this world or in the world of religion, it is true that fear is the sure cause of degradation and sin. It is fear that brings evil. And what causes fear? Ignorance of our own nature.[40]
>
> Weakness leads to all kinds of misery, physical and mental. Weakness is death. There are hundreds of thousands of microbes surrounding us, but they cannot harm us unless we become weak, until the body is ready and predisposed to receive them. There may be a million microbes of misery, floating about us. Never mind! They dare not approach us; they have no power to get a hold on us, until the mind is weakened. This is the great fact; strength is life; weakness is death; strength is felicity, life eternal, immortal; weakness is constant strain and misery; weakness is death.[41]
>
> We reap what we sow. We are makers of our own fate. None else has the blame, none has the praise.[42]
>
> Do you know how much energy, how many powers, how many forces are still lurking behind that frame of yours? What scientist has known all that is in man? Millions of years have passed since man first came here, and yet but one infinitesimal part of his powers has been manifested. Therefore, you must not say that you are weak. How do

[40]CW III:160. [41]CW II:3. [42]CW II:224.

> you know what possibilities lie behind that degradation on the surface? You know but little of that which is within you. For behind you is the ocean of infinite power and blessedness.[43]
>
> Men are taught from childhood that they are weak and sinners. Teach them that they are glorious children of immortality, even those who are the weakest in manifestation. Let positive, strong, helpful thought enter into their brains from very childhood. Lay yourselves open to these thoughts, and not to weakening and paralyzing ones. Say to your own minds, "I am He [pure, free, immortal spirit]," "I am He [pure, free, immortal spirit]."[44]

Swami Vivekananda had the capacity to appreciate greatness in any form. In judging races as well as individuals his principle was "each is great in his own place." "Each race has a peculiar mission to fulfill in the life of the world," says he.[45] A king or a farmer, a monk or a householder, each has his own status. Each and everything has to be viewed from its particular position. He saw a person's strong points, degraded though he might be, and appraised him accordingly. He would not cut the ground under anybody's feet, loose though it might be, but lead him to firmer ground from where he stood. "Do not destroy anyone's faith," says Sri Ramakrishna.

Like the world's great religious reformers Vivekananda's method was to fulfill and not to destroy. He wanted a country's progress on the basis of her own greatness, past and present. Never did he think of future India as the replica of her glorious past. "What he himself wanted was to see the strength of that old India finding new application and undreamt of expression, in the new age," says Sister Nivedita.[46]

As a close observer of Swami Vivekananda's personality, she has mentioned an incident illustrative of his aptitude to recognize greatness anywhere.

[43]CW II:299-300.
[44]CW II:87.
[45]CW III:108.
[46]Sister Nivedita, *The Master as I Saw Him,* p.241.

> One day, in the course of my voyage to England, when he had been telling me, with the greatest delight, of the skilled seamanship and exquisite courtesy of the Turk, I drew his attention to the astonishing character of his enthusiasm. His mind seemed to turn to the thought of the ship's servants, whose childlike devotion to himself had touched him deeply. "You see I love our Mohammedans!" he said simply as if accused of a fault. "Yes!" I answered, "but what I want to understand is this habit of seeing every people from their strongest aspect. Where did it come from? Do you recognize it in any historical character? Or is it in some way derived from Sri Ramakrishna?" Slowly the look of puzzled surprise left his face. "It must have been the training under Ramakrishna Paramahamsa," he answered.[47]

Apropos of this characteristic of Swami Vivekananda Romain Rolland remarks:

> That which emerges most clearly is his *universal* sense. He had hopes of democratic America, he was enthusiastic over the Italy of art, culture, and liberty — the great mother of Mazzini. He spoke of China as the treasury of the world. He fraternized with martyred Babists of Persia. He embraced in equal love the India of the Hindus, the Mohammedans, the Buddhists. He was fired by the Mogul Empire: when he spoke of Akbar the tears came into his eyes. He could comprehend and defend the grandeur of Genghis Khan and his dream of Asiatic unity. He made Buddha the subject of magnificent eulogy: "I am the servant of the servants of Buddha. . . ."[48]

With this universal sympathy, with this lively interest in all that is great and good, Swami Vivekananda was completely detached from his surroundings. This is corroborated by the statements of several eye-witnesses. I quote below what Sister Nivedita writes from her own experience:

> The outstanding impression made by the Swami's bearing, during all these months of European and American life, was one of almost

[47] *Ibid.*, p.228.

[48] Romain Rolland, *The Life of Vivekananda and the Universal Gospel*, p. 149, footnote 1.

complete indifference to his surroundings. Current estimates of value left him entirely unaffected. He was never in any way startled or incredulous under success, being too deeply convinced of the greatness of the Power that worked through him, to be surprised by it. But neither was he unnerved by external failure. Both victory and defeat would come and go. He was their witness. . . .

He moved fearless and unhesitant through the luxury of the West. As determinedly as I had seen him in India, dressed in the two garments of simple folk, sitting on the floor and eating with his fingers, so, equally without doubt or shrinking, was his acceptance of the complexity of the means of living in America or France. Monk and king, he said, were obverse and reverse of a single medal. From the use of the best to the renunciation of all, was but one step.[49]

As a knower of Brahman, Swami Vivekananda lived on both transcendental and normal planes. He had only the semblance of the ego. His "I-consciousness" was ever united with Supreme Consciousness. Fully established in the knowledge of the Blissful Self, the ground of all diversity, he moved unaffected from one condition of life to another, no matter how great the difference between the two might be. As noted by Śrī Śaṅkarācārya: "Neither pleasure nor pain, nor good nor evil ever touches the knower of Brahman who always lives without the body-idea."[50] With his all-embracing love for the living he maintains evenness of mind with regard to the nonliving.

The life and the message of Swami Vivekananda point to the fact that there can be unity among men on the widest scale despite all differences. The world-unity which is the crying need of the age has to be achieved not by exclusion or uniformity but by unison, by following the principle of unity in variety. The one and the same Ideal Reality — Pure Being-Consciousness-Bliss — holds all multiplicity; the same Divine Being who controls the universe dwells in the hearts of all individuals as the inmost self. This

[49]Sister Nivedita, *The Master as I Saw Him*, pp. 217-18.
[50]VC 545.

central truth is the key to the explanation of all facts. To realize the Divinity is the supreme end of human life. From any situation in life a person can proceed towards this Goal following his own line of development according to his or her psychophysical constitution. One expression of life does not contradict another as long as it is in conformity with the highest Ideal. All other ideals of life should be subordinate to this supreme One. Religion promises to lead to It directly. All human values — all that are necessary and desirable — art, literature, science, philosophy, ethics, politics, economics can contribute to the attainment of the highest Good, the Divine perfection.

In his inaugural message on the Swami Vivekananda Birth Centenary, January 17, 1963, Swami Madhavananda, at that time the President of the Ramakrishna Math and Mission, rightly observed on Vivekananda's life and message:

> In his comprehensive message, science and religion, reason and faith, the secular and the sacred, the modern and the ancient, and the East and the West became unified, and he himself was the personification of this union. His life and message have given the necessary impetus for the ushering in of a new era in the history of the civilization of man.

CHAPTER V

A CLASSIFIED SURVEY OF SWAMI VIVEKANANDA'S MESSAGE

The selections under each heading are so arranged as to form a unified statement offering clues to the solution of modern man's basic problems in individual and collective life.

1. Humanity must progress as a whole. Unity in variety, not uniformity, is the pattern for world-culture. There is no inherent conflict between science and religion, between reason and faith, or between poetry and philosophy.
2. Each individual has to move toward the Highest Ideal, God, from where he is, along his own line of development.
3. The final solution of human problems rests on the individuals' moral and spiritual life.
4. The goal of civilization is the same as the goal of religion.
5. Faith in himself is the secret of a man's growth. It is the source of all strength. Man's development means the unfoldment of his potential capacities.
6. "Education is the manifestation of the perfection already in man."
7. "Religion is the manifestation of the divinity already in man."
8. Each religion is an approach to one and the same Supreme Being variously conceived.
9. Harmony of religions is the crying need of the day. It is essential to the peace and the progress of the world.
10. The spiritual oneness of mankind is the foundation of morality. The vision of this unity is the way to universal love and bliss.

11. The ideal of religion must penetrate and inspire all spheres of life with the recognition of the spiritual solidarity of the universe.
12. The ideal and the practice are interrelated.
13. God can be directly worshipped by serving man.

1. *Humanity must progress as a whole. Unity in variety, not uniformity, is the pattern for world-culture. There is no inherent conflict between science and religion, between reason and faith, or between poetry and philosophy.*

One atom in this universe cannot move without dragging the whole world along with it. There cannot be any progress without the whole world following in the wake, and it is becoming clearer every day that the solution of any problem can never be attained on racial, or national, or narrow grounds. Every idea has to become broad till it covers the whole of this world, every aspiration must go on increasing till it has engulfed the whole of humanity, nay, the whole of life, within its scope.[1]

We want today that bright sun of intellectuality, joined with the heart of Buddha, the wonderful, infinite heart of love and mercy. This union will give us the highest philosophy. Science and religion will meet and shake hands. Poetry and philosophy will become friends. This will be the religion of the future, and if we can work it out, we may be sure that it will be for all times and peoples.[2]

Just as in the same society some individuals want to control the external nature, and others the internal, so, among races, some want to control the external nature, and others the internal. Some say that by controlling internal nature we control everything. Others that by controlling external nature we control everything.

[1]CW III:269. [2]CW II:140.

Carried to the extreme both are right, because in nature there is no such division as internal or external. These are fictitious limitations that never existed. The externalists and the internalists are destined to meet at the same point, when both reach the extreme of their knowledge. Just as a physicist, when he pushes his knowledge to its limits, finds it melting away into metaphysics, so a metaphysician will find that what he calls mind and matter are but apparent distinctions, the reality being One.[3]

Modern science has really made the foundation of religion strong. That the whole universe is one is scientifically demonstrable. What the metaphysicians call "being," the physicist calls "matter," but there is no real fight between the two, for both are one.[4]

2. *Each individual has to move toward the Highest Ideal, God, from where he is, along his own line of development. Take man where he stands, and from there give him a lift.*[5]

All the men and women, in any society, are not of the same mind, capacity, or of the same power to do things; they must have different ideals, and we have no right to sneer at any ideal. Let every one do the best he can for realizing his own ideal. Nor is it right that I should be judged by your standard or you by mine. The apple tree should not be judged by the standard of the oak, nor the oak by that of the apple. To judge the apple tree you must take the apple standard, and for the oak, its own standard.[6]

Unity in variety is the plan of creation. However men and women may vary individually, there is unity in the background. The different individual characters and classes of men and women are natural variations in creation. Hence, we ought not to judge them by the same standard or put the same ideal before them. Such

[3]CW I:133.
[4]CW VII:48.
[5]CW II:382.
[6]CW I:39.

a course creates only an unnatural struggle, and the result is that man begins to hate himself and is hindered from becoming religious and good. Our duty is to encourage every one in his struggle to live up to his own highest ideal, and strive at the same time to make the ideal as near as possible to the truth.[7]

Through high philosophy or low, through the most exalted mythology or the grossest, through the most refined ritualism or arrant fetishism, every sect, every soul, every nation, every religion, consciously or unconsciously, is struggling upward, towards God; every vision of truth that man has, is a vision of Him and of none else.[8]

3. *The final solution of human problems rests on the individuals' moral and spiritual life.*

It is a change of the soul itself for the better, that alone will cure the evils of life. No amount of force, or government, or legislative cruelty will change the conditions of a race, but it is spiritual culture and ethical culture alone that can change wrong racial tendencies for the better.[9]

But the basis of all systems, social or political, rests upon the goodness of men. No nation is great or good because Parliament enacts this or that, but because its men are great and good. . . . Religion goes to the root of the matter. If it is right, all is right.[10]

Great indeed are the manifestations of muscular power, and marvellous the manifestations of intellect expressing themselves through machines by the appliances of science; yet, none of these are more potent than the influence which spirit exerts upon the world.[11]

I direct my attention to the individual, to make him strong, to teach him that he himself is divine, and I call upon men to make

[7]CW I:39.
[8]CW II:381.
[9]CW III:182.
[10]CW V:122.
[11]CW III:137.

themselves conscious of this divinity within. That is really the ideal — conscious or unconscious — of every religion.[12]

It is a man-making religion that we want. It is man-making theories that we want. It is man-making education all round that we want. And here is the test of truth — anything that makes you weak physically, intellectually, and spiritually, reject as poison, there is no life in it, it cannot be true. Truth is strengthening. Truth is purity, truth is all-knowledge; truth must be strengthening, must be enlightening, must be invigorating.[13]

4. *The goal of civilization is the same as the goal of religion.*

This universe is simply a gymnasium in which the soul is taking exercise; and after these exercises we become gods. So the value of everything is to be decided by how far it is a manifestation of God. Civilization is the manifestation of that divinity in man.[14]

Civilization, true civilization, should mean the power of taking the animal-man out of his sense-life — by giving him visions and tastes of planes much higher — and not external comforts.[15]

A nation may conquer the waves, control the elements, develop the utilitarian problems of life seemingly to the utmost limits, and yet not realize that in the individual, the highest type of civilization is found in him who has learned to conquer self.[16]

The more advanced a society or nation is in spirituality, the more civilized is that society or nation. No nation can be said to have become civilized, only because it has succeeded in increasing the comforts of material life by bringing into use lots of machinery and things of that sort . . . In this age, as on the one hand people have to be intensely practical, so on the other hand they have to acquire deep spiritual knowledge.[17]

[12]CW V:117.
[13]CW III:224.
[14]CW V:232.
[15]CW IV:230.
[16]CW IV:196.
[17]CW VI:417-18.

India has to learn from Europe the conquest of external nature, and Europe has to learn from India the conquest of internal nature. Then there will be neither Hindus [Indians] nor Europeans — there will be the ideal humanity which has conquered both the natures, the external and the internal. We have developed one phase of humanity, and they another. It is the union of the two that is wanted. The word freedom which is the watchword of our religion really means freedom physically, mentally, and spiritually.[18]

5. *Faith in himself is the secret of a man's growth. It is the source of all strength. Man's development means the unfoldment of his potential capacities.*

The ideal of faith in ourselves is of the greatest help to us. If faith in ourselves had been more extensively taught and practiced, I am sure a very large portion of the evils and miseries that we have, would have vanished. Throughout the history of mankind, if any motive power has been more potent than another in the lives of all great men and women, it is that of faith in themselves. Born with the consciousness that they were to be great, they became great.[19]

We can see that all the difference between man and man is owing to the existence or non-existence of faith in himself. Faith in ourselves will do everything. I have experienced it in my own life, and am still doing so, and as I grow older that faith is becoming stronger and stronger. He is an atheist who does not believe in himself. The old religions said that he was an atheist who did not believe in God. The new religion says that he is the atheist who does not believe in himself. But it is not selfish faith, because the Vedanta, again, is the doctrine of Oneness. It means faith in all, because you are all.[20]

[18]CW V:146. [19]CW II:299. [20]CW II:299.

Love for yourselves means love for all, love for animals, love for everything, for you are all one. It is the great faith which will make the world better. I am sure of that. He is the highest man who can say with truth, "I know all about myself." Do you know how much energy, how many powers, how many forces, are still lurking behind that frame of yours? What scientist has known all that is in man? Millions of years have passed since man first came here, and yet but one infinitesimal part of his powers has been manifested. Therefore, you must not say that you are weak. How do you know what possibilities lie behind that degradation on the surface? You know but little of that which is within you. For behind you is the ocean of infinite power and blessedness.[21]

The tree comes out of the seed, goes back to the seed; the beginning and the end are the same. The earth comes out of its cause and returns to it. We know that if we find the beginning we can find the end. *E converso,* if we find the end we can find the beginning. If that is so, take this whole evolutionary series, from the protoplasm at one end to the perfect man at the other, and this whole series is one life. In the end we find the perfect man, so in the beginning it must have been the same. Therefore, the protoplasm was the involution of the highest intelligence. You may not see it, but that involved intelligence is what is uncoiling itself until it becomes manifested in the most perfect man.[22]

Follies there are, weakness there must be, but remember your real nature always — that is the only way to cure the weakness, that is the only way to cure the follies.[23]

I may be a little bubble of water, and you may be a mountain-high wave; never mind! The infinite ocean is the background of me as well as of you. Mine also is that infinite ocean of life, or power, of spirituality, as well as yours.[24]

Losing faith in one's self means losing faith in God.[25]

[21]CW II:299.
[22]CW II:208-9.
[23]CW III:377.
[24]CW III:376.
[25]CW III:376.

6. *"Education is the manifestation of the perfection already in man."*

The end and aim of all training is to make the man grow.[26]

Like fire in a piece of flint, knowledge exists in the mind; suggestion is the friction which brings it out.[27]

What we say a man "knows," should in strict psychological language, be what he "discovers" or "unveils"; what a man "learns" is really what he "discovers," by taking the cover off his own soul, which is a mine of infinite knowledge. We say Newton discovered gravitation. Was it sitting anywhere in a corner waiting for him? It was in his own mind; the time came and he found it out. All knowledge that the world has ever received comes from the mind; the infinite library of the universe is in your own mind. The external world is simply the suggestion, the occasion, which sets you to study your own mind, but the object of your study is always your own mind. The falling of an apple gave the suggestion to Newton, and he studied his own mind. He rearranged all the previous links of thought in his mind and discovered a new link among them, which we call the law of gravitation. It was not in the apple nor in anything in the centre of the earth. All knowledge therefore, secular or spiritual, is in the human mind. In many cases it is not discovered, but remains covered, and when the covering is being slowly taken off we say "we are learning," and the advance of knowledge is made by the advance of this process of uncovering.[28]

We have but one method of acquiring knowledge. From the lowest man to the highest Yōgin, all have to use the same method; and that method is what is called concentration. The chemist who works in his laboratory concentrates all the powers of his mind into one focus, and throws them on the elements, and the elements stand analyzed, and thus his knowledge comes. The astronomer

[26]CW II:15.
[27]CW I:26.
[28]CW I:26.

has also concentrated the powers of his mind, and brought them into one focus; and he throws them on to objects, through his telescope; and stars and systems roll forward, and give up their secrets to him. So it is in every case; with the professor in his chair, the student with his book, with every man who is working to know.[29]

The more this power of concentration, the more knowledge is acquired, because this is the one and only method of acquiring knowledge. Even the lowest shoeblack, if he gives more concentration will black shoes better; the cook with concentration will cook a meal all the better. In making money, or in worshipping God, or in doing anything, the stronger the power of concentration, the better will that thing be done. This is the one call, the one knock, which opens the gates of nature, and lets out floods of light. This, the power of concentration, is the only key to the treasure-house of knowledge.[30]

Education is not the amount of information that is put into your brain and runs riot there, undigested, all your life. We must have life-building, man-making, character-making, assimilation of ideas. If you have assimilated five ideas and made them your life and character, you have more education than any man who has got by heart a whole library.[31]

What you want is character, strengthening of the will. If I teach you, therefore, that your nature is evil, that you should go home and sit in sackcloth and ashes and weep your lives out, because you took certain false steps, it will not help you, but will weaken you all the more, and I shall be showing you the road to more evil than good. If this room is full of darkness for thousands of years and you come in and begin to weep and wail, "Oh, the darkness," will the darkness vanish? Strike a match and light comes in a moment. What good will it do you to think all your lives, "Oh, I have done

[29]CW II:388-89.

[30]CW II:389.

[31]CW III:302.

evil, I have made many mistakes." It requires no ghost to tell us that. Bring in the light and the evil goes in a moment. Build up your character, and manifest your Real Nature, the Effulgent, the Resplendent, the Ever-Pure, and call It up in everyone that you see.[32]

7. *Religion is the manifestation of the Divinity already in man.*

Each soul is potentially divine. The goal is to manifest this Divinity within, by controlling nature, external and internal. Do this either by work, or worship, or psychic control, or philosophy, by one or more or all of these — and be free. This is the whole of religion. Doctrines, or dogmas, or rituals, or books, or temples, or forms, are but secondary details.[33]

Teach yourselves, teach every one his real nature, call upon the sleeping soul and see how it awakes. Power will come, glory will come, goodness will come, purity will come, and everything that is excellent will come when this sleeping soul is roused to self-conscious activity.[34]

Aye, let every man and woman and child, without respect of caste or birth, weakness or strength, hear and learn that behind the strong and the weak, behind the high and the low, behind every one, there is that Infinite Soul, assuring the infinite possibility and the infinite capacity of all to become great and good. Let us proclaim to every soul — "Arise, awake and stop not till the goal is reached."[35]

Religion is realization; not talk, nor doctrine, nor theories, however beautiful they may be. It is being and becoming, not hearing or acknowledging; it is the whole soul becoming changed into what it believes. That is religion.[36]

[32]CW II:355.
[33]CW I:257.
[34]CW III:193.
[35]CW III:192.
[36]CW II:394.

8. *Each religion is an approach to one and the same Supreme Being variously conceived.*

In all religions we travel from a lesser to a higher truth, never from error to truth. There is Oneness behind all creation, but minds are very various. "That which exists is One, sages call It variously." What I mean is that one progresses from a smaller to a greater truth. The worst religions are only bad readings of the truth.[37]

To the Hindu, then, the whole world of religions is only a traveling, a coming up, of different men and women, through various conditions and circumstances, to the same goal. Every religion is only evolving a God out of the material man, and the same God is the inspirer of all of them. Why, then, are there so many contradictions? They are only apparent, says the Hindu. The contradictions come from the same truth adapting itself to the varying circumstances of different natures.[38]

If there is ever to be a universal religion, it must be one which will have no location in place or time; which will be infinite, like the God it will preach, and whose sun will shine upon the followers of Kṛṣṇa and of Christ, on saints and sinners alike; which will not be Brāhmiṇic or Buddhistic, Christian or Mohammedan, but the sum total of all these, and still have infinite space for development; which in its catholicity will embrace in its infinite arms, and find a place for, every human being, from the lowest grovelling savage not far removed from the brute, to the highest man towering by the virtues of his head and heart almost above humanity, making society stand in awe of him and doubt his human nature. It will be a religion which will have no place for persecution or intolerance in its polity, which will recognize divinity in every man and woman, and whose whole scope, whose whole force, will be centered in aiding humanity to realize its own true, divine nature.

[37]CW V:132.

[38]CW I:16.

Offer such a religion and all the nations will follow you.[39]

Holiness, purity and charity are not the exclusive possessions of any church in the world, and . . . every system has produced men and women of the most exalted character. In the face of this evidence, if anybody dreams of the exclusive survival of his own religion and the destruction of the others, I pity him from the bottom of my heart, and point out to him that upon the banner of every religion will soon be written, in spite of resistance: "Help and not Fight," "Assimilation and not Destruction," "Harmony and Peace and not Dissension."[40]

9. *Harmony of religions is the crying need of the day. It is essential to the peace and the progress of the world.*

No civilization can long exist unless this idea enters into it. No civilization can grow, unless fanaticism, bloodshed and brutality stop. No civilization can begin to lift up its head until we look charitably upon one another, and the first step towards that much-needed charity is to look charitably and kindly upon the religious convictions of others. Nay more, to understand that not only should we be charitable, but positively helpful, to each other, however different our religious ideas and convictions may be.[41]

Religion is the greatest motive power for realizing that infinite energy which is the birthright and nature of every man. In building up character, in making for everything that is good and great, in bringing peace to others, and peace to one's own self, religion is the highest motive power, and therefore, ought to be studied from that standpoint. Religion must be studied on a broader basis than formerly. All narrow, limited, fighting ideas of religion have to go. All sect ideas and tribal or national ideas of religion must be given

[39]CW I:17.
[40]CW I:22.
[41]CW III:187.

up. That each tribe or nation should have its own particular God, and think that every other is wrong, is a superstition that should belong to the past. All such ideas must be abandoned.

As the human mind broadens, its spiritual steps broaden too. The time has already come when a man cannot record a thought without its reaching to all corners of the earth; by merely physical means we have come into touch with the whole world; so the future religions of the world have to become as universal, as wide.

The religious ideals of the future must embrace all that exists in the world and is good and great, and, at the same time, have infinite scope for future development. All that was good in the past must be preserved; and the doors must be kept open for future additions to the already existing store. Religions must also be inclusive, and not look down with contempt upon one another, because their particular ideals of God are different.[42]

If there ever is going to be an ideal religion, it must be broad and large enough to supply food for all these minds. It must supply the strength of philosophy to the philosopher, the devotee's heart to the worshipper; to the ritualist, it will give all that the most marvellous symbolism can convey; to the poet, it will give as much of heart as he can take in, and other things besides. To make such a broad religion, we shall have to go back to the time when religions began and take them all in.

Our watchword, then, will be acceptance, and not exclusion. Not only toleration, for so-called toleration is often blasphemy, and I do not believe in it. I believe in acceptance. Why should I tolerate? Toleration means that I think that you are wrong and I am just allowing you to live. Is it not a blasphemy to think that you and I are allowing others to live? I accept all religions that were in the past, and worship with them all; I worship God with every one of them, in whatever form they worship Him.[43]

[42]CW II:67.
[43]CW II:371-72.

10. *The spiritual oneness of mankind is the foundation of morality. The vision of this unity is the way to universal love and bliss.*

The rational West is earnestly bent upon seeking out the rationality, the *raison d'être* of all its philosophy and its ethics; and you all know well that ethics cannot be derived from the mere sanction of any personage, however great and divine he may have been. Such an explanation of the authority of ethics appeals no more to the highest of the world's thinkers; they want something more than human sanction for ethical and moral codes to be binding, they want some eternal principle of truth as the sanction of ethics. And where is that eternal sanction to be found except in the only Infinite Reality, that exists in you and in me and in all, in the Self, in the Soul? The infinite oneness of the Soul is the eternal sanction of all morality, that you and I are not only brothers — every literature voicing man's struggle towards freedom has preached that for you — but that you and I are really one. This is the dictate of Indian philosophy. This oneness is the rationale of all ethics and all spirituality.[44]

We have always heard it preached, "Love one another." What for? That doctrine was preached, but the explanation is here. Why should I love every one? Because they and I are one. Why should I love my brother? Because he and I are one. There is this oneness, this solidarity of the whole universe. From the lowest worm that crawls under our feet to the highest beings that ever lived — all have various bodies, but are the one Soul. Through all mouths, you eat; through all hands, you work; through all eyes, you see. You enjoy health in millions of bodies, you are suffering from disease in millions of bodies. When this idea comes and we realize it, see it, feel it, then will misery cease, and fear with it. How can I die? There is nothing beyond me. Fear ceases, and then alone

[44] CW III:188-89.

comes perfect happiness and perfect love. That universal sympathy, universal love, universal bliss, that never changes, raises man above everything. It has no reactions, and no misery can touch it, but this little eating and drinking of the world always brings a reaction. The whole cause of it is this dualism, the idea that I am separate from the universe, separate from God. But as soon as we have realized that, "I am He, I am the Self of the universe, I am eternally blessed, eternally free," — then will come real love, fear will vanish, and all misery cease.[45]

11. *The ideal of religion must penetrate and inspire all spheres of life with the recognition of the spiritual solidarity of the universe.*

The ideals of religion must cover the whole field of life, they must enter into all our thoughts, and more and more into practice.[46]

Religion, to help mankind, must be ready and able to help him in whatever condition he is, in servitude or in freedom, in the depths of degradation or on the heights of purity; everywhere, equally, it should be able to come to his aid. The principles of Vedanta, or the ideal of Religion, or whatever you may call it, will be fulfilled by its capacity for performing this great function.[47]

The power of religion, broadened and purified, is going to penetrate every part of human life. So long as religion was in the hands of a chosen few, or of a body of priests, it was in temples, churches, books, dogmas, ceremonials, forms, and rituals. But when we come to the real, spiritual, universal concept, then, and then alone, religion will become real and living; it will come into our very nature, live in our every movement, penetrate every pore of our society, and be infinitely more a power for good, than it has ever been before.[48]

[45]CW II:412-13. [46]CW II:289-90. [47]CW II:298-99. [48]CW II:68-69.

12. *The ideal and the practice are interrelated.*

The principle is seldom found perfectly expressed in the practical, yet the ideal is never lost. On the one hand, it is our duty never to lose sight of the ideal, whether we can approach it with sensible steps, or crawl towards it with imperceptible motion; on the other hand, the truth is, it is always looming in front of us — though we try our best to cover its light with our hands before our eyes.

The life of the practical is in the ideal; it is the ideal that has penetrated the whole of our lives, whether we philosophize, or perform the hard everyday duties of life. The rays of the ideal, reflected and refracted in various straight or tortuous lines, are pouring in through every aperture and windhole, and consciously or unconsciously, every function has to be performed in its light, every object has to be seen transformed, heightened, or deformed, by it. It is the ideal that has made us what we are, and will make us what we are going to be. It is the power of the ideal that has enshrouded us, and is felt in our joys or sorrows, in our great acts or mean doings, in our virtues and vices.

If such is the power of the ideal over the practical, the practical is no less potent in forming the ideal. The truth of the ideal is in the practical. The fruition of the ideal has been through the sensing of the practical. That the ideal is there is a proof of the existence of the practical somehow, somewhere. The ideal may be vaster, yet it is the multiplication of little bits of the practical. The ideal mostly is the summed-up, generalized, practical units.

The power of the ideal is in the practical. Its work on us is in and through the practical. Through the practical, the ideal is brought down to our sense-perception, changed into a form fit for our assimilation. Of the practical we make the steps to rise to the ideal; on that we build our hopes; it gives us courage to work.

One man who manifests the ideal in his life is more powerful than legions, whose words can paint it in the most beautiful colors, and spin out the finest principles.[49]

13. *God can be directly worshipped by serving man.*

We have to cover everything with the Lord Himself, not by a false sort of optimism, not by blinding our eyes to the evil, but by really seeing God in everything. Thus we have to give up the world, and when the world is given up, what remains? God. What is meant? You can have your wife; it does not mean that you are to abandon her, but that you are to see God in the wife. Give up your children; what does that mean? To turn them out of doors, as some human brutes do in every country? Certainly not. That is diabolism; it is not religion. But see God in your children. So, in everything. In life and in death, in happiness and in misery, the Lord is equally present. The whole world is full of the Lord. Open your eyes and see Him. This is what Vedanta teaches.[50]

Look upon every man, woman and every one as God. You cannot help anyone; you can only serve: serve the children of the Lord, serve the Lord Himself, if you have the privilege. If the Lord grants that you can help any one of His children, blessed you are; do not think too much of yourselves. Blessed you are that that privilege was given to you, when others had it not. Do it only as a worship.[51]

You may invent an image through which to worship God, but a better image already exists, the living man. You may build a temple in which to worship God, and that may be good, but a better one, a much higher one, already exists, the human body.[52]

[49]CW IV:231-32.
[50]CW II:146.
[51]CW III:246.
[52]CW II:311.

From highest Brahman to the yonder worm,
And to the very minutest atom,
Everywhere is the same God, the All-love;
Friend, offer mind, soul, body, at their feet.

These are His manifold forms before thee,
Rejecting them, where seekest thou for God?
Who loves all beings, without distinction,
He indeed is worshipping best his God.[53]

[53]CW IV:429.

CHAPTER VI (Supplement)

SWAMI VIVEKANANDA'S BROTHER DISCIPLE, SWAMI BRAHMANANDA, AS A SPIRITUAL TEACHER

1. *An object of love and veneration of the entire Ramakrishna Order, Swami Brahmananda nurtured the Ramakrishna Math and Mission founded by Swami Vivekananda.*

Perhaps no religious heads have ever been so highly revered, so dearly loved, so devotedly served and so implicitly obeyed by their brother-disciples, lay as well as monastic, and also by the entire body of seekers of Truth drawn by the message of Sri Ramakrishna, as were Swami Vivekananda or Swami Brahmananda. His brother-disciples' reverence for Swami Brahmananda very nearly amounted to adoration. To them he was the very image of their Master. He was their chosen "king," their beloved "Maharaj." Gradually he became known throughout the Order by the epithet "Maharaj," lit. a great King. Swami Vivekananda always held him in very high esteem. He called him "a mountain of spirituality." He sought his counsel in all important matters. He vested him with sole authority over the Order founded by himself, saying: "Everything belongs to you, Raja, I am nobody." He looked upon him as the veritable son and successor of Sri Ramakrishna. It was also his desire that so long as Rakhal lived, no other of his *gurubhais* (brother-disciples) would be elected President of the Ramakrishna Order.

The Ramakrishna Math and Mission, the religious and philanthropic institution inaugurated by Swami Vivekananda, was consolidated and developed by Swami Brahmananda. Swami Vivekananda laid the foundation; Swami Brahmananda built the edifice. What Swami Vivekananda left in an infant state was reared to full maturity under the fostering care of his brother-disciple Swami Brahmananda, whose transcendental spiritual characteristics had installed him in the sonship of Sri Ramakrishna. Swami Vivekananda with his dynamic personality, eloquent voice, lucid exposition fought against materialism, agnosticism, and atheism, and made religion acceptable to humanity in general. Swami Brahmananda with his characteristic quietness set out to mould the lives of those who, in response to Swami Vivekananda's inspiring message and clarion call, gathered around Sri Ramakrishna's name and ideal. His gentle personality, shining beside the flaming figure of Swami Vivekananda, may sometimes go unnoticed, but its greatness and glory cannot but be appreciated.

2. *His brother-disciple Swami Ramakrishnananda's deep reverence for Swami Brahmananda. He escorted him during his tour in South India.*

Of all the gurubhais Swami Ramakrishnananda's love for and devotion to Maharaj were most marked. In October, 1908, Swami Ramakrishnananda, the Head of the Madras Center at the time, came all the way from Madras to Puri to escort Maharaj.

To Swami Ramakrishnananda, Maharaj was the veritable child of Sri Ramakrishna. In fact, he made no distinction between the father and the son. He was often heard to say: "He who has seen the son has seen the father." Once, in Madras Math, Maharaj wanted to eat fruits, but unfortunately there was no fruit in the Ashrama at the time to offer him. Just then a devotee brought some apples, grapes, bananas, etc., to be offered to Sri Ramakrishna. But Swami Ramakrishnananda at once offered half of them to Maharaj with the gentle remark: "To offer these fruits to Maharaj is as good as offering them to Sri Ramakrishna, for Sri Ramakrishna eats through his mouth." He kept the other half for Sri Ramakrishna to be offered to Him at the time of daily worship.

While Swami Brahmananda was staying in the Madras Math as the guest of Swami Ramakrishnananda, one day a gentleman of a high position who had heard Swami Vivekananda's eloquent speeches, asked Swami Ramakrishnananda who was escorting him to Maharaj's room, "Will not this Swami lecture?" Then Swami Ramakrishnananda said, "This Swami does not lecture. One or two words drop from his lips and we spin them out into a lecture."

While staying at the Madras Math, Swami Brahmananda noticed that there was no proper arrangement for the ceremonial performance of the evening service. It was he who introduced it there. Every evening after the ceremonial worship he would hold an assembly of devotees in which scriptures were read and devotional songs were sung in chorus. Along with others Maharaj himself would play on some musical instrument in accompaniment.

In December, 1908, he went on a pilgrimage to Rameswar accompanied by Swami Ramakrishnananda, Swami Dhirananda, Swami Vishuddhananda, Swami Ambikananda and C. Ramaswami Aiyangar. On reaching the sacred spot, Maharaj went straight to the temple from the railway station and worshipped the presiding deity, Śrī Rāmeśwara Śiva. Maharaj and his party stayed there nearly a week in a bungalow belonging to the Raja of Ramnad. Many an inhabitant of the place came to seek his instruction and blessing. Maharaj received them all with utmost kindness and love. On his way back to Madras he stopped at Madura to worship the Goddess Mīnākṣī. Here Maharaj had a wonderful spiritual experience which is beyond description. He realized the living presence of the Divine Mother in the temple. As he was escorted to the *sanctum sanctorum,* he stood before the image firm and motionless gazing at the lotus-feet of the Goddess. Soon his whole body began to tremble in ecstasy. Tears trickled down his cheeks. Swami Ramakrishnananda held his arms around him to prevent a fall. Others stood by watching. This spiritual mood lasted nearly an hour after which Maharaj gradually came down to the plane of normal consciousness. He spent a few days at Madura visiting notable historical places. Thence he returned to Madras direct.

From Madras, in January, 1909, Maharaj went to Bangalore to open the new Ashrama there. The elite of the town including the officials of Mysore State attended the opening ceremony. They all assembled under a Durbar Samiana (canopy) set up for the occasion. Mr. V.P. Madhava Rao, C.I.E., at that time the Dewan of Mysore State, presented the key of the Ashrama to Maharaj on behalf of the public with a short but impressive speech, to which Maharaj gave a suitable reply. It was on this occasion that Maharaj spoke before the public for the first and last time. The speech lasted about fifteen minutes, but it made an excellent impression on the audience. Though he generally felt very shy to participate in a function which had a public character, this time he stood firm like a rock while speaking, as he humorously said afterwards to some of the devotees.

After a week's stay at Bangalore, Maharaj returned to Madras. In March he went to Conjeevaram and remained there for three or four days. He worshipped the Goddess Kāmākṣī and visited the temple several times during his short stay there. He also visited Śiva Kāñcī and Viṣṇu Kāñcī. He was greatly charmed with the sanctity of the temples and the beauty of the images. In Madras some of its residents approached him for religious instruction. Justices Krishnaswami Aiyar and Sundaram Iyer and other leading men came to pay their respects to him.

3. *Maharaj introduced Śrī Rāma-nāma Kīrtanam and Kālī Kīrtanam as a form of devotional practice.*

In Madras he heard the Rāma-nāma chant of Southern India for the first time and was much fascinated by it. It at once occurred to him that it could be set to a more melodious tune and sung by the monks of the Order in chorus, in accompaniment with musical instruments, as a form of devotional practice. Since then Rāma-nāma Saṅkīrtanam has been introduced into the Ramakrishna Math and its branches. Now it is sung in almost all the Centers of the Order once a fortnight, usually on the eleventh lunar day; many devotees attend.

Similarly, Maharaj introduced Kālī Kīrtanam, choral songs, in praise of the Divine Mother Kālī. It is usually sung on the new moon day in accompaniment with different musical instruments. Monastics and householders as well participate in the chant.

4. *His relationship with his brother-disciples was marked by mutual love and reverence as testified by Swami Premananda.*

Swami Premananda used to say: "When I hear that brother Rakhal is going to be absent from the Math, I feel a void within myself." But this reverence of the brother-disciples was not characterized by rigid solemnity. It was blended with the intimacy and sweetness of genuine love. Maharaj also in his turn looked upon them as the chosen sons of the Master and gave them all the honor and love relative to such an attitude. Truly, in this divine relationship of the gurubhais veneration was mingled with affection, service with devotion, intimacy with regard, obedience with dignity, command with tenderness, faith with understanding, and admiration with conviction.

One can imagine from this what reverence, love, faith and service Maharaj commanded from others who were attracted by the name and personality of Sri Ramakrishna and his disciples. They vied with one another to do him homage and service. His word was the divine command. Even to be in his presence was a blessing. A kind look, a word, or a touch was a benediction, an inspiration to be treasured forever in memory.

5. *Complete freedom from self-consciousness was a mark of his greatness. His deep feeling for the young monastics who joined the Order.*

The secret of this unique position was perhaps his childlike simplicity and impersonality of nature. He was really a divine child — a veritable son of the Lord. He was a master without any idea of mastery, a ruler without any feeling of rulership. He was rarely heard to talk about himself. In all his conversations he seldom referred to his own deeds and accomplishments. Though the supreme leader of a religious organization of most rapid and extensive growth, with multifarious activities in India and abroad, he was never seen to command but to suggest. Indeed, he was an agent without the conceit of the doer in him. In the language of the *Bhagavad-gītā* he found inaction in action and action in inaction.[1]

Swami Premananda, who was for many years in charge of the Belur Monastery, once wrote in the course of a private letter: "Though an agent, one should live like a non-agent. The character of Swami Brahmananda has made me realize this to some extent." In fact, though a master in all outward appearance Swami Brahmananda had an attitude of service towards those under him. He looked after their physical needs and comforts with parental care. He could not bear the idea that young sannyāsins should hazard their health by undergoing too much austerity and make

[1]BG IV:18. "He who sees inaction in action, and action in inaction, he is wise among men, he is tranquil-minded and a doer of all actions [that is, he has achieved the end of all actions, which is freedom]."

themselves unfit for the spiritual pursuits for which they had left their hearth and home. Decent food, clothes, etc., on the other hand, he thought, would maintain their physical and mental vigor intact and enable them to make a strenuous effort to attain to the Goal. He wanted to give them all the facilities for spiritual development.

In conducting the activities of the Order, the mere management and extension of work had far less claim on his attention than the individual spiritual growth of the members engaged in the work. The thought of their spiritual advancement was always uppermost in his mind. He would not appoint a monastic to a work that would hamper his spiritual growth in any way, though from the consideration of the work itself that would have been the right step.

The real growth of a religious order, he knew within himself, rests on the spiritual progress of each individual member. Thus, by promoting the spiritual culture of the individuals, he furthered the growth of the Order as a whole without making any conscious effort for it. His life is a lesson for the leaders who, in their solicitude for the expansion of an association, lose sight of the well-being of the individuals and thus defeat their own purpose.

Beneath all this there was a perennial flow of love with a silent equable course unknown and unnoticed. There was not the least turbulence in it. The lover and the loved seemed to be equally unconscious of its existence. Gently and quietly it made its way into the hearts of all who gathered around him, and held them under its sway. Swami Premananda once wrote in the course of a letter: "As the Master had completely won Maharaj and the rest of his disciples by his supreme love, so Maharaj has in his turn made the sons of others his own by his wonderful love. At his bidding they go anywhere and everywhere and exert themselves to the verge of death simply because of his love."

6. *His love and regard for the devotees and holy men (sādhus) made him the center of attraction wherever he went.*

His noble, genial, loving nature made him the center of attraction wherever he went. People of heterogeneous temperaments gathered around him, not always for the sake of religion but for the pleasure of his blessed company. He looked after their personal and family welfare and gratified them by presents of flowers, fruits, vegetables, a piece of cloth or a tidbit according to their needs and liking. These tokens of love, trifling as they often were, testified only to those who received them, the depth of his love and its genuineness. He took great delight in feeding others with the delicacies which they liked the most. At Benares and Kankhal he sumptuously fed a number of up-country sādhus with Bengali sweets and dishes the like of which they said they had never tasted before.

As a matter of fact, there was constant festivity wherever he went. A circle of devotees and admirers formed itself at every place and fulfilled every wish of this chosen child of the Lord. Indeed, in his life was verified the truth of the following text of one of the Purāṇas: "Those who realize the eternal presence of the Lord in their hearts are endowed with perpetual good and beauty, and their life is imbued with an eternal festive joy."[2]

7. *Seldom did he give formal talks as a spiritual teacher. Usually he maintained a jovial childlike attitude, but behind it there was an undercurrent of deep spiritual feeling and transcendental aloofness.*

Never did he pose as a religious preacher or teacher. He did not talk much on spiritual matters, either because he held them too high and sacred, or because his gentle nature oftentimes shrank

[2]There are eighteen Purāṇas included in Hindu scriptures.

from the attitude of a teacher. Seldom in his life did he give a formal discourse on religion. Whenever he spoke on it, he did it in a mood of inspiration in the course of ordinary conversation. If a serious question was put to him, he would generally avoid it, humorously pointing to a learned junior Swami who happened to be nearby as the fit person to answer it. At times with his usual sense of humor, he would introduce a light topic or tell a joke, in the course of which he would disclose a spiritual truth or give a hint or suggestion which would solve the doubt of the questioner and even change his outlook on life forever. These were matters of almost everyday occurrence. To all appearance, he was as merry and playful as a child and possessed an inexhaustible fund of jokes in which he often indulged. Sometimes he would take a special fancy for someone, no matter what his social rank or condition or age was, and treat him as his own playmate.

Behind all gaiety and jollity, however, there was an undercurrent of spiritual consciousness which nothing could thwart or impede. Many a time it was observed that while he was indulging in jokes and merriment, an expression of genuine religious feeling by any one among the audience would bring about a sudden and complete change in his jovial mood. His soft, cheerful countenance would appear grave and solemn and a perfect serenity would fill the atmosphere. His natural inwardness of mind also exhibited itself in the occasional moods of absorption into which he passed while listening to a random conversation as well as in his dignified and sober demeanor which commanded willing reverence.

But the ceaseless flow of spiritual consciousness was all the more apparent in his transcendental aloofness. Though in the body, he was not of the body. He loved all, he mixed with all, he had an interest in everything; yet his mind soared far and beyond. Perchance, to describe the indescribable, things floated in his consciousness not as bubbles of no worth, but as manifestations of the same Reality. He viewed things neither in the grossness of limited forms nor in the homogeneity of pure existence. With name and form he realized the infinitude of each. Thus, though living apart as a spectator, he had an ineffable love and sympathy for all. This witness-like attitude was so remarkable a feature of his personality that it could not escape even casual notice. Thus observes Sister Devamata in her *Days in an Indian Monastery:* "Wherever he [Swami Brahmananda] went, people came in large numbers to bow at his feet and beg his blessing; but it seemed to reach his consciousness only impersonally, as if it had merely a casual acquaintance with the one who was being honored."[3]

8. *As an instructor of spiritual courses.*

In spite of his wonted reserve he liked to commune with earnest seekers of Truth. If anyone had real trouble or difficulty in spiritual life, he was ever ready to help him. To many he gave private instruction, but only after he had been convinced of their sincerity and earnestness. His attitude in this respect has been best described by himself. One day he said to an intimate group of devotees: "There are many who request me to bless them. I cannot help laughing within myself when I hear them. They don't do as I instruct them. On the contrary, the moment they leave my presence, they follow their wonted course. They want to attain spiritual realization without the necessary exertion. Don't you see when such people come, I usually while away the time in aimless talk — in cracking jokes and making fun? What is the use of tiring myself for nothing, in speaking of spiritual practices to people who won't follow them? I speak of higher matters only to a very few, who I think would take my word and act up to it. But even they don't follow the instructions fully and properly."

[3]Sister Devamata, *Days in an Indian Monastery* (La Crescenta, Calif.: Ananda Ashrama, 1927), pp. 152-53.

Besides giving general and individual religious instruction to earnest seekers of Truth he gave spiritual initiation to a selected few. After a period of probation, he also gave sannyāsa and brahmacarya every year to selected candidates for monastic life, usually on the birthday anniversaries of Sri Ramakrishna and Swami Vivekananda. These memorable ceremonies of formal admission into the Holy Order were held mostly at Belur Math. Benares, Bhubaneswar, Madras, Bangalore and certain other places also witnessed the blessed functions. Besides, he gave a Tāntrika form of sannyāsa called *pūrṇābhiṣeka* to a few householders who were especially qualified for it.

9. *As a giver of individual spiritual instruction suited to the pupil's own line of development. The relationship between the Preceptor and the pupils.*

But in the matter of giving initiation (dīkṣā), in accepting one as a true disciple, he was particularly strict and discriminative. He refused almost all when they approached him for the first time. If he found anyone worthy of it, he would give him a preparatory lesson after the seeker's persistent prayer for four or five years. The final initiation would come, in some cases, seven to ten years later, after the seeker's steadiness and earnestness had been fully tested and his eagerness for Truth roused to the extreme. But once Maharaj accepted him as a disciple he would stand by him until the disciple would reach the Goal. The following words of his reveal the status of the speaker himself: "He is the best guru, who, whether his physical body stands or falls, will see that every one of his disciples attains liberation. The speciality of this age is that even after the disappearance of his physical body, the guru appears in flesh to his disciples to guide and bless them."

He loved his disciples in spite of their faults and weaknesses. If any of them went astray under the influence of deep-seated wrong tendencies (saṁskāras), he would not reproach or despise him, but like a fond mother feel for him more deeply, watch him inwardly and bless him all the more. Sometimes he would send for him and call him to his side not to warn or chastise him but to wean him from the evil course by making him feel the holy attraction of his personality and infusing into him sufficient spiritual strength to fight against the *saṁskāras* (inborn wrong tendencies). He could ill brook any criticism of a beloved disciple from others.

In giving initiation he took into consideration particularly the seeker's spiritual aptitude, his yearning for the highest Good, and never thought of his position, rank, learning or sex. Monks and householders, men and women, the high and the low in the social rank, equally shared his grace in this respect. While men of worldly supremacy without spiritual inclination were summarily dismissed, he very willingly initiated an ordinary person in whom he discerned any real spiritual inkling.

He once initiated one of the menials in the service of an admirer of his. While Maharaj was at Bangalore, K. L. Datta, the then Accountant-General of Madras, who happened to be there at the time, paid him occasional visits. He had great regard for Maharaj and used to send him certain delicacies from a Bengali home through a servant of his, probably a Nepalese young man. Maharaj perceived the religious inclination of the boy and talked with him on spiritual matters whenever he came. The youth in his turn realized Maharaj's holy influence, but he did not dare to ask for his grace. One day Maharaj called him to the shrine room and gave him initiation.

He initiated his disciples according to the individual's spiritual trend. Every man has to grow spiritually and realize the Truth in his own way as determined by his inherent tendencies. Maharaj's psychic faculty was wonderfully developed. Some of his visions and experiences testify to this. He could perceive the spiritual inclinations and possibilities of the person he was going to initiate and prescribed for him the only course suitable for him. Before he gave initiation he would find out by meditation the *Iṣṭa* (Chosen Deity), and *mantra* (corresponding mystic formula) of the disciple, that is to say, the mode of practice and the Ideal appropriate to his own spiritual nature. Thus he guided each of his disciples in his particular line of spiritual development. This is a task which only the gurus of exceptional spiritual powers, those who come to earth to fulfill a divine mission, are capable of doing. An ordinary guru tries to lead his disciples along the path by which he himself has received spiritual illumination, but this cannot suit one and all. Maharaj laid special stress on the choice of the practical course by the guru, according to the disciple's spiritual characteristics.

"Regarding spiritual practices," he remarked, "the same rule will not be applicable to all. We must know the peculiar tendencies of each individual before any spiritual instruction can be given for his guidance. If the instruction goes against the particular bent of one's nature, not only will it do one no good, but may even give rise to harmful consequences. It is, therefore, very essential that the guru should study closely the individual tendencies and characteristics of his disciples, and give instructions in such a way as will readily appeal to their respective temperaments. In this matter no individual can be told in the presence of others what particular path he should follow. I have seen in the case of the Master how he would take each individual disciple aside and give him in private the special instructions necessary for him."

Yet Maharaj did not bind any of his disciples with hard and fast rules of conduct. Nor did he lead him by the hand at every step. But he gave him sufficient freedom to cultivate his innate spiritual consciousness and realize the Truth for himself. He did not give him any direct order but recommended to him certain courses of action which would help his spiritual growth. "I give freedom to all," he said once. "I want every individual to advance along his own line. But when I find that he is not able to do so, I come to his aid."

As a rule, he did not give initiation unless he was divinely inspired to do so and until he had a clear vision of the seeker's Iṣṭa and mantra. Once, at Travencore, a railway employee, who was an Aiyanger by birth, prayed to him for initiation. Maharaj made no objection. But a day or two after, he said that he could not find out his Iṣṭa and mantra, so he asked him to wait. Then Maharaj went to Cape Comorin to visit the temple of the Goddess Kanyā-Kumārī. The same gentleman also joined the party. There at Cape Comorin his Iṣṭa revealed Himself to Maharaj, who then gladly initiated him.

There are also cases of persons receiving initiation from him in a dream. Their number is, of course, very small. Some of them had not even seen Maharaj before. They had been attracted only by his name. The present writer had the occasion to know two of them directly. One of them was a devout young woman who had heard about Maharaj but had never seen him personally. After the dream-vision, she sought the earliest opportunity to go to the physical presence of Maharaj for confirmation. From her hometown she went to Calcutta. As she approached Maharaj, who was then seated with his gurubhais at Balaram Bose's drawing room, she recognized him at first sight, though he was not identified to her by anyone. After others had left she narrated the dream-incident to him. Maharaj asked her not to disclose the mantra, which he found out for himself and told her later, perhaps to convince her of the reality of the dream.

The other recipient was a young man who forgot the mantra as he woke up. Later he approached Maharaj in person for initiation. Maharaj told him to wait. When the young man received initiation several years later, he at once recalled the mantra he had received in his dream and found to his joy and surprise that the present mantra was the same as the one he had received in his dream.

10. *He helped the seekers of Truth in diverse ways.*

Maharaj helped the seekers of Truth in diverse ways. As he stayed in different places during his long tours, many a weary traveller in the pathless forest of life came to him, mysteriously drawn as it were, for consolation, encouragement, guidance and benediction.

It so happened in Madras that a Vaiṣṇava devotee who earned his living by popular talks on God *(Hari-Kathā),* was greatly attracted by Maharaj's spiritual personality. He had been seeking a guru for a long time. Though he had great veneration for Maharaj he still could not prepare his mind to receive initiation from Maharaj, who belonged to the Śaṅkara Order of Sannyāsins, while he himself was an orthodox Vaiṣṇava by birth and culture. One day he besought Maharaj for his blessing so that he might soon find a guru of the same religious faith as himself. Maharaj was gracious to him and the man went away buoyed up with assurances he had received. Long after Maharaj had left Madras, the same man one day came to the Madras Math bare-footed in the garb of a Vaiṣṇava ascetic. It was known on inquiry that through the grace of Maharaj he had met a *siddha* (one who has reached the Goal) Vaiṣṇava guru, who was pleased to initiate him into his long-cherished line of *sādhanā* (spiritual discipline).

11. *His interpretation of religion was based on reason. He strongly emphasized regular spiritual practice with firm determination to realize the Truth.*

In explaining religion Maharaj always appealed to reason. His interpretation of it was natural and rational. He invariably urged his hearers first to understand and then to accept. In a certain period of his life he went so far as to say that Truth revealed to the mind which is laid open to It being uninfluenced by any religious idea or sentiment, carries with It a greater force of conviction than that perceived by the mind which starts with preconceived ideas. Though he himself did not take an active part in religious discussions, lectures and discourses, he attended them with interest and recommended them to those who had aptitude for them. Study and writing also received their due share of encouragement. But the greater stress was always laid on individual spiritual practice. As the most intimate form of sādhanā he believed this to be a direct aid to Self-realization.

He repeatedly urged all who came to him for spiritual instruction, to struggle heart and soul to realize the Truth for themselves and attain the peace and bliss eternal in this very life. He was never tired of reminding them of this supreme Goal of human life. His daily conversations were full of exhortations for sādhanā. Practice and realization were the burden of his talks. We reproduce here one of his discourses delivered before the monks at Belur Math one morning in December, 1915.

12. *The following discourse delivered by him before the monks at Belur Math testifies to what we have said above.*

". . . There *is* God. There *is* religion. These are not mere words or ethical conventions. He *does* exist. He can be seen. He can be realized. There is nothing more real than He. Fanaticism is not good. You have to be calm, sober and self-controlled." (As he uttered these words, an electric current as it were passed through the audience.)

"You should practice meditation four times daily, in the early morning, in the forenoon after bath, in the evening and at midnight. You have left your hearth and home with a view to realize God. With single-minded devotion you should strive to attain to Him even at the cost of life. Be crazy, so to speak, for God-realization. Simply to drag on an existence is the most miserable life. This way you will gain neither this nor that — neither God nor the world. Both will be lost. If you cannot fix your mind on Him, practice hard. Do not give up practice, even if the mind does not like to dwell on Him. Read the *Bhagavad-gītā* at least one chapter every day. I have seen myself that if I read the *Gītā,* when the mind is low, all the impurities are at once swept away.

"Everyday you will have to poke the mind, 'Why have we come here? How is the day spent? Do we really seek God? If so, what are we doing?' Let us be sincere, let us say to ourselves with a clear conscience, whether we are faithful to the ideal, whether we are working in such a way as to reach the Goal. The mind will try to deceive us. We must throttle it so that it may not play false. You should hold fast to Truth. You must be pure. The purer you are, the greater will be the steadfastness of your mind. You will be able to detect and destroy the subtle tricks of the mind. Who are the foes? One's own senses. Only those are friends, which are under control. The more one can discover one's weaknesses by self-introspection and remove them, the more rapid will be one's progress in spiritual life.

"Practice hard. In the beginning the mind takes hold of gross objects. Through the practice of meditation and japa it learns to perceive the finer and subtler things. Winter is the proper season for practice. Now you are in the prime of life. Sit down saying like the Buddha: 'Let my body be withered on this seat. Let skin, bone and flesh be dissolved. My body will not move from this seat without attaining Illumination, which is difficult to attain even in many cycles of existence.'

"See once for all if God really exists or not. A little of *titikṣa* (endurance), such as to live on one meal on the new-moon day or on the eleventh lunar day, is good. Give up all random talk and gossiping and think of Him constantly, whether you bathe, eat, rest or work — at all times. If you do so, you will find that

Kuṇḍalinī[4] is being awakened. There is nothing like constant remembrance of God. The veils of māyā will fall off one by one. You will find what a wonderful treasure there lies within you. You will become self-effulgent.

"Days are passing. What are you doing? These days cannot be revoked. Pray to Sri Ramakrishna. He is still with us. If anyone prays to him sincerely, he shows the way. Do not forget him. If you do so, you will be ruined. 'Thou art mine, I am thine,' — let this be your only thought. Having taken to this mode of life, if you do not practice meditation and japa and try hard to merge your mind in Him, you will suffer much — your mind will hanker after lust and gold."

These words of exhortation of Swami Brahmananda remind us of his own struggle for God-realization in the early days of his monastic life of complete renunciation, particularly during his pilgrimages as a penniless itinerant monk. Truly speaking, this was the formative period of his life as a spiritual teacher.

13. *His own struggle for God-realization in the early stage of his monastic life, particularly during his pilgrimages as an itinerant monk for nearly six years, along with his varied experiences, was preparatory to his life as a spiritual teacher.*

After the Mahāsamādhi of Sri Ramakrishna (August 16, 1886), one of his disciples, Gopal Senior (who was even older than the Master), along with a few of the young disciples, started a monastery (Math) at Baranagore in a rented house in the suburb of Calcutta, not far from Dakshineswar. Gradually the other young disciples joined and the total number rose to sixteen. The entire brotherhood was inspired by the spiritual ideal of God-

[4]Kuṇḍalinī — Literally "the coiled up." It means the latent spiritual force in every human individual located at the end of the canal within the spinal column. See Swami Vivekananda's *Rāja-Yōga,* chaps. IV & V, "The Psychic Prāṇa."

realization set up by the Master. Days and nights passed in study, prayer, meditation, and so forth.

Before long they performed the ceremony for formal Sannyāsa (monasticism) according to the scriptural regulations of Śṛṅgerī Math in South India founded by Śaṅkara's disciple Sur-eśvarācārya, from which Math Sri Ramakrishna's monastic guru, Tōtā Purī, had his spiritual lineage. Henceforth, the disciples of Sri Ramakrishna came to be known by their monastic names — Naren (Swami Vivekananda), Rakhal (Swami Brahmananda), Yogin (Swami Yogananda), Baburam (Swami Premananda), Tarak (Swami Shivananda), Gopal Senior (Swami Advaitanan-da), Sashi (Swami Ramakrishnananda), Sarat (Swami Saradananda), Latu (Swami Adbhutananda), Hari (Swami Turiyananda), Gangadhar (Swami Akhandananda), Subodh (Swami Subodhananda), and so on.

In the course of a few months, they grew tired of living together in one place. Less than a year after the disappearance of the Master many of the disciples left the monastery one by one for pilgrimages as itinerant monks. Only Sashi (Swami Ramakrishnananda) with a few of his gurubhais continued to stay in the Math beside the sacred relics of the Master as well as some of his belongings, and carried on the daily worship steadily from the beginning of the Math.

Swami Brahmananda set out on the Parivrājaka life in the latter part of 1888. Swami Vivekananda wanted one of his brother disciples to accompany Maharaj, whose intense spiritual mood would make it difficult for him to secure daily food and the bare necessities by alms. Accordingly, Swami Subodhananda accom-panied Swami Brahmananda. Together they travelled mostly on foot to many places in Southern and Northern India such as Vaidyanath, Varanasi, Omkarnath on the River Narmada (where Śrī Śaṅkarācārya met his guru Gōvindapāda), Bombay, Dwarka, Vetpuri, Sundama-puri, Junagar, Mt. Girnar, Ahmedabad,

Pushkar, and then came back to Brindavan. From there Swami Subodhananda went out on a pilgrimage to the Himalayas.

After staying some time at Brindavan, Maharaj went to Kankhal. There some of his gurubhais, e.g., Swami Vivekananda, Swami Saradananda, Swami Turiyananda, met him. Later, accompanied by Swami Turiyananda, Maharaj travelled to a number of places in the Punjab for about two years, such as Jwalamukhi, Kangra, Pathankot, Baijnath, Gopalpur, Guzranwala, Montgomery, and Multan. Then they visited Karachi and Bombay and later came to Mt. Abu in Rajputana.

In many places of pilgrimage there are monasteries and rest houses. Since they travelled mostly on foot they stayed for short or long periods in solitary places which they found suitable for spiritual practice. For instance, at Omkarnath on the River Narmada, Maharaj was seated in deep meditation for several days at a stretch and at Mt. Abu also he practiced intense tapasyā.

In the course of their pilgrimages Swami Turiyananda and Swami Brahmananda came to Brindavan and stayed there for several months. Here Maharaj underwent intense tapasyā. He used to sit for meditation from early evening until nine o'clock. Then from nine o'clock until twelve midnight he would rest. Then again from midnight until dawn he would practice meditation. The Vaiṣṇava saint Vijaykrishna Goswami, who had seen Sri Ramakrishna a number of times and had great reverence for him, was living at Brindavan at the time. When he came to know that Maharaj had no mosquito curtain he himself brought one and fixed the same over his bed. It is to be noted that Brindavan was infested with mosquitos. When he learned that Maharaj was undergoing intense spiritual practice he told him one day, "Sri Ramakrishna loved you as his very son. Did he not give you all that you need? Then why do you behave like a beggar spending all night in meditation?" Swami Brahmananda replied, "It is true that He graciously gave me all that I need. Still, what I attained through his grace [the supraconscious experiences] I want to have within my capacity to reach from the normal level."

Later from Brindavan Swami Brahmananda, accompanied by Swami Turiyananda, went to Ayodhya. Meanwhile Swami Vivekananda had attended the Parliament of Religions in Chicago (Sept. 1893) with great success, and fervently preached Vedanta in America. More than once he wrote to his brother disciples at the Monastery, which had already been removed from Baranagore to Alambazar, that Maharaj and his other brother-disciples should return from their itineracy to the Monastery and start work for the benefit of the people. After visiting one or two more places, Swami Brahmananda, along with Swami Turiyananda and Swami Shivananda, returned to Alambazar Math early in 1895.

Here, too, Maharaj continued his spiritual practice in the same strain. During the daytime he was mostly engaged in counting his beads. In these days his appearance was remarkably sober and serene. An ineffable radiance shone over his face. His eyes were wonderfully lustrous. His very person seemed to emanate spirituality. Several young ardent souls had by this time joined the Monastery being attracted by the all-renouncing ideals of Sri Ramakrishna and his disciples. Many other earnest seekers of Truth occasionally came to the Math to associate with the monks. Sometimes Maharaj would sing devotional songs in a rapturous mood to those who came in close contact with him. One of his favorite songs in those days began as follows (we give an English rendering): "Pledge the very life, O mind. Can priceless gems be found in ankle-deep water? Dive into the bottomless depths, if you want to take hold of the Real Man."

14. *Practical wisdom of Swami Brahmananda.*

Let us resume our main theme. With his childlike gaiety and transcendental spiritual attainments Maharaj possessed great practical wisdom. He had true business-like tactfulness. He directed the varied affairs of the vast organization with rare intelligence, ability and foresight. His wise suggestions astonished the experienced workers of the field. In book-publication, in engineering, in financial and legal affairs he exhibited as keen an understanding and judgment as in religious matters. Some of his lay devotees holding distinguished positions in society frequently sought his advice even in matters relating to their profession or occupation.

As the supreme head of a large organization he had to face occasional disputes and controversies in which the contending parties seemed to have equal claim to truth and reason. Some of them proved momentous, but Maharaj settled these invariably to the satisfaction of all. By a single stroke he could most ingeniously save the situation. Sometimes in settling an affair he would adopt the policy of "wait and see" and let matters take their own course, though at times to the discontent of the persons concerned. But it was found more often than not that the course of events naturally took a favorable turn and the difficulties disappeared of themselves.

He was extremely strict in the management of public funds. He always insisted that any sum whatsoever received for a specified object should be scrupulously devoted to that particular purpose. Extreme care was taken in the keeping of accounts. The monks in charge of these accounts were asked to deal with all in monetary affairs on strict business principles without any distinction.

He had a keen insight into the tendencies and capacities of men and women and never failed to choose the right person for the right place. He could therefore place full confidence in them and gave them complete freedom in their respective positions. He only helped them from behind the scenes. This naturally evoked their best energies and latent virtues. If they made any mistake he would not chastise them openly, but gave them necessary instructions individually. His words not only gave them conviction but had an impelling force. He was their leader, friend and guide in one.

15. *His balanced attitude toward various activities at the Math.*

With his characteristic evenness of mind he maintained a balanced attitude in all matters. He had no bias towards a particular course, thing or person. He possessed a wonderful sense of proportion. Reason, devotion, and work found full play in his life. Though a constant supporter of meditation and contemplation as essentials to Self-realization, he paid due attention to the performance of ceremonial worship, humanitarian deeds, and devotional singing. He recognized the necessity and value of all these according to an individual's temperament, capacities, and circumstances.

The annual pūjās and other ceremonials introduced into the central Monastery at Belur Math from the very beginning were strictly observed by him all along. Under his auspices the *Durgā Pūjā* (worship of the ten-handed Divine Mother Durgā), was celebrated with an image in distant Kankhal and Madras. The birthday celebrations of Sri Ramakrishna, Swami Vivekananda and of other great personages, such as Śrī Kṛṣṇa, the Buddha, Jesus Christ and Śrī Caitanya, evoked the same zeal and devotion in him. He took great pains to see that all the rites connected with a religious function were strictly observed according to the rules laid down in the Śāstras. Without these forms and ceremonials religious life loses much of its charm, freshness and vivacity, and spirituality is likely to turn into formalities and dry intellectualism.[5]

16. *His view of the Philanthropic Work conducted by the Order.*

[5]See Appendix A, the author's article on "Folk Festivals in India."

In the service of humanity he laid greater stress on the attitude of the worker than on the nature of the work or the mere performance of it. It is the spiritual outlook of the worker which turns the work into worship. Therefore he wanted everyone to cultivate the true spirit of the servant of the Lord residing in all. As regards his own attitude toward service, who can sound the depth of the feeling of one who dedicated his life, heart and soul, to the cause; who forsook his most favorite pursuit of solitary sādhanā and the joy of samādhi to be the builder of an organization which was to embody the twin ideals of renunciation and service in the world, from its foundation to the mature stage of development; to be at the helm of all affairs during the most critical period of its growth, unto the last day of his life? Yet, he was so reticent about himself that it was hardly possible to get any clue to this mainspring of action.

But the spirit sometimes asserted itself in spite of himself. Those who had the privilege of knowing him most intimately will recall occasions on which he would be restless at the sight of the sufferings of others and would not be at peace until they were relieved of their misery. Nothing but the realization of the Self in all can give such deep sympathy, heart-felt compassion and intense feeling. To attain the true spirit of sevā (service), the development of one's spiritual nature is essentially necessary. He, therefore, urged the aspirants to make earnest efforts to cultivate spirituality along with philanthropic deeds. Mere work unaided by devotional practice, contemplation or reflection proves mechanical and has a tendency to make the mind outgoing. Again, one cannot resort to spiritual practice with profit, unless one has attained sufficient purity of mind. Only those whose minds are purified can undertake service to their own advantage as well as to the benefit of others. Simultaneous performance of sevā (service) and sādhanā (spiritual practice) is what he as a general rule prescribed for the seekers of Truth.

17. *This is evidenced by his own words.*

In an informal meeting of the residents of the Math at Belur held in February, 1916, he spoke as follows on the value and necessity of philanthropic work:

"I hear that some of you think that the activities of the Mission are only hindrances to spiritual culture, that one cannot make spiritual progress if one undertakes such work as famine relief and the like and that Swami Premananda and myself are not in favor of them. These are all wrong notions. You have failed to comprehend our attitude. Indeed, I repeatedly tell you and even now I emphasize that whatever work you have to do, be it famine relief or any other, you must contemplate on God, you must practice meditation, etc., in the morning and in the evening as well as at the end of the work. Of course, it is a different thing if you miss a day or two under the pressure of work. We heard Swamiji frequently say that we should work as well as worship, do work and meditate as well.

"Can anyone practice meditation day and night? Therefore one must do disinterested work. Otherwise one will be engrossed with vain and evil thoughts. Is it not then better to do good work? You will find that the *Bhagavad-gītā* and other Śāstras (scriptures) have strongly emphasized this truth. I also say so from my own experience. I have also worked hard for the Math. If you like you may inquire of Sarat Maharaj (Swami Saradananda) and Baburam Maharaj (Swami Premananda). [Both of them were present at the meeting.] At the command of Swamiji, how many times I had to go to such uninviting places as the attorney's office! Nowadays you get your train fare and food wherever you go. But then there was no certainty about food, drink and rest, still we had to work 'for the good of many, for the happiness of many.'

"Don't you see what a terrible war [the First World War] is raging before your eyes? They are laying down their lives, rich and poor, young and old, leaving behind their wives and all pleasures of life, for no higher cause than the saving of their respective countries, while you have surrendered your body and mind to Sri Ramakrishna abandoning your homes, friends and relations, etc., for a far superior object, i.e., the realization of God and the good of humanity — still you murmur against work! Swamiji used to say to us: 'Even if you think that this one life of yours is going to be spent in vain for the good of many, what does it matter? Who knows how many lives have been spent in vain? Why fear if one life is spent in doing good to the world?' Indeed, there is nothing to fear. It is said in the Śāstras that work without attachment leads us to God. We find in the *Bhagavad-gītā,* 'Verily, Janaka and others attained to perfection by work alone.'[6] Surely, a man reaches the Supreme by doing work without attachment.

"Once Swamiji said to us: 'You see, the young boys of these days who will join the Math, will not be able to devote themselves to meditation and such other practices day and night, hence the necessity to start various forms of humanitarian work.' If one can always engage oneself in prayer, meditation, study, etc., that is well and good; but that is not practically possible, so in the long run one becomes idle. Besides, you see, a good work must produce a good result. That itself will clear the path of your liberation. I have observed that those who have steadily performed meditation, study, etc., along with work adhering to a particular place, are soaring high like rockets in the spiritual firmament.

"Have you not seen whenever a number of sādhus like you have undertaken a work with unity of purpose, with your hearts set on God, how many great deeds have been performed by you and are still being performed? It is you who are showing to the world what great ends can be achieved even by a handful of men, if there is unity among them. You will reap the benefit of a lack of *japa* (repetition of God's name), if you can feed those who are

[6]BG III:20.

dying of starvation. Only giving food will not do, you will have to teach them, you will have to educate them. You must know it full well that he who will shirk work, will deceive himself."

18. *His love of music. He emphasized the regular singing of devotional songs in chorus and the recitation of hymns to gods and goddesses.*

As to his love of music, we have seen how he participated in it in his early days. He was specially fond of devotional songs and encouraged spiritual aspirants both to sing and to listen to them as aids to spiritual practice. They give a zest to austere spiritual life. They relax and soothe the nerves. We have already mentioned that the regular performance of choral songs in praise of Rāma and Kālī and also the chanting of hymns to gods and goddesses were introduced by him in the various Centers of the Ramakrishna Order. These have been a special feature of the Ramakrishna Math and Mission Centers and have fostered in them a pleasant atmosphere in spite of strenuous public activities and the responsibilities involved in them. The adoration of different gods and goddesses has considerably fostered the Order's spirit of religious harmony, which Maharaj like a true child of Sri Ramakrishna always maintained in his life and deeds. Later in life he used to listen to devotional songs and hymns almost every day sung by the monastics who had specialized in music and generally accompanied him in his travels. During his stay in different places musical soirées were sometimes arranged by the local devotees for his pleasure, in which adepts in vocal and instrumental music considered it their blessed privilege to display their skill in his holy presence.

19. *His versatile talents.*

His aesthetic sense was really very highly developed. He was a man of refined taste. He could appreciate art and beauty in all forms. Persons with literary skill of no mean order sometimes came to him with their manuscripts and read to him selected passages for his approval and highly valued his suggestions for improvement. One of them, a Bengali playwright of considerable repute, thus testifies to Maharaj's dramatic insight:

"One day I received from Maharaj one or two instructions relating to the essentials of dramatic composition and was astonished to find that he had mastered the dramatic art as well. I have gathered much valuable information from the best dramatists, but none of them explained to me in such few words the secrets of dramatic art."

Even in devising plans for a building, his advice was sought by many of the devotees. His daily habits and way of living also exhibited a fine taste and culture. In later life he lived in moderate comfort. His stalwart physical frame, robust by nature, had grown so tender and susceptible that it could not bear any hardship, strain or irregularity. His nerves also had become extremely delicate and fine. His physique had to be looked after with utmost care by one or two monks whose duty it was to attend on him. It seemed to have imbibed the fineness of his spiritual nature. The articles of his daily use were kept in their exact places and in perfect order. His clothing and all other things under his care always appeared fresh and tidy. It was happily expressed by one of Sri Ramakrishna's most intimate lay disciples that he would make brass look like gold. His majestic personality combined with his cultured style of living gave a royal air to his ways and movements.

Maharaj had a great liking for plants and trees. In whatever place he lived for a considerable time, it was his pastime to plant orchards, flower-beds, fruit and vegetable gardens. He took personal care of them. He enjoyed their growth and beauty as they existed in nature. He looked upon them as Nature's offering to the

Virāṭ (Omnipresent Being). A flower blooming on the tree would give him more delight than one plucked and presented to him. He could not bear that the trees should be so shorn of their produce as to lose their natural charm, even for the sake of the pūjā. Once a monk at Belur Math was scolded by him for doing such violence to the trees while gathering flowers for the daily worship of Sri Ramakrishna.

Maharaj could instinctively find out the peculiar needs of a tree or plant and devise the necessary nutriment. In this way he turned a dying plant into a luxuriant one with profuse flowers or fruits as the case might be. Sometimes by a special treatment he astonishingly improved the size, color and fragrance of the products. He successfully transplanted some of the best plants from one part of India to another. Certain monasteries of the Order have thus come to possess, more or less, exotic plants and trees.

The domestic animals of the monastery, such as cows and dogs, also received great care and attention from him. There was one pet cow at Belur Math which used to come at his call to receive food from his hand. One of his favorite dogs is said to have expired out of grief for him when he had to leave it at Belur Math on the occasion of his journey to Kankhal.

20. *Concluding remarks.*

With all these virtues of head and heart he was remarkably unassuming and unassertive. A dignified reserve was an outstanding feature of his personality. He wore as it were the profound calmness of the sea. Just as the sea holds in its bosom the immense wealth of vegetation, living creatures, and precious pearls, and yet may appear solemn and tranquil, so he looked serene and sober with all the hidden treasures within him. But this reticence, far from being the effect of self-conscious will, was characterized by the natural simplicity and sweetness of self-forgetfulness. His personality was gentle but potent in its influence like the quiet power of Nature. Smoothly and silently she brings about each moment incalculable changes on the face of the universe. He, too, like a guiding power, unseen and unperceived, directed the course of each active organ of this mighty Organization. His sphere of influence was not confined within the monastic circle, but extended far beyond even the entire body of lay devotees, disciples, friends, and admirers. Indeed, his personality was so impersonal that it could be felt rather than described. It worked upon the human soul through the silent forces of its blessedness and purity.

His very presence was an inspiration. Those who had the privilege of being in his personal contact knew full well how unconsciously their minds were raised beyond the ordinary level — a fact which they realized more and more deeply, the more they were away from him.

APPENDIX A

THE BUDDHIST SCRIPTURES

The earliest collection of the Buddhist tenets is the Pāli *Tipiṭaka* (*Tripiṭaka* in Sanskrit), "The Three Baskets," which contain an elaborate account of the Buddha's life and teachings. These three are (1) the *Vinaya Piṭaka* (Discipline Basket), (2) the *Sutta-Piṭaka* (Sermon Basket), and (3) the *Abhidhamma Piṭaka* (Metaphysical Basket). The *Vinaya Piṭaka* sets various rules and ordinances to be observed by the Buddhist Order as stated by the Buddha himself on different occasions. The *Sutta Piṭaka* presents the sermons and the discourses in prose and verse delivered by the Buddha and some of his disciples. The *Abhidhamma Piṭaka* dwells on abstruse philosophy, psychology, and ethics. The Buddha delivered his message in Pāli, the dialect of the people among whom he lived. Pāli is akin to Sanskrit, being derived from it.

The Buddha did not write any book. Shortly after his Parinibbāṇa, which occurred in 544 B.C. according to Theravāda ("The Doctrine of the Elders"), the whole body of the Buddhist monks held a council at Rajagriha for the collection and preservation of his teachings in as pure form as possible. It is said that the contents of the *Vinaya Piṭaka* and the *Sutta-Piṭaka* and of the *Abhidhamma Piṭaka* in part were gathered from the words of the elders and settled at the First Buddhist Council. There were further deliberations on the tenets at the Second and the Third Buddhist Council before they were finally adopted. The Second Council was convened at Vesali about a century after the First. The Third was held at Pataliputra (near modern Patna) in 247 B.C. under the patronage of the Emperor Aśōka. For some centuries the whole collection was traditionally handed down orally from teachers to pupils. The complete scripture was compiled in the form of books for the first time in Ceylon in 29 B.C., "with all the detailed classifications that are not obtained in the Pāli *Tipiṭaka* of the Theravāda School."

The *Tipiṭaka* texts constitute the Buddhist canonical literature in Pāli. The commentaries on the *Piṭakas* and other Pāli works belong to the non-canonical literature. Both the schools of Buddhism — the Mahāyāna (lit. "The Great Vehicle") as well as the Hīnayāna (lit. "The Small Vehicle") — recognize the Piṭaka canons. The Mahāyāna has been predominant in the northern countries, such as Tibet, China, Korea, Japan, and is also called "The Northern School." The Hīnayāna has been predominant in southern countries, such as Ceylon, Burma, Thailand, Cambodia, and is also called "The Southern School." Besides the Pāli canonical literature the two schools have other sacred works in Pāli and in Sanskrit. The Mahāyāna School has a vast literature including five biographies of the Buddha, e.g., (1) The *Mahāvastu* (in mixed Sanskrit), (2) The *Lalitavistara* (in mixed Sanskrit), (3) The *Buddhacarita* (in pure Sanskrit poetry), (4) The *Nidānakathā* (in pure Pāli), (5) The *Abhiniṣkramaṇa-sūtra* (in mixed Sanskrit, now extant in Chinese translation).

APPENDIX B

THE VEDIC SCRIPTURES

The source of the religio-philosophical system known as "Hinduism" is the Veda, which is in all probability the most ancient of the religious records of the world. The primary meaning of the term *Veda* (lit. knowledge, from the Sanskrit root *vid,* to know) is suprasensuous knowledge. Secondarily, it means the original literary expression of this knowledge. There are four Vedas: the *Ṛk,* the *Yajuḥ,* the *Sāma,* and the *Atharva.*

Each Veda has two main sections: the Saṁhitā and the Brāhmaṇa. The Saṁhitā is the collections of hymns, prayers, benedictions, and sacrificial formulae. The Brāhmaṇa consists of the explanatory texts on the Saṁhitā and are primarily in prose. To the Brāhmaṇa proper are added the Āraṇyakas and the Upaniṣads, which are also treated as independent books. The Āraṇyakas (lit. Forest-books) dwell on the symbolic meanings of the fire-sacrifices for the purpose of meditation in forest retreats. The Upaniṣads dwell particularly on the knowledge of the ultimate Reality and its attainment. Of the one hundred and eight extant Upaniṣads about twenty are widely read. Śaṅkarācārya wrote commentaries on ten of them: *Īśa, Kena, Kaṭha, Praśna, Muṇḍaka, Māṇḍūkya, Aitareya, Taittirīya, Chāndōgya* and *Bṛhadāraṇyaka.*

The classical commentators on the Vedic texts recognize no chronological development of religious thought in them. The gradations of religious ideals noticeable in the Saṁhitā, the Brāhmaṇa, the Āraṇyaka, and the Upaniṣad are supposed to be due to the fact that the four sections were intended to be studied in the four successive stages of an individual's life, brahmacaryya (the student's life of study and celibacy), gārhasthya (the married life of a householder), vānaprastha (the life of retirement in the forest), and sannyāsa (the monastic life).

In the Saṁhitā part of the *Ṛg-Veda,* which is the earliest according to the modern scholars, there are gradations of religious ideas from popular polytheism to highly philosophical monism. But this is not a sure indication of the gradual evolution of religious consciousness of the Indo-aryans, as is generally assumed. In all probability higher and lower ideas suited to different grades of people prevailed simultaneously. Whatever might have been the popular conceptions of the deities mentioned in the Vedas, such as Indra (god of rain), Varuṇa (god of sky), Mitra (sun-god), Vāyu (god of wind), Agni (god of fire), etc., to the Vedic seers they were neither supernatural beings nor deified forces and phenomena of nature, but different manifestations of Nondual Brahman, "the One without a second." Indeed, the prevailing note of the Saṁhitā part is not polytheism, henotheism, or even monotheism, but absolute monism or nondualism.

APPENDIX C

FOLK FESTIVALS IN INDIA

The Hindu socio-religious life is very rich in festivals. "Thirteen festivals in twelve months" is a common saying in India. Most of these festivals are observed by all Hindu sects in all parts of India in some way or other. Each festival has, however, acquired some local color and form. There are also local festivals prevalent in different provinces and among different communities. There is no fundamental difference between the folk festivals and the festivals of the cultured except the difference of forms and features. The same festivals are observed by the cultured and the uncultured as well, but not in the same way. Those festivities in which the common folk take the initiative and give expression to their natural tendencies and capacities, their ideas and sentiments, can be counted as folk festivals.

These festivals did not, perhaps, originate with the common people. Some are mentioned in the classical literature of the Hindus and the Buddhists. It is a general tendency of the human spirit to seek relaxation and self-expression without restraint. According to one of the Purāṇas, Rāma, the Prince of Ayodhya, while living in exile in the woods of Chitrakuta with his wife Sītā and brother Lakṣmaṇa celebrated the spring festival, which is the principal folk festival in the present-day India. Later on, the spring festival became associated with the early life of Śrī Kṛṣṇa in

An address given by Swami Satprakashananda at the Folklore Conference of the National Folk Festival Association held under the auspices of the University College, Washington University, Saint Louis, on Wednesday, May 27, 1955. Printed in "Midwest Folklore," vol. VI, no. 4, 1956, published by Indiana University, Bloomington, Indiana.

Brindavan. In Bengal it has acquired additional religious significance being the birth anniversary of Śrī Caitanya, who lived from A.D. 1485 to 1533, and is worshipped by many as an Incarnation of Divine Love.

All Hindu festivals have some religious background. But secular elements are also noticeable in them. The people try to amuse themselves in various ways and give expression to their love of freedom, beauty, and joy. Sometimes they seem to forget the religious significance of the occasion and indulge in rude songs and behavior.

Each festival is held on a certain day of the lunar fortnight. So the day of its observance does not fall on the same calendar date every year, but varies from the solar day as does the Christian festival of Easter.

The festivals are observed in homes, in temples, and in public places, in various ways. An invariable element of the celebration is the worship of God in one or another aspect. On certain occasions clay images of the Deity, sometimes larger than life-size, are made by professional artists. They are ceremonially installed by the priests and elaborate worship is performed with the offering of flowers, fruits, incense, lights, sandal paste, and cooked food. Fasting and feasting also form a part of the celebration. Of course, it is the devout who usually observe the fast, the rest enjoy the feast.

Devotional songs sung in chorus to the accompaniment of instrumental music form an important part of the celebration. Drums and cymbals are the two very popular musical instruments of India. There are drums of many different sizes and shapes. Cymbals, too, vary in shape and size. Dance follows the songs in some cases. The Sanskrit word *saṅgīt,* which is usually translated as *music,* includes vocal music, instrumental music, and dance. In the National Folk Festival in this country there is a predominance of dancing; in Hindu festivals there is a predominance of song and instrumental music over dancing.

A prominent feature of certain festivals is the street procession, which is attended by all classes of people. It is a long pageantry of persons carrying flags, bunting, gorgeous umbrellas, of caparisoned horses and elephants, of bedecked chariots and thrones, of groups of singers and players enacting religious scenes, and so forth. It is mentioned in the *Bhāgavatam* that there were festivities at the nativity of Śrī Kṛṣṇa. The streets and archways of Vraja (Brindavan) were decorated with flags and festoons. The houses were beautified. The bards sang, the Brāhmins chanted the Vedic hymns, the musicians played, the dancers danced. Even the cattle were washed and adorned. The cowherds of Vraja came in a procession gayly dressed carrying presents in their hands. Even in these days a procession is held in some places to commemorate the occasion. This traditional way of jubilation and ostentation is perhaps common to all humanity. Street processions are still prevalent in India on festive occasions, including marriages and triumphs.

Bonfires, firecrackers, and illumination also go with some celebrations. On a new moon night in late autumn every house is illuminated with garlands of lights, so to say. It is called *dewāli* (from the Sanskrit *dīpāvalī*), the festival of lights.

Colorful fairs are held on some occasions. Many popular handicrafts and art productions are exhibited, or presented there for sale.

Women attend public celebrations, but do not take part in them. They usually busy themselves with decorating the homes, and arranging for the feast and the worship of the Deity. Sometimes they join with their relatives and neighbors, sing songs, and make fun. Grandmothers often tell stories to the children relative to the occasion.

The festivals have various sources. Some are connected with the worship of the Deity, in the form of Śiva, who represents the static aspect of the Supreme Being, or Durgā, the Divine Mother, representing the dynamic aspect of the Divinity, or Viṣṇu, the all-gracious Preserver of the Universe. The festival of Śiva is observed on the fourteenth day of the dark fortnight in early spring with complete fast and night-long vigil and worship. It is near the vernal equinox. The festival of the Divine Mother, Durgā, is observed close to the autumnal equinox at the harvest home. The car festival of Viṣṇu is held around the summer solstice when the southward journey of the sun begins.

One festival is particularly connected with the movement of the sun. It is held at the time of the winter solstice, when the passage of the sun into the sign of Capricornus in the zodiac begins. Its name *makara saṁkrānti* signifies the event. It is also called *Uttarāyaṇa saṁkrānti,* which means the beginning of the northward journey of the sun. The people, however, observe the festival with deep religious feeling. They immerse themselves in the Ganges at dawn and give alms.

There are festivals commemorative of the birthdays of Rāma, Kṛṣṇa, and other God-men. The birth anniversary of Rāma is held on the ninth day of the bright fortnight in late spring and that of Kṛṣṇa on the eighth day of the dark fortnight in early autumn. Some are occasioned by certain events in the life of Kṛṣṇa or Rāma. According to some, the Hōli festival in spring is connected with the killing of a demon by Śrī Kṛṣṇa. It is also called Dōl, the swing festival which represents one of His pastimes in Brindavan in full moon light. Another swing festival is held in the bright fortnight at the end of the rainy season. It is said that the worship of the Divine Mother, Durgā (the destroyer of distress), was initiated by Rāma during his exile. He worshipped the ten-handed Goddess, invoking Her blessings for the success of his campaign against the ten-headed demon, Rāvaṇa, the King of Ceylon, who had stolen his wife.

Among the folk festivals in India two are prominent. One is the spring festival called Hōli or Dōl, the other is Rāma-līlā. On the former occasion, every laborer, farmer, and servant leaves work for two days and feels free from the shackles of life. They form large parties and go from place to place playing drums, singing songs, and occasionally dancing. Some even drink and use rude language, of course, among themselves. One common practice of this celebration is to throw red or pink powder at one another. The heads and faces of the participants become so besmeared with powder that one cannot recognize even his own houseboy, unless one is clever enough to look closely into his eyes. On the following day they squirt colored water with syringes. In some places two parties of singers stand facing each other on platforms raised for the purpose and sing aloud responsive choruses. Each party includes as many as a hundred singers.

Rāma-līlā is a kind of primitive performance dramatizing the scenes from the life of Rāma. This is held usually on the occasion of Dashara, which is the truly national festival of the Hindus. It is the tenth day of the worship of the Divine Mother, Durgā, in autumn. In some places, Durgā is worshipped in the image on the seventh, the eighth, and the ninth day of the bright fortnight. Then, on the tenth day, the day of Dashara, the image is carried by men in a gala procession in the evening and immersed in some lake, or river, or in the sea, as the case may be. On this occasion every junior pays his respects to his elders. Every visitor at home or in the business place is entertained with sweetmeats. Presents are given to friends and relatives. The employers feed the employees and present gifts to them. Everywhere there is an exchange of greetings. Even the poorest man puts on new clothes for the occasion. Joyousness and cordiality fill the atmosphere.

Rāma-līlā is usually held in the evening in the open air in a public place. Sometimes it continues ten or twelve days. Men, women, and children attend the play with great joy and devotion. The characters of the Rāmāyaṇa, in which the life of Rāma is depicted, have furnished the Hindus with ethical ideals in all spheres of life. There is hardly any Hindu man or woman, who has not received moral or religious inspiration from this great Sanskrit epic. There are several popular versions of the book in different vernaculars, which the common people read or listen to.

Rāma was the eldest son of the King Daśaratha of Ayodhya (modern Oudth). He was the heir-apparent to the throne, but was sent into exile for fourteen years through the machinations of his stepmother, who wanted to secure the kingdom for her son, Bhārata. The old king died out of grief for Rāma. Bhārata did not sit on the throne, but placed Rāma's wooden sandals there and ruled the kingdom on his behalf. Rāma's devoted wife, Sītā, and his faithful stepbrother, Lakṣmaṇa, followed him into the forest. They moved southward and lived happily among natural surroundings. One day, in the absence of Rāma and Lakṣmaṇa, Sītā was stolen and carried away by the demon king, Rāvaṇa, to his golden kingdom in Ceylon. The mighty Rāvaṇa tried in all possible ways to win the hand of Sītā, but she was unflinching in her devotion to her husband. Rāma rallied a large army of monkeys (probably the aborigines of India), of whom Hanuman was the chief. With their help he finally defeated Rāvaṇa, rescued Sītā, and returned to Ayodhya on the expiration of the term of exile. He gave the kingdom of Ceylon to Rāvaṇa's brother, Bibhīṣaṇa.

The person who plays the part of Rāma's ally and devotee, Hanuman, appears wearing a monkey mask and a long curly tail. Occasionally he climbs trees and jumps from branch to branch. He also carries on his head paper-made mountains, which represent the heaps of rocks that were used in building the bridge between India and Ceylon over which Rāma marched with his monkey troops. Women's parts are played by boys who have girlish features and who wear female dress. Towards the end of the festival, a huge effigy of the ten-headed demon King, Rāvaṇa, the vanquished foe of Rāma, which is made of paper and bamboos, is burnt with shouts of rejoicing.

In Bengal there is a folk festival associated with the worship of Śiva. It is held in early summer and called Gajan. In almost every neighborhood in some cities, a small building is reserved for the purpose. It also serves as a meeting place for amusement. At the time of the festival, Śiva is worshipped there in the image. Every household sends its offering of flowers, fruits, and sweets. After the performance of the worship, one of the devotees appears in the guise of Śiva and another (usually a boy) in the guise of his consort, Gaurī. They move from house to house and dance. In the evening, someone puts on the guise of Kālī and dances with swords in hands. Several such parties come out on the occasion. Besides these, people organize groups of singers, who dramatize religious scenes and visit different places. The songs are composed by their leaders.

Apart from being a source of amusement, the folk festivals have proved to be a great educational force for the masses. By providing them opportunities to work together for a common cause, the festivals make them public-spirited, and strengthen the bond of union among them. The various functions call forth their artistic talents, literary abilities, poetic powers, and capacities for organized work. Their songs and literary compositions have a natural flavor, free from artificiality, full of grace, spontaneity, and beauty. Many folk poems, songs, and sayings have acquired literary status and have become the common property of the nation. In some places, poetasters organize parties of singers. A popular pastime is to watch two opponent poetasters carry on debate in extempore verses for hours. The followers of each sing a refrain from time to time.

The fairs held at the festivals give the people an occasion to develop their skill in making toys and other handicrafts. Their aesthetic sense is also cultivated through the decorations that form an invariable part of the celebrations. Women have developed a special art of painting, which is called *alpina.* Their paint is rice powder mixed with water and their brush is a little piece of rag held by the fingers. With this simple equipment they make exquisite diagrams, draw lotuses and other figures, and decorate the floors and walls, the porches and door sills, and even the courtyard for the occasion.

So far I have dealt with the festivals of the Hindus, who form the bulk of Indian population. But no account of the folk festivals of India can be complete without mentioning the Muslim festivals. The most notable of the folk festivals of the Mohammedans is Moharrum, which is also the name of the first lunar month of the Muslim year, in which it is celebrated. It is held in commemoration of the martyrdom of Hassan and Hussein, the two grandsons of the Prophet Mohammad. Both of them suffered tragic deaths at the hands of their rival claimants to the Caliphate, the supreme leadership of the Muslim world. Mohammad did not have a son. His daughter, Fatima, married his cousin, Ali, who succeeded in being the Caliph, but was assassinated by an opponent. After Ali's death, his eldest son, Hassan, declared himself as the Caliph, but was killed by his father's rival. Then came the turn of his younger brother, Hussein. On the plain of Karbela in Iraq, he was entrapped, along with his young son and followers, by a vast army of his enemy, Yezid. There first his son and then he died tragic deaths.

The Shias and the Sunnis form the two primary divisions of the Mohammedans. It is mainly the Sunnis who observe a period of mourning during the first ten days of the month of Moharrum. On the tenth day a procession is held. Hundreds of Mohammedans, wailing and beating their breasts, carry a large paper-made mausoleum of Hassan and Hussein, called Tazia, along the streets to a place called Karbela. Many Hindus attend this festival. Many Mohammedans also attend Hindu festivals.

There is an interconnection of folk lore and culture lore. They penetrate each other. It may sound strange to many, if I say that the caste system has not culturally segregated the lower classes among the Hindus. Originally, it was based on the principle of the division of labor according to inborn tendencies and acquired capacities. The purpose was not to keep down the lower classes but to let each rise to a higher level, through the performance of duties on hand. The Brāhmin was the ideal of the society; the Śūdra was expected to rise by gradual stages to Brāhminhood. Various ethnic groups and cultural units were incorporated into Hindu society on the same principle.

The present caste division determined by parentage is a deviation from the original pattern. Religious and social reformers from Buddha down to Mahatma Gandhi have rebelled against it. It has been the constant endeavor of the great leaders to reach the individuals at their own level. With this end in view they have devised various methods to accommodate the high metaphysical truths and life-attitudes to the psychophysical status of the common folk. Mythology and rituals have developed mainly from these efforts. Itinerant monks have also carried religious teachings and ideals to the doors of all.

As a result, saints, seers, and poets have arisen from the lowest ranks. They are adored by Brāhmins as well as by Pariahs. Some of the Vedic seers such as Kavas, Mahīdās, were Śūdras by birth. The *Mahābhārata* (the other Sanskrit epic) records the words of wisdom of a hunter-sage (dharma-vyādha). In the *Rāmāyaṇa* there is the story of the scavenger-prince, Guhaka, who was a dear friend and devotee of Rāma, an Incarnation of God. The saint Kavīr was a weaver, Ravidās a cobbler, Senā a barber, Nāma-deva of Marwar a carder of cotton, Tukārāma of Maharashtra a farmer, to mention just a few out of numerous instances. Among women also there have been numberless seers and sages from the Vedic time up to the present age.

The common folk usually receive metaphysical truths and even historical events through their imagination and feelings. They have a tendency to interpret all these in figurative languages. As a result, legends weave around spiritual and historical truths. The fables that have clustered around the personalities and the teachings of Kṛṣṇa, Buddha, Śaṅkara, and other religious leaders and have found admittance into standard literature are mainly the contributions of the mass mind. Though not historically true, they illustrate moral and spiritual principles.

APPENDIX D

THE ORIGIN AND THE RESTORATION OF THE HANDWRITTEN MANUSCRIPT OF SWAMI VIVEKANANDA'S "SONG OF THE SANNYĀSIN"

The poem "Song of the Sannyāsin" was composed by Swami Vivekananda offhand in a state of inspiration one afternoon at Thousand Island Park on the St. Lawrence River. He was living at Miss Elizabeth Dutcher's cottage with a group of students (including Miss Dutcher) where he held daily classes from Wednesday, June 19, 1895, until Tuesday, August 6, 1895.

The incident is thus noted by Sister Christine, a devoted student, who was present at the time: "There were twelve of us and it seemed as if Pentecostal fire descended and touched the Master. One afternoon, when he had been telling us of the glory of renunciation, of the joy and freedom of those of the ochre robe, he suddenly left us, and in a short time he had written his 'Song of the Sannyāsin,' a very passion of sacrifice and renunciation."[1]

The draft of the poem in Swamiji's handwriting was miraculously restored over sixty years later in September 1955. It happened this way. The cottage where the Swamiji lived was bought by The Ramakrishna-Vivekananda Center of New York and was being remodeled in the spring of 1948. The original manuscript of the poem, the existence of which nobody was aware at the time, had been thrown outside the house with some rubbish and was picked up by Mr. Harold Kohl, a young electrician, who

[1]Swami Vivekananda, *Inspired Talks,* 11th ed. (Madras, India: Sri Ramakrishna Math, 1974), p. 24.

regularly attended the services at the Ramakrishna-Vivekananda Center with his family. Familiar with the name of Swami Vivekananda, he recognized the importance of the manuscript, but for some reason known only to himself, did not speak to anyone about it for seven years. In September, 1955, he brought the manuscript to Swami Nikhilananda in New York and handed it over to him. A facsimile of that manuscript follows.

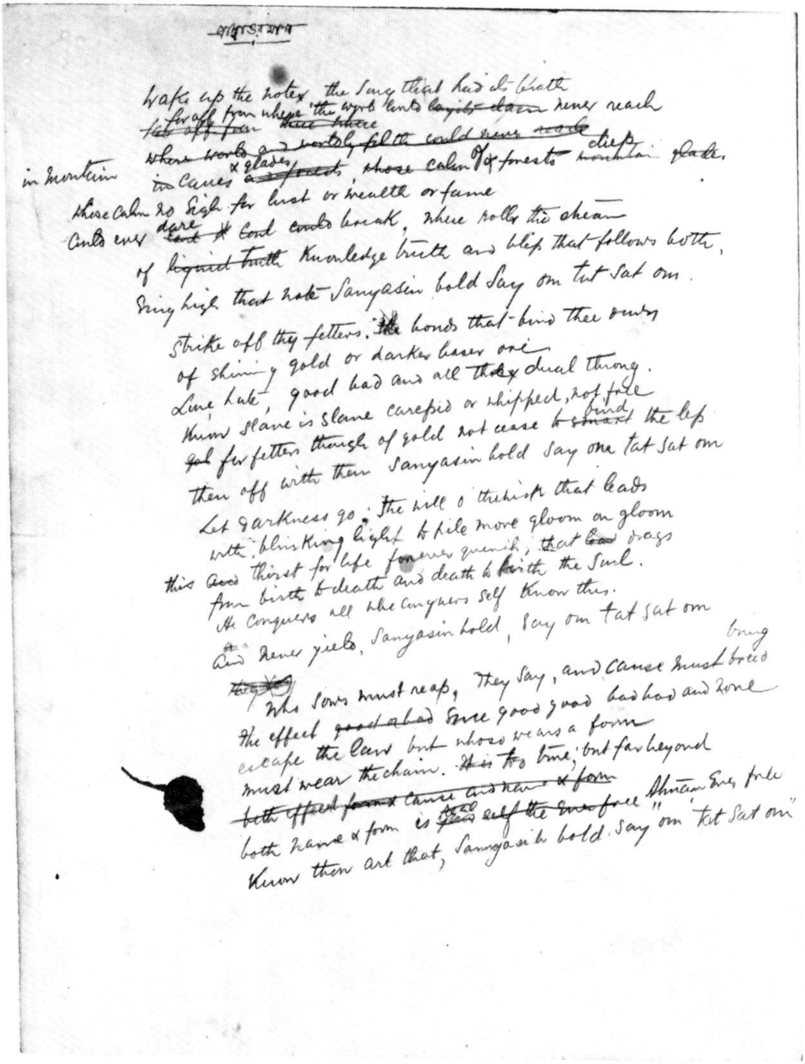
Wake up the note! the song that had its birth
far off from where the worldly taints never reach
far off from
in Mountain in Caves & glades, whose calm of forests deep glade.
whose calm no sigh for lust or wealth or fame
Could ever dare lust & Gold could break, where rolls the stream
of liquid truth Knowledge truth and bliss that follows both,
Sing high that note Sanyasin bold Say Om tat Sat Om.

Strike off thy fetters. bonds that bind thee down
of shining gold or darker baser ore
Love hate, good bad and all the dual throng.
Know slave is slave caressed or whipped, not free
for fetters though of gold not cease to smart bind the less
Then off with them Sanyasin bold Say Om tat Sat Om

Let darkness go: the will o' the wisp that leads
with blinking light to pile more gloom on gloom
this Good thirst for life forever quench, that drags
from birth to death and death to birth the Soul.
He conquers all who conquers self Know this.
And never yield, Sanyasin bold, Say Om tat Sat Om

Who sows must reap, they say, and cause must breed bring
The effect good or bad Since good good bad bad and none
escape the law but whoso wears a form
must wear the chain. but far beyond
both name & form is Atman ever free
Know thou art that, Sannyasin bold. Say "Om 'Tat Sat Om'"

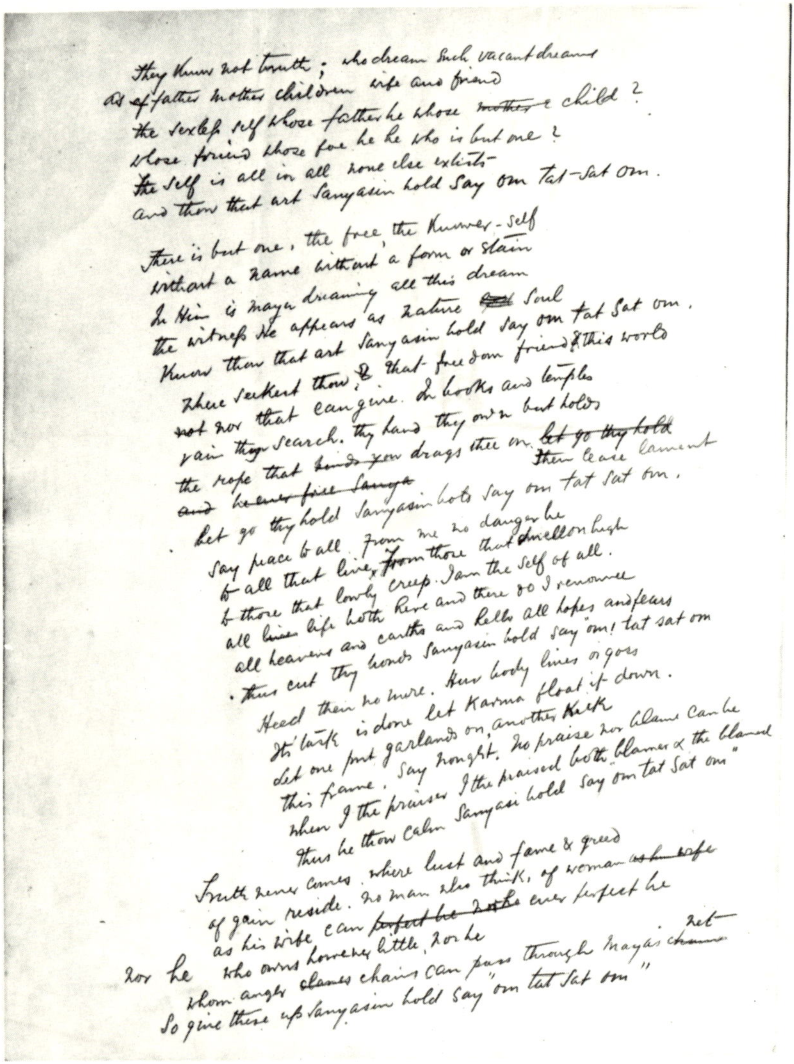

They know not truth; who dream such vacant dreams
As of father mother children wife and friend
The sexless self whose father he whose child?
Whose friend whose foe he he who is but one?
The self is all in all none else exists
And thou that art Sanyasin hold Say Om Tat-Sat Om.

There is but one, the free, the knower-self
Without a name without a form or stain
In Him is Maya dreaming all this dream
The witness He appears as nature soul
Know thou that art Sanyasin hold Say Om tat Sat Om.
Where seekest thou? That freedom friend this world
nor that can give. In books and temples
vain thy search. Thy hand thy own but holds
the rope that drags thee on. Then cease lament
and let go thy hold Sanyasin hold Say Om tat Sat Om.
Say peace to all. From me no danger be
to all that live. To those that dwell on high
to those that lowly creep. I am the self of all.
All life both here and there do I renounce
all heavens and earths and hells all hopes and fears
thus cut thy bonds Sanyasin hold Say Om! tat sat om
Heed then no more. How body lives or goes
Its task is done let Karma float it down.
Let one put garlands on, another kick
this frame. Say nought. No praise nor blame can be
when I the praiser I the praised both blamer & the blamed
Thus be thou calm Sanyasin hold Say Om tat Sat Om"
Truth never comes where lust and fame & greed
of gain reside. No man who thinks of woman
as his wife can ever perfect be
Nor he who owns however little, nor he
whom anger chains can pass through Maya's net
So give these up Sanyasin hold Say "Om tat Sat Om"

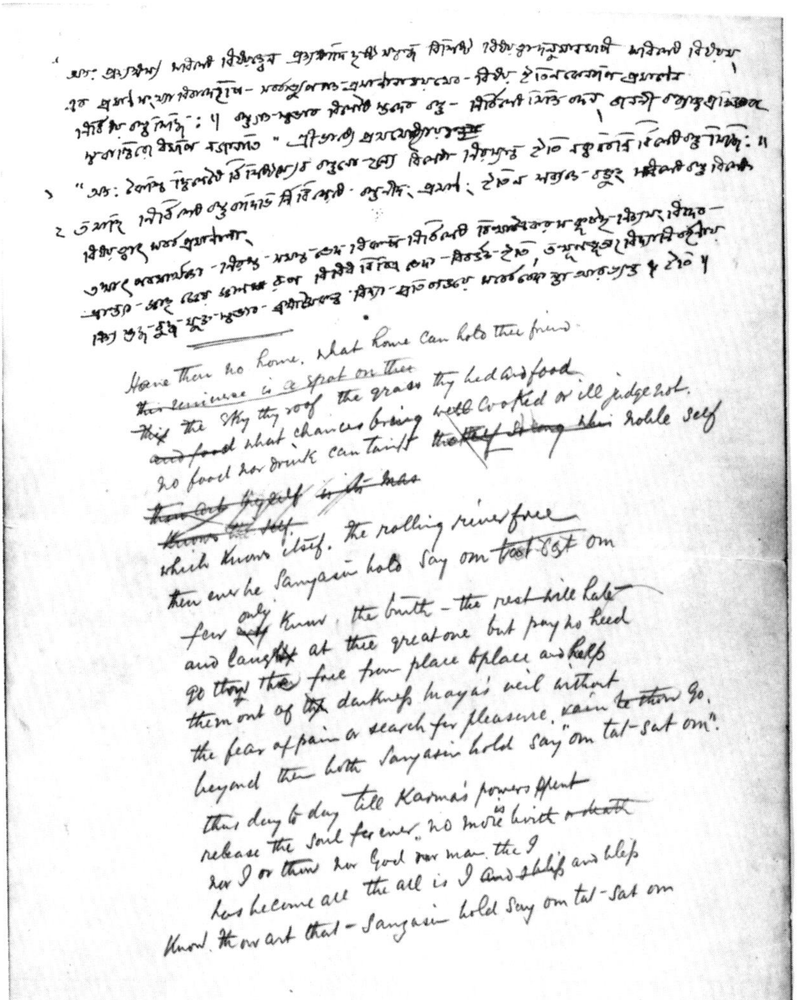

Have then no home, what home can hold thee friend
~~thi universe is a spot on thee~~
this the sky thy roof, the grass thy bed and food
~~and food~~ what chance brings well cooked or ill judge not
no food nor drink can taint ~~that~~ ~~of Atong~~ thy noble self
~~thou art thyself in its max~~
~~knows its self~~
which knows itself. The rolling river free
then ever be Sanyasin hold say om ~~tat sat~~ om

few ~~only~~ know the truth — the rest will hate
and laugh at thee great one but pay no heed
go thou ~~there~~ free from place to place and help
them out of ~~the~~ darkness maya's veil without
the fear of pain a search for pleasure. ~~vain to them go~~
beyond then both Sanyasin hold say "om tat-sat om".

Thus day to day till Karma's powers spent
release the soul forever. "no more birth or death
nor I or thou nor God nor man. the I
has become all the all is I and bliss and bless
know. thou art that — Sanyasin hold say om tat-sat om

SONG OF THE SANNYĀSIN

Wake up the note! the song that had its birth
Far off, where worldly taint could never reach;
In mountain caves, and glades of forest deep,
Whose calm no sigh for lust or wealth or fame
Could ever dare to break; where rolled the stream
Of knowledge, truth, and bliss that follows both.
Sing high that note, sannyāsin bold! Say,
"Ōm Tat Sat, Ōm!"

Strike off thy fetters! Bonds that bind thee down,
Of shining gold, or darker, baser ore —
Love, hate; good, bad; and all the dual throng.
Know slave is slave, caressed or whipped, not free;
For fetters, though of gold, are not less strong to bind;
Then off with them, sannyāsin bold! Say,
"Ōm Tat Sat, Ōm!"

Let darkness go, the will-o'-the-wisp that leads
With blinking light to pile more gloom on gloom.
This thirst for life, for ever quench; it drags
From birth to death, and death to birth, the soul.
He conquers all who conquers self. Know this
And never yield, sannyāsin bold! Say,
"Ōm Tat Sat, Ōm!"

"Who sows must reap," they say, "and cause must bring
The sure effect: good, good; bad, bad; and none
Escape the law — but whoso wears a form
Must wear the chain." Too true; but far beyond
Both name and form is Ātman, ever free.
Know thou art That, sannyāsin bold! Say,
"Ōm Tat Sat, Ōm!"

They know not truth, who dream such vacant dreams
As father, mother, children, wife and friend.
The sexless Self — whose father He? whose child?
Whose friend, whose foe is He who is but One?
The Self is all in all — none else exists;
And thou art That, sannyāsin bold! Say,
"Ōm Tat Sat, Ōm!"

There is but One — The Free — The Knower — Self!
Without a name, without a form or stain.
In Him is Māyā, dreaming all this dream.
The Witness, He appears as nature, soul.
Know thou art That, sannyāsin bold! Say,
"Ōm Tat Sat, Ōm!"

Where seekest thou? That freedom, friend, this world
Nor that can give. In books and temples, vain
Thy search. Thine only is the hand that holds
The rope that drags thee on. Then cease lament.
Let go thy hold, sannyāsin bold! Say,
"Ōm Tat Sat, Ōm!"

Say: "Peace to all! From me no danger be
To aught that lives. In those that dwell on high,
In those that lowly creep — I am the Self in all.
All life, both here and there, do I renounce,
All heavens and earths and hells, all hopes and fears."
Thus cut thy bonds, sannyāsin bold! Say,
"Ōm Tat Sat, Ōm!"

Heed then no more how the body lives or goes.
Its task is done: let karma float it down.
Let one put garlands on, another kick
This frame: say naught. No praise or blame can be
Where praiser, praised, and blamer, blamed are one.
Thus be thou calm, sannyāsin bold! Say,
"Ōm Tat Sat, Ōm!"

Truth never comes where lust and fame and greed
Of gain reside. No man who thinks of woman
As his wife can ever perfect be;
Nor he who owns the least of things, nor he
Whom anger chains, can ever pass through māyā's gates.
So give these up, sannyāsin bold! Say,
"Ōm Tat Sat, Ōm!"

Have thou no home. What home can hold thee, friend?
The sky thy roof, the grass thy bed, and food
What chance may bring — well cooked or ill, judge not.
No food or drink can taint that noble Self
Which knows Itself. Like rolling river free
Thou ever be, sannyāsin bold! Say,
"Ōm Tat Sat, Ōm!"

Few only know the truth. The rest will hate
And laugh at thee, great one; but pay no heed.
Go thou, the free, from place to place, and help
Them out of darkness, māyā's veil. Without
The fear of pain or search for pleasure, go
Beyond them both, sannyāsin bold! Say,
"Ōm Tat Sat, Ōm!"

Thus, day by day, till karma's powers, spent,
Release the soul for ever. No more is birth,
Nor I, nor thou, nor God, nor man. The "I"
Has All become, the All is "I" and Bliss.
Know thou art That, sannyāsin bold! Say,
"Ōm Tat Sat, Ōm!"[1]

[1]See Appendix E, the story of how the practice of renunciation and austerity turned a king into a saint.

APPENDIX E

HOW A KING BECAME A SAINT

Over a thousand years ago there lived in the Province of Khorasan in Eastern Persia a king known far and wide for his bounty and piety. Ready to acknowledge excellence of any type, the king used to give freely to all who would approach his royal presence to display their skill and achievements.

While travelling through the distant parts of his dominion incognito in order to see the condition of his people, he showed as much zeal to visit persons of eminence as places of importance. Off and on one might see him with an attendant or two treading on the winding paths of a village on his way to a humble cottage, the dweller in which was known to be an artist, a scholar, or a sage. It was, indeed, a rare sight to see a magnificent princely figure squatting on the floor listening with rapt attention to the words of wisdom and experience from a venerable old man, wrinkled with age, and with piercing eyes and a prominent forehead.

His court was the frequent resort of men of extraordinary gifts and attainments. Himself a lover of learning and culture, he would not only converse long hours with them, but would also devote what time he could secure from his kingly engagements to the study of religion and philosophy, for which he had a special aptitude. It was his daily program to listen to holy texts, expounded and interpreted by the court scholar.

Thus, the course of events went on smoothly until the day when fortune gave a new turn to his life. His kingdom, vast as it was, was invaded by a neighboring king, who succeeded in wresting a considerable portion of his dominion. The king had not sufficient wealth in his treasury, already drained by his lavish gifts, to make a mighty effort for the restoration of the lost territory. Deeply mortified, he retired to the inner apartments of his palace and was not in a mood to appear before the court.

The grey-haired minstrel was advised to approach the king in his affliction. In vain did he try to assuage his feelings. "It does not behove thee, O my lord," said the bard with tenderness and humility, as he was going to take leave of the king, "to grieve for what is lost beyond recovery, inasmuch as thou hast the highest esteem for ancient lore which extols perfect equanimity under all storm and stress of circumstances." The words moved the king and no sooner was the musician gone than he fell into the following train of thoughts: "Truly, I have discussed the religious texts with full alacrity and have marveled with felicity at the excellence of virtues related therein. How is it, then, that in practice I lag far behind and seem to have acquired little in actual life? Do not the scriptures serve to make us sober and calm in a crisis? Have they not sufficient motive power to direct our lives to truth and virtue? Or do they give only a momentary impetus to the mind?"

Thus embarrassed, the king was brooding over the question and could not come to a decision. He called for the court scholar, who presented himself immediately. The king related to him the difficulty he was in and asked for a solution. "You are versed, O scholar," continued the king, "in all the scriptures. Day after day you have explained to me the golden truths and the beautiful tenets they propound. Yet you have failed to implant these ideas in my mind; I am not above troubles and tribulations." The scholar, unable to give a conclusive answer all at once, begged for a day's time. "Very well," said the king in vexation, "but if you fail tomorrow, you need not appear before me ever again." The next day, the king was at the height of expectation at the appointed hour; but the scholar did not appear. The morning hours of the king's audience had passed, the afternoon period of interview was also almost over. The king called his other courtiers one by one and demanded from each a solution of the problem. Each offered an explanation as well as he could, but none was convincing and cogent enough to satisfy the king's understanding.

Meanwhile, the court scholar had been at home pondering the question over and over again, without any inclination to take his usual food and drink. Now, he had a young daughter possessed of rare talents and devoted to study and meditation. She had taken a vow of life-long celibacy and acquired through the help of her father a sound knowledge of religious ideas and ideals. Understanding her father to be in a plight, she wanted to know the reason. The father, who had great faith in her attainments, recounted to her all that had passed between him and the king. "I will solve the difficulty, O father," cried out the maiden, "just finish your meal and then take me to his royal presence."

With the last glimmer of the setting sun, when the courtiers had just taken leave of the king, the father and the daughter entered the palace and presented themselves before his royal presence. "What conclusion have you come to?" exclaimed the king, as soon as his eyes fell upon the scholar. "If it so pleases your Lord, my daughter will offer a solution," answered the scholar meekly, while both were making obeisance to the king. The king, who had heard much about the exceptional nature and conduct of the youthful virgin and had confidence in her merits and abilities, turned to her and said, "Speak out, O maiden, your decision."

"With your Lord's permission, I shall solve the problem by action and not by words," replied the maiden.

"You may do as you choose," granted the king.

Then she begged for two pieces of cord, which were forthwith brought to her. Her next prayer was that none but her father and herself would be with the king while she answered the question. This being granted, even the personal attendant of the king having left the hall, she implored, "Do not take amiss, O king, O my father, what I am going to do now, until you have seen the end of it." Then with much grace and modesty she proceeded to her father and tied him hand and foot to a pillar of the hall. In the same way she bound the king to an opposite pillar. Then she requested her father to go and unfasten the king. "How can that be," cried her father, "I am bound myself, how can I release another?" Then she loosened the bonds of her father and asked him to untie those of the king. At once he rushed to the king and rescued him in a moment. The daughter said, "Pray forgive me, O king, O my father, assuredly you understand me."

"Certainly, you have taught us a good lesson," the king observed, "a sinking man cannot save another who is drowning. Your father and I are both caught up in the meshes of the world; how can one rescue the other? But the question is not wholly concerning your father," continued the king, "it relates to the scriptures as well. Can they not make man wise and spiritual?"

At this the maiden spoke as follows: "The scriptures help us to a considerable extent by presenting before us a correct view of life and things, but they do not go a long way in developing our inner nature. It is the living personalities, the embodiments of spiritual ideals, that can ignite our lives with spirituality in the same way a lamp can light another lamp. In books we come across words and names describing principles and virtues, which do not actually exist there. It is the great personages who exemplify the precepts. So if you want to acquire true greatness and virtues, you must not seek them in books but in persons who demonstrate all that is good and great." The king's eyes were opened. He amply rewarded the scholar and his daughter before they took leave of him.

All night long the idea revolved in his mind and did not allow him a wink of sleep. Where and how to find a sage who could enkindle in him the light of spirituality was the burning question with the king. At last he recalled having heard in his youth about a great saint who lived in the remote province of Ajmer in India. "I must go in search of him even at the cost of life," resolved the king. At the dead of night before the cock's crow the king slipped out of the royal mansion, unknown and unnoticed, with no other possession but a drinking-pot, a pillow, and a small ruby. The vessel was made of gold and the pillow of velvet, being the articles of daily use in the royal household. The ruby was tied up in a corner of his robe for future provision.

The lustrous Venus was gleaming in the eastern sky when the king hastened out of his capitol into the meadow beyond. For a time there was a hush all over nature. Gradually the eastern horizon was ablaze with the splendor of the rising sun. A gentle breeze was blowing, carrying the sweet smell of wild flowers and the melodious song of birds. With the glorious birth of a new day, there loomed before his mind's eye a realm of celestial light and beauty. Buoyed up with hope and joy, he journeyed on and on through woods, and fields, and habitations of men, till at noon he came to a rivulet, where he stopped for rest.

As he was going to draw water from the sparkling stream with his vessel of gold, he noticed on the other side an old man scorched by the midday sun drinking his fill with joined palms. He thought: "There is no need of this bowl. I can do without it. Why shall I carry and guard it?" Then and there he threw the golden vessel down into the stream. Then he allayed his thirst with palmfuls of water and laid his head on the velvet pillow for a nap. When he awoke he saw under a tree nearby another man lying asleep with his head placed on his arms and snoring loudly from time to time. At once the king cast away the pillow, saying: "This is unnecessary and burdensome."

Soon the western sky was aglow with the rays of the setting sun. The king was too tired to resume his journey, yet, it was necessary to proceed to the next village to find a resting-place for the night. His path lay through the woods. Happily the moon shone bright overhead. As he was passing through a grove, something like a ruby seemed to glitter on the ground in the chequered moonlight. Attracted by its luster, the king stooped to lay his hand on it, when, lo, a peal of mocking laughter carried by the rustling wind burst upon his ears. He looked up and saw a horseman riding by. To the king's extreme shame and sorrow, what glittered like a gem proved to be nothing but vile saliva just spat out by the rider while chewing spice-reddened betel-leaf. He muttered, "I have given up my kingdom. I have renounced all worldly possessions. I have even cast aside the last two things I carried with me as essential for life. Still my mind turns to trivial stones. Why is it?" The king was not long in such reveries, when the ruby tied up in a part of his cloth flashed into his memory. "This is the last little thing that still binds my heart to what people call treasures," said the king with a sigh of relief, as he threw the ruby away.

The next morning he felt refreshed and relieved of his burden, and commenced journeying with renewed energy. Day in and day out he travelled over hills and valleys, plains and deserts with no other possession but an all-absorbing yearning for his objective. Towns and villages, and people of different types filled his mind with new experiences and relieved the fatigue of the journey. He walked on and on depending entirely on such food and shelter as chance would bring. His hardships and privations knew no bounds, but fortified with strong determination, he came victorious through them all.

At last the much-desired city of Ajmer came into view. His heart throbbed with joy. His long-cherished hope was going to be realized. He inquired about the abode of the saint and hastened on till he reached the entrance.

"What brings you here, sir?" said an aged disciple of the saint, as he entered the courtyard. "I have come seeking an interview with the sage," was the king's reply.

"He lives as a recluse and does not appear before strangers."

"Kindly bear him the message that the King of Khorasan is at his door waiting for initiation into monastic life."

"Two swords cannot be in the same scabbard," was the saint's reply forthwith conveyed to the king, who could hardly make out the significance of this remark.

He was bewildered and insisted on knowing its meaning so the disciple stated: "You profess to be the King of Khorasan and at the same time you presume to be an ascetic. How can that be? Two contrary forms of self-consciousness cannot exist in the same individual. You must give up all worldly pretensions before you can feel or realize yourself as a humble monastic, a devotee of the Lord — as a seeker of truth and truth alone. It is this feeling — this inner attitude — which is the mainspring of spiritual life."

The king acknowledged his fault and begged permission to stay in the hermitage rendering such services as might be required of him, until he would be considered fit for initiation. With the saint's permission he was allowed to stay. He was assigned the duty of a cowherd. Day after day he tended the cattle in a neighboring pasture ground. Five long years glided by. He had not even seen the saint. One day he sent word that his discipleship might be favorably considered. "Not yet," was the reply borne to the king.

Now, it was his regular practice to study books and make notes at night after the day's toil. It so happened one evening that on his return to the hermitage from the fields, he found to his great sorrow that the book containing his precious notes had been taken away and spoiled during his absence by one of the charity-boys. He immediately punished the culprit for his misdeed. When the news of the incident reached the saint he remarked, "You see, the time of his acceptance as a disciple has not yet come; he cannot forgive and forget the wrong done to him." It was decided that the king should henceforth live on one meal a day as a penance.

Three more years passed. At the close of the eighth year he was much emaciated. The rigors of the new way of life had told on his magnificent health. But he bore all its severities calmly and quietly. The disciples of the saint took pity on him and pleaded for him. But the only answer they could elicit from the saint was "Wait and see." A few days later, it so happened that one of the cows in the care of the king was missing and could not be found after careful search. He was held responsible and had to go without food as punishment. The king, although he had stood proof against all humiliations, was so distressed with hunger as to mutter in agony, "Ah, my kingdom, little dost thou know that thy king is starving to death!" When the matter was brought to the notice of the saint, he observed, "The time is not yet ripe, you see. He is not free from the vanity of his royal position." The king was allowed to have his regular meals. But it was enjoined that he should henceforth carry on his head a load of grass every evening when returning from the field.

Years rolled on; the king had to go through the same round of duty day after day. His body and mind were thoroughly disciplined. His power of endurance increased to the full. He seemed to be perfectly accommodated to his mode of life. There was a peaceful serenity about him and a graceful demeanor marked all his movements. It was now his twelfth year in the hermitage. One morning the saint inquired about him and was fully satisfied with the report he received as to his conduct and character. "Let him, however, pass through an ordeal," said the saint. "As he comes down the mountain slope at dusk with the load of grass on his head, let one of you try to give him a fall and watch what happens." The saint's order was enacted the same evening. One of the disciples in disguise approached the king under cover of darkness and purposely stumbled on his stick, as though unawares. The king fell down; but instead of being provoked, he asked the offender if he had been hurt and begged to be pardoned.

When the saint was informed of this, he was so happy that he ordained that no tasks should henceforth be imposed on the king;

he should be given all the relief and comfort the hermitage could afford. The new situation, far from making him indolent and ease-loving, gave him new opportunities for self-restraint and self-culture. His active life was followed by an ardent life of contemplation. He would sit long hours morning and evening absorbed in meditation.

One evening as he was returning to the hermitage from the meadow, he found that the boy who took care of the cows was being severely beaten by the owners of an adjacent cornfield, which the cows had entered and seriously damaged. He at once hurried to the spot, but the blows went on notwithstanding his remonstrances. In his attempt to protect the boy he was struck on the head and was bleeding profusely. As soon as the news reached the hermitage some of the brothers ran up to the place of occurrence, caught hold of the culprits, and brought them with their hands tied behind their backs to the king for punishment. Instead of accusing them he blamed himself for being the unfortunate cause of their sad plight, and implored his brother-monks to release them at once. "Are we not children of the same Lord?" he cried out, "What right have we to punish our brothers? I love my brothers regardless of what they do unto me."

As soon as the saint heard of this he ran up to the king and clasped him to his heart, saying, "Thou art already a monk, a monk in spirit, not a mere ascetic by vow. What need is there of formal initiation for thee." With these words, the saint held him by the hand and escorted him to the solitary shelter reserved for him.

The story illustrates how the practice of renunciation and austerity turns the human mind from the search for the temporal to the search for the Eternal.

Indeed, self-sacrifice and self-restraint provide the key to man's inner development, such as intellectual, moral, spiritual.

To seek God, the Eternal One, is the privilege of human life.

To realize God is the Goal of human life.

BIBLIOGRAPHY I

ENGLISH WORKS QUOTED FROM AND CONSULTED IN THIS BOOK

Bapat, P.V., ed. *2500 Years of Buddhism.* Delhi, India: Government of India, Publications Div., 1959.

Burke, Marie Louise. Swami Vivekananda in America New Discoveries. Rev. 2d ed. Calcutta: Advaita Ashrama, 1966.

Burtt, Edwin A., ed. *The Teachings of the Compassionate Buddha.* New York: New American Library, Mentor Book, 1955.

Devamata, Sister. *Days in an Indian Monastery.* La Crescenta, Calif.: Ananda Ashrama, 1927.

Eliot, Sir Charles. *Hinduism and Buddhism: An Historical Sketch.* 3 vols. New York: Barnes and Noble, 1921.

Ferm, Virgilius, ed. *Religion in the Twentieth Century.* New York: Philosophical Library, 1948.

Hiriyanna, M. *The Essentials of Indian Philosophy.* London: George Allen and Unwin, 1949.

Jeans, Sir James H. *Physics and Philosophy.* New York: Macmillan Co., 1944.

Nikam, N.A., and McKeon, Richard, eds. and trans. *The Edicts of Aśōka.* Chicago: University of Chicago Press, Phoenix Books, 1959.

Nikhilananda, Swami, ed. *The Gospel of Sri Ramakrishna.* New York: Ramakrishna-Vivekananda Center, 1942.

Nivedita, Sister. *The Master as I Saw Him.* 10th ed. Calcutta: Advaita Ashrama, 1970.

Oldenberg, Hermann. *Buddha, His Life, His Doctrine, His Order.* London: Williams and Norgate, 1882.

Radhakrishnan, S. *Eastern Religions and Western Thought.* 2d ed. London: Oxford University Press, 1940.

Radhakrishnan, S. *Indian Philosophy.* 2d rev. ed, 2 vols. London: George Allen and Unwin, 1929-31.

Radhakrishnan, S., and Moore, Charles A., eds. *A Source Book In Indian Philosophy.* Princeton, N.J.: Princeton University Press, 1957.

Ramakrishna Mission Institute of Culture. *The Cultural Heritage of India.* 2d rev. ed, 4 vols. Calcutta: Ramakrishna Mission Institute of Culture, 1953-62.

Ramakrishna Vedanta Centre. *Swami Vivekananda in East and West.* London: Ramakrishna Vedanta Centre, 1968.

Rolland, Romain. *The Life of Vivekananda and the Universal Gospel.* 4th impr. Calcutta: Advaita Ashrama, 1953.

Saradananda, Swami. *Sri Ramakrishna, the Great Master.* Translated by Swami Jagadananda. Madras: Sri Ramakrishna Math, 1952.

Scofield, C.I., ed. *The Holy Bible.* New York: Oxford University Press, 1917.

Vivekananda, Swami. *The Complete Works of Swami Vivekananda.* 8 vols. Mayavati, India: Advaita Ashrama, 1922-51.

Vivekananda, Swami. *Letters of Swami Vivekananda.* 3d ed. Calcutta: Advaita Ashrama, 1970.

BIBLIOGRAPHY II

SANSKRIT AND PĀLI WORKS QUOTED FROM AND REFERRED TO IN THIS BOOK

Advaita-siddhi by Madhusūdana Sarasvatī. With 'Gauḍa-Brahmānandī,' 'Siddhi-Vyākhyā,' and other commentaries. Ed. with critical notes by Mm. Ananta-kṛṣṇa Śāstrī. Bombay: Nirnaya Sagar Press, 1937.

Amara-kōśa (Sanskrit lexicon in poetry in three books) by Amara-siṁha, the court scholar of King Vikramāditya, 4th Century, A.D. Ed. by N. G. Sardesai and D. G. Padhye, Poona, 1940.

Aṅguttara-nikāya of Sutta-piṭaka (Sacred Books of the Buddhists) ed. by Bhikshu J. Kashyapa (Devanagari Pali Series, Nalanda), 4 vols., Nalanda, 1960.

Aṣṭasāhasrikā-Prajñāpāramitā, (1) ed. by R. L. Mitra, Bibliotheca Indica, Calcutta 1888; (2) ed. by P. L. Vaidya, Buddhist Sanskrit Text, No. 4, Darbhanga, 1960; (3) English trans. by Edward Conze, Bibliotheca Indica, Calcutta, 1958.

Bhagavad-gītā (Śrīmad)

(1) (Sanskrit edn.) Text with Śaṅkara's commentary (with Ānandagiri's gloss) and the commentaries of Nīlakaṇṭha, Śrīdhara, Madhusūdana Sarasvatī, and two others. Nirnaya Sagar Press, Bombay, 1936.

(2) Text with Eng. trans. of Śaṅkara's commentary by A. Mahadeva Sastry. Published by V. Ramaswamy Sastrulu & Sons, Madras, 1929.

(3) Text with Eng. trans., comments & index by Swami Swarupananda. Advaita Ashrama, Mayavati, Himalayas, 1948.

(4) Text with Eng. trans. and Eng. rendering of Śrīdhara's gloss by Swami Vireswarananda. Sri Ramakrishna Math, Mylapore, Madras, 1948.

Bhāgavatam (Śrīmad) (also known as Bhāgavata Purāṇam) by Kṛṣṇa-dvaipāyana Veda-vyāsa (in Beng. character). Sanskrit text with Śrīdhara Swāmī's commentary ((Bhāvārtha-dīpikā." Bangavasi Press, Calcutta, 1927.

Bodhicaryāvatāra of Śānti Deva, ed. by P. L. Vaidya, Buddhist Sanskrit Text Series No. 12, 1960; trans. into Hindi and published along with the Sanskrit text by Santibhiksu Sastri, Lucknow, 1955.

Brahma-sūtras of Bādarāyaṇa (Sanskrit edn.) with the commentary of Śaṅkara and the sub-commentaries — "Bhāṣya-ratnaprabhā," "Bhāmatī," and "Nyāya-nirṇaya" of Śrī Gōvindānanda, Vācaspati, and Ānandagiri. Nirnaya Sagar Press, Bombay, 1934.

Buddhacarita of Aśvaghōsha included in *Buddhist Mahāyāna Texts*. Trans. by E. B. Cowell, New York: Dover Publications, Inc., 1969.

Dhammapada, The

(1) Trans. by Prof. F. Max Müller (Sacred Books of the East, Vol. X, Part I) Oxford, 1881.

(2) Trans. by Venerable Bhikkhu Buddharakkhita. Bangalore: Maha Bodhi Society, 1959.

(3) Trans. by Narada Thera. London: John Murray, 1954.

(4) Trans. by Irving Babbitt. New York: Oxford University Press, 1936.

(5) Trans. by S. Radhakrishnan. London: Oxford University Press, 1950.

Itivuttaka. One of the fifteen books of Khuddaka-Nikāya of Sutta-Piṭaka. *The Tripiṭakas* (41 vols.). The Buddhist Scriptures in Pāli. Gen. Ed. Bhikkhu J. Kashyap, published on the occasion of the 2500th anniversary of the Mahāparinirvāṇa of the Buddha, Pali Publication Board (Bihar Government) 1956.

Mahābhārata of Kṛṣṇa-dvaipāyana Veda-vyāsa. Sanskrit Epic of eighteen parvas (sections). Trans. into Eng. by Pratap Chandra Ray. Bharata Press, Calcutta, 1893.

Majjhima-nikāya (Pāli book), ed. by V. Trenckner and Lord Chalmers, 3 vols. London: Pali Text Society, 1888-99.

Mahāparinibbāṇa suttanta included in *Dīgha-Nikāya,* ed. T. W. Rhys Davids, J. Estlin Carpenter, 3 vols. London: Pali Text Society, 1908-11.

Māṇḍūkya-kārikā by Gauḍapāda — with Śaṅkara's com. and Ānanda-giri's gloss. Ananda Ashrama Sanskrit Series, 1928.

Rāmāyaṇa of Vālmīki (Seven Kāṇḍas or sections) ed. by Prof. P. P. Subrahmanya Sastri. Srirangam: Sri Vani Vilas Press. Of the two epics in Sanskrit (the Mahābhārata and the Rāmāyaṇa) the Rāmāyaṇa is the earlier.

Sutta-Nipāta of the Sutta-piṭaka. New edn. by Dines Andersen and Helmer Smith. London: Pali Text Society, 1913.

Upaniṣads — Sanskrit edns.

(1) *Ten Upaniṣads* — Text with Śaṅkara's commentary. Pt. I includes Īśa, Aitareya, Kaṭha, Kena, Chāndōgya, Taittirīya, Praśna, Māṇḍūkya, and Muṇḍaka. Pt. II includes Bṛhadāraṇyaka. Ashtekar and Co., Poona, 1927-29.

(2) The above ten Upaniṣads — each a separate volume with Śaṅkara's commentary and Ānandagiri's gloss. Ananda Ashram Sanskrit Series, Ananda Ashram, Poona.

Bṛhadāraṇyaka — Sanskrit text with Eng. trans. of Śaṅkara's commentary by Swami Madhavananda. Advaita Ashrama, Mayavati, Himalayas, 1934.

Bṛhadāraṇyakōpaniṣad-bhāṣya-vārttikam — by Sureśvarācārya with Ānandagiri's commentary "Śāstra-prakāśika" — in three parts. Ananda Ashram Sanskrit Series, Ananda Ashram, Poona, 1934.

Chāndōgya — Text with Eng. trans. and copious notes by Swami Swahananda. Sri Ramakrishna Math, Mylapore, Madras, 1956.

Eight Upaniṣads (excluding Bṛhadāraṇyaka & Chāndōgya) in two vols. — Sanskrit text with Eng. trans. of Śaṅkara's commentary by Swami Gambhirananda. Advaita Ashrama, Calcutta.

Māṇḍūkya

(1) with Gauḍapāda's kārikā, Śaṅkara's commentary and Ānandagiri's gloss. Ananda Ashram Sanskrit Series, Ananda Ashram, Poona, 1928.

(2) with Gauḍapāda's kārikā and Eng. trans. of Śaṅkara's commentary with notes by Swami Nikhilananda. Sri Ramakrishna Math, Mylapore, Madras, 1956.

Śvetāśvatara

(1) (Beng. edn.) Text and commentary (attributed to Śaṅkara) with explanation by Pandit Durgacharana Samkhya-Vedanta-tirtha. Calcutta, 1931.

(2) with Sanskrit text, Eng. trans. and comments by Swami Tyagisananda. Sri Ramakrishna Math, Mylapore, Madras, 1937.

(3) included in *The Upanishads*, vol. II — Eng. trans. of text with notes and explanations based on Śaṅkara's commentary by Swami Nikhilananda. Harper & Bros. Publishers, New York, 1952.

Vedānta-paribhāṣā by Dharmarājā Adhvarīndra

(1) Edited by M. Anantakṛṣṇa Śāstrī with introduction and commentary "Paribhāṣā-prakāśikā," University of Calcutta.

(2) with Rāmakṛṣṇa Adhvarīndra's commentary "Śikhāmaṇi" and Amaladās' gloss "Maṇiprabhā." Sri Venkatesvara Press, Bombay, 1911.

(3) (Eng. edn.) Text with explanation and notes by Saratchandra Ghosal, and with a preface by Hirendranath Datta. White Lotus Publ. Co., Calcutta.

Vedic Scriptures

Ṛg-Veda Saṁhitā with Sāyaṇa's commentary:

(1) Ed. by F. Max Müller, 4 vols. London: Oxford University Press, 1890. Chowkhamba Sanskrit Series, Varanasi, India, 1966.

(2) Ed. by Sontakke, Kashikar, and others, with exhaustive Index, 5 vols. Poona, Vaidika Samsodhana Mandala, 1933-51.

Ṛg-Veda Saṁhitā (Text with exhaustive Index), ed. by Sreepada Sarma Satavalekara, Svadhyaya-mandala, Paradi, Surat, India.

Ṛg-Veda Saṁhitā with Sāyaṇa's commentary, vols. I-V. A new critical edition based on old unused manuscripts of the commentary. Vaidika Samsodhana Mandala, Poona, India.

Yajur-Veda Saṁhitā

(1) The Kṛṣṇa (Black) Yajur-Veda — Taittirīya Saṁhitā with the commentary of Sāyaṇa, vols. I-VIII. Ananda Ashrama, Poona, India.

(2) The Śukla (White) Yajur-Veda — Yajur-Veda Saṁhitā (Mādhyandina recension). Text with exhaustive Index, Satavalekara Edn., Svadhyaya-mandala, Paradi, Surat, India.

Sāma-Veda Saṁhitā — Tāṇḍya-Mahābrāhmaṇa with the commentary of Sāyaṇa, in two volumes. Edited with notes, Introd., etc. by Pandit A. Chinnaswami Sastri, Professor, Benares Hindu University.

Atharva-Veda Saṁhitā (Text with exhaustive Index) — edited by Sreepada Sarma Satavalekara, Svadhyaya-mandala, Paradi, Surat, India.

Viveka-cūḍāmaṇi by Śrī Śaṅkarācārya (1) *The Works of Śaṅkara,* vol. X. Sri Vanivilas Press, Srirangam (2) Sanskrit text with Eng. trans., notes and index by Swami Madhavananda. Advaita Ashrama, Mayavati, Himalayas, 1944.

INDEX

Abhedananda, Swami, 129
Advaita Vedanta, 98, 112-13; principal tenets of, 113-14
Akhandananda, Swami, 130
Aśōka, Emperor, spread Buddhism, 39-40

Brāhma Samāj, 73, 74
Brahman: basis of all, 66; Nirguṇa, 113; reality of, 63-64; Saguṇa, 112; two kinds of, 66-67
Brahmananda, Swami (Maharaj), 81, 91, 92, 130, 131, 132; discourse on spiritual practice and realization, 193-95; early monastic life, 195-98; love of music, 204; love for others, 184, 185; personality of, 183-84, 185-87, 206-7; on philanthropic work, 201-4; practical wisdom of, 198-99; as spiritual teacher, 187-91; versatile talents of, 205-6; was highly revered, 178, 179-80, 182
Buddha: basic teachings of, 29-32; basis of teachings, 33-34; Eightfold path of, 31; Four Noble Truths of, 29-30; life story, 27-29; made religion dynamic, 38; names of, 23-24; on non-resistance of evil (Parable of the Saw), 32; organized monastics, 25
Buddhism: decline of, 43-46; deficiencies of, 51; doctrines of momentariness and no-self, 48-49; four schools of, 48; Hīnayāna — Mahāyāna, 43, 48, 210; image-worship in, 46; scriptures of, 209-10; variant of Hinduism, 34-36

Concentration, 168

Dependent Origination, Buddhist theory of, 30
Duties and debts, fivefold, 57-58

Edicts of Aśōka, 26 n, 39
Eightfold Path, Buddha's, 31

Faith, in oneself, 17, 165-66

God: seeing and serving in all, 90, 105, 106, 115, 152-53, 176; Self within, 17-18
Goodwin, J.J., 88, 127
Gōvindapāda, 53

Hinduism: early spread of, 41; term explained, 63, 63 n; and Vedanta, 112
Holy Mother (Sri Sarada Devi), 124

India: origin of word, 63 n; at time of Sri Ramakrishna, 74-75, 119-20
Īśvara, 68-69

Jīva, identity with Brahman, 68-69

Karma: and devotion leads to Liberation, 102; differences between Śaṅkara's and Vivekananda's views, 99-101, 103
Karma-yōga, 104, 105

Life, human, goal and background of, 21, 140

Man: divinity of, 17; goodness of, 16
Māyā, 67-68
Monotheistic Vedanta, 61, 62, 63, 112, 113
Morality, 15-16; closest to spirituality, 18, 19; foundation of, 173; unselfishness basic virtue of, 18

Nirvāṇa, 23, 30-31
Nivedita, Sister, 86, 92, 126; on Swamiji's detachment, 157-58; on Swamiji's love for humanity, 151; on Swamiji's seeing the best in all, 157
Nondualism. *See* Advaita Vedanta

Pāli canons, 42-43
Parliament of Religions, Swami Vivekananda at, 83-84
Perception, sense, limits of, 65-66

Rāma, story and festival of, 217-18
Ramakrishna Math and Mission, 91, 111, 129
Ramakrishna Order: inception, 80; founding of, 82; organizing of, 91
Ramakrishna, Sri: on free soul living in world, 107, 108-9; disciples of, 196: India at time of, 74-75, 119-20; last illness, 80-81; life briefly described, 115-18; message summed up, 76, 120-21; significance of his message, 121-23; Swami Vivekananda's early visits to, 72-73; training of Swami Vivekananda, 76-79
Ramakrishna-Vivekananda Movement: distinctness from traditional Vedanta, 114-15; influence of, 132-34
Ranti Deva, prayer of, 109
Religion: manifestation of divinity, 17, 169; universal truths underlying, 20, 140; universality, harmony of, 144-47, 170-72
Renunciation, 136
Rolland, Romain, on Swamiji's universal sense, 157

Samādhi, 23, 139
Śaṅkara: debate with Maṇḍana Miśra, 56; early life and mission of, 52-53; established four monasteries, 59; fivefold duties and debts of, 57-58; on illumined souls, 139; on Īśvara-jīva relation, 69; monastic order of, 26; nondualism of compared to Buddhism, 50-51; stressed rationality, 52; substance of his Advaita philosophy, 63-69; teachings and writings of, 53-55, 58, 60-61; view of karma compared to Vivekananda's, 99-101, 103
Saradananda, Swami, 91, 129, 132
Self-interest, enlightened, insufficiency of, 15
Sevier, Mr. and Mrs., 86, 88, 93, 126, 131
Strength, necessity of, 90, 154-56
Śūnyatā (voidness), 24, 48, 49
Śūnya-vāda (theory of voidness), 48, 49

Tripiṭakas (Pāli canons), 42
Truths: Four Noble, 29-30; universal, 20-21, 140
Turiyananda, Swami, 21, 108, 109, 130

United Nations, 14
Unity, spiritual, 140-41

Vedanta: Advaita, 98, 112-13; principal tenets of, 113-14; distinction between Śaṅkara's and Ramakrishna-Vivekananda's, 107; and Hinduism, 112; schools of, 61-63, 112-13
Vedas, 211-12
Vivekananda, Swami: activities for reconstruction of India, 89-92, 128-31; the Buddha and Śaṅkara meet in, 69-71; comprehensiveness of his message, 94-95, 136-37; death of, 93-94, 131-32; detachment of, 157-58; differs with Śaṅkara's view of karma, 99-101, 103; divergences from classical Vedanta, 96-97; early life and meetings with Ramakrishna, 71-74; in England, 86, 87, 126, 127; experiences nirvikalpa samādhi, 80-81, 139; first trip to America and

work there, 83, 85, 126; organizes Ramakrishna Order, 91; at Parliament of Religions, 83-84; saw best in all, 157; second trip to America, 92, 130; significance of mission, 88, 128; "Song of the Sannyāsin," origin, copies of, 223-27; training under Sri Ramakrishna, 76-79

Quoted: on acceptance of other religions, 146; on civilization as manifestation of divinity, 164; on development of the individual, 16, 17, 154, 163-64; on education, knowledge, and concentration, 167-69; on faith in oneself, 17, 165-66; on foundation of morality, 173-74; on goodness of individuals, 154, 163-64; on his rebirth to worship God, 22, 108; on individual progress, 162-63; on Karma-yōgī, 104; on mission of disciples, 89; on potential divinity of all, 71, 135, 148, 149, 154, 169; on practice and the ideal, 175; on progress of humanity as a whole, 161; on real nature of the soul, 19; on religion as realization, 85; on renunciation, 136; on seeing and serving all as God, 90, 105, 106, 152-53, 176; on spiritual and cultural unity, 140-44; on strength and freedom, 90, 154-56; on universal love, 151

Work, as worship, 105, 115

World: appears through māyā, 67-68; reality of, 64, 66; unification of, 14, 15, 21, 158

On his first visit to America Swami Vivekananda arrived on the steamer Empress of India, *which docked in Vancouver, British Columbia, on July 25, 1893 (see frontispiece). This painting of the ship, by artist Robert Banks, is one of a series of historic scenes commissioned for the British Columbia Centennial in 1971. It was originally published in a calendar by the B.C. '71 Centennial Committee, and is reproduced with their kind permission.*